# Numbers

A Commentary for Children

Herein is Love
COMMENTARY SERIES

# Numbers

## A Commentary for Children

### Nancy E. Ganz

Shepherd Press
Wapwallopen, PA

Herein is Love: Numbers
©2006 by Nancy Ganz

ISBN 09767582-2-9

Unless otherwise noted, Scripture quotations are from The Holy Bible, New
International Version (NIV) , ©1972, 1976, 1984 by the International Bible
Society.

Italics or bold text within Scripture quotations indicate emphasis added.

Graphic layout & design by Tobias' Outerwear for Books (www.tobiasdesign.com)
Typesetting by Andrew MacBride

Cover Artwork: *The Bright Morning Star* by Nicora Gangi—www.machairastudio.com

Printed in the United States of America

To my daughter, Natanyah

# CONTENTS

# Acknowledgements

First of all, I thank my husband, Richard L. Ganz, whose enthusiasm for my writing never wanes.

Once again I am greatly indebted to Matthew Henry for his commentaries, which continue to inspire me in my studies of God's Word.

I thank Jim Peterson, who keeps the computers running smoothly, and Stas Jesionka, who irons out any technical problems with my books.

I also thank the team at Shepherd Press, especially Richard Irvin for all his personal encouragement to this author.

Finally, I thank Nicora Gangi Manwaring for another beautiful landscape that is perfect for another one of my books. This particular piece of art— *The Bright Morning Star*—is part of my own private collection of her work. This picture has hung beside my bed for many years and it is the dawn I see each morning when I first open my eyes. I am glad that I can share this spectacular sight with the readers of my book. The Old Testament blesses us with this prophecy of the coming Christ: "A star will come out of Jacob" (Numbers 24:17). In the New Testament we read of its ultimate fulfillment in Jesus, who says of Himself: "I am the bright Morning Star" (Revelation 22:16).

# INTRODUCTION

The Book of Numbers opens with these words: "The LORD spoke to Moses. He said: 'Take a census of the whole Israelite community . . . listing every man by name, one by one . . . number by their divisions all the men in Israel. . . .'" (Numbers 1:1–3). The LORD of Hosts is concerned with counting and listing, numbering and recording, and we see this work of God throughout his Holy Word, not just in the book called *Numbers*. From the beginning of the Bible to its end, we see God involved in these activities. Long lists of numbers are part of God's wonderful Word. They are even part of his glorious gospel.

How does the Bible begin? In the opening verses of Genesis, God numbers the days of creation, and each day's number becomes its name: the first day, the second day, the third day . . . until the seventh day, the Sabbath Day, the holy day of rest (Genesis 1:1–2:3).

How does the Bible end? In the Bible's final book we see the number of all things brought to perfection. Revelation is riddled with numbers of symbolic significance. Again and again the numbers of perfection are revealed: 3, 7, 10, 12 (or 3 fours), 24 (or 2 twelves), 144 (or 12 twelves), and 1,000. In Revelation we see these numbers:

o The 7 lampstands, which are the 7 churches (Revelation 1:20).
o The 7 stars, which are the 7 angels (Revelation 1:20).
o The 24 elders seated on the 24 thrones (Revelation 4:4).
o The 4 living creatures, and each of the 4 living creatures had 6 wings with eyes all around, even under his wings (Revelation 4:8).
o The Lamb, who was worthy to take the scroll and open its 7 seals.
o The Lamb with his 7 horns and 7 eyes, which are the 7 spirits of God (Revelation 5:1–10).
o The myriads of angels, who worshipped the Lamb, "numbering thousands upon thousands, and ten thousand times ten thousand" (Revelation 5:11).
o The opening of the 7 seals (Revelation 6).
o The 4 angels standing at the 4 corners of the earth, holding back the 4 winds of the earth (Revelation 7:1).
o The number of those who had the seal of the living God: 144,000 – 12,000 from each of the 12 tribes of Israel—a number representing perfection (Revelation 7:4–8), who were the "great multitude that no one [except God] could count" (Revelation 7:9).
o "The angels who had the seven trumpets" (Revelation 8:6).
o The 3 angels (Revelation 14:6–13).
o The 7 angels with the 7 plagues in the 7 golden bowls (Revelation 15–16).
o The Holy City, the New Jerusalem, coming down out of heaven from God with its gates and its walls, its foundations and its dimensions, all carefully numbered, measured and recorded that we might know that it was a place of perfection:

> *It had a great, high wall with twelve gates, and with twelve angels at the gates. On the gates were written the names of the twelve tribes of Israel. There were three gates on the east, three on the north, three on the south and three on the west. The wall of the city had twelve foundations, and on them were the names of the twelve apostles of the Lamb.*
>
> *(Revelation 21:12–14)*

o The city measured 12,000 × 12,000 × 12,000 stadia—a city of perfection, the city of God.

Revelation also speaks about a mysterious number, a number of imperfection, which belongs to the beast who blasphemes God. The Bible says that the mark of the beast is "the name of the beast or the number of his name. This calls for wisdom. If anyone has insight, let him calculate the number of the beast, for it is man's number. His number is 666" (Revelation 13:17–18).

There is only one book in the Bible called Numbers, but numbers fill the Scriptures. Think about Exodus: This book deals with the Ten Plagues, a number which corresponds with the actual number of plagues, but which also represents the perfection of God's judgment (Exodus 7–11); the Ten Commandments, a number which represents the perfection of God's Law (Exodus 20); and the exact dimensions of the Tabernacle (Exodus 26–27), which is "a copy and shadow of what is in heaven," the perfect Tabernacle, "the true Tabernacle set up by the Lord, not by man" (Hebrews 8:2).

Think also of Leviticus: This book deals with the precise number of sacrifices to be offered each year, a staggering number. Often the number of sacrifices required on a certain holy day was a perfect number, such as seven or ten. While the vast numbers of these sacrifices demonstrate their own imperfection, nonetheless their numerical symbolic significance points to the perfection of Christ's sacrifice, "because by one sacrifice he has made perfect forever those who are being made holy" (Hebrews 10:14).

Now let us think about Numbers: Why has God recorded these long lists of numbers? Why did God command a census to be taken twice, both recorded in the book of Numbers? What was the purpose of each census then, and why is it important for us to know about these numbers now? How can a census record from thousands of years ago possibly have any relevance for us today? Why, of all the things in the world to study, would you study this?

The Bible says of itself that, "All Scripture is God-breathed and is useful for teaching" (II Timothy 3:16), so we know that even the record of an ancient census must have value for us.

What was God's purpose in commanding that a census be taken?

1. The census was used to collect the "temple tax," the money necessary for the upkeep of the Tabernacle. The LORD said to Moses, "When you take a census of the Israelites to count them, each one must pay the LORD a ransom for his life at the time he is counted. . . . Each one who crosses over to those already counted is to give a half shekel . . . All who cross over, those twenty years old or more, are to give an offering to the LORD. Receive the

atonement money from the Israelites and use it for the service of the Tent of Meeting. It will be a memorial for the Israelites before the LORD, making atonement for your lives" (Exodus 30:11–14, 16).

2. The census was necessary for the organization of the nation's army. This was the first step that each man took to become a soldier. Being counted in the census was his enlistment into Israel's army. By faith, in obedience to the LORD's direct command to take a census, an army was being formed for the conquest of Canaan.

3. The census was the inheritance list. (If you have ever been involved in dividing up an inheritance, you know how important those lists are.) Whoever was named on the census list, which was the army list, that man and his family received an inheritance in the Promised Land.

4. The existence of Israel was based upon the promises God made to Abraham, Isaac and Jacob. God promised Abraham: "I will make you into a great nation and I will bless you . . . I swear by myself . . . I will surely bless you and make your descendants as numerous as the stars in the sky and as the sand on the seashore" (Genesis 12:2; 22:15, 17). God also promised Isaac, "I will bless you and increase the number of your descendants" (Genesis 26:24). The same promise was repeated to Jacob; God said, "Your descendants will be like the dust of the earth . . . Be fruitful and increase in number. A nation and a community of nations will come from you" (Genesis 28:14; 35:11). Who can count the stars in the sky or the sand on the seashore or the dust of the earth? God promised Abraham, Isaac and Jacob to make their descendants so numerous that they could not be counted.

In the counting of the hundreds of thousands of soldiers in Israel we see the LORD fulfilling his Word. By faith, Abraham believed God's promise, "and so from this one man, and he as good as dead, came descendants as numerous as the stars in the sky and as countless as the sand on the seashore" (Hebrews 11:12). Moses himself said to the Israelites, "The LORD your God has increased your numbers so that today you are as many as the stars in the sky. May the LORD, the God of your fathers, increase you a thousand times and bless you as he has promised" (Deuteronomy 1:10–11).

5. The census of Israel long ago upon the earth was a shadow or a picture for us of the gathering of the great and glorious army of heaven, "that great multitude of saints, whose names are written in the Lamb's Book of Life" (Revelation 21:2). God's heavenly army is numbered and listed and

sealed tribe by tribe, the number of each tribe totalling 12,000, which is not a literal number, but a number representing perfection (see Revelation 7:1–8). The Israel of God numbers 12,000 × 12 or 144,000—not an actual number, but a symbolic number of perfection. This army of heaven is the final, ultimate fulfillment of God's promise.

The LORD promised Abraham that he would be "a father of many nations" and his wife Sarah would be "the mother of nations" (Genesis 17:5–6, 16). God also promised Jacob that he would be the father, not just of one nation, but "a community of nations" (Genesis 35:11).

God planned to justify the Gentiles by faith and announced the gospel in advance to Abraham: "All nations on earth will be blessed through you" (Genesis 12:3; 13:15; 24:7). "So those who have faith [in Christ] are blessed along with Abraham, the man of faith" (Galatians 3:7–9). The blessing given to Abraham would encompass the whole world through Jesus Christ. We see that the census of Israel in Numbers was just a small earthly glimpse of that great heavenly host that one day would be gathered from all nations on earth.

6. We cannot number all the wonderful works that God has done (Psalm 40:5). We see only the faintest glimmer of who he is and count only the smallest fraction of what he does. But God knows everything about us. God knows us better than we know ourselves. He sees every moment of our lives from beginning to end, and he knows us to the very depths of our souls (Psalm 139:1–16). "Nothing in all creation is hidden from God's sight" (Hebrews 4:13).

God keeps track of human beings because he loves them, just as parents keep careful watch over their little ones. The holy God tells us to look into the night sky filled with stars and he asks us: "To whom will you compare me? Who is my equal? Who created all these? He who brings out the starry host one by one, and calls them each by name. Because of his great power and mighty strength, not one of them is missing" (Isaiah 40:25–26). This same God, who "counts the number of the stars and calls them each by name" (Psalm 147:4), also gives life to his people one by one, and names them, and watches over their lives, so that not one of them is missing.

Jesus taught us that even the little birds are not forgotten by God, so we need not fear that God will forget us. We must not be afraid, for one human being is worth infinitely more to God than whole flocks of sparrows or a whole world full of beautiful birds. Jesus said, "Even the very hairs of your head are all numbered. So don't be afraid" (Matthew 10:29–31; Luke 12:6–7). Do you know the number of hairs on your own head? Have you ever tried to count them? You see, God knows us better than we know ourselves and he keeps far better records of our lives than we do. He hears our sighs; he knows our grief; he feels our pain; he counts our tears; he numbers our journeys; he remembers our sorrows.

God also sees our many sins, but when we believe in Jesus Christ he forgives them all. Not one of our troubles is insignificant to God. We can pray: "O God . . . record my lament. Number my wanderings. List my tears on your scroll and save them in your bottle. Are they not in your book?" (Psalm 56:8). Not a single tear falls from our eyes that God does not see and count. Do we realize how great God's LOVE is for us? Do we realize how wonderful it is to be counted by the LORD? The numbering of the soldiers in Israel's army was another demonstration of God's great love for his people.

7. God knew the number of soldiers in Israel's army, and he knew each one of them by name, but Moses did not have this information. God commanded Moses to take a census of the soldiers in Israel and to keep a written record of that census because every individual soldier in Israel's army was important.

The Israelites were not to be like Cain, who belonged to the Evil One, and said, "Am I my brother's keeper?" (Genesis 4:9). Taking a census—counting the soldiers and listing their names—was a way for the nation to keep watch over the lives of their "brothers" in the army. To keep track of the men who were risking their lives for the community demonstrated love toward them. "We love because God first loved us. And he has given us this command: Whoever loves God must also love his brother" (I John 4:19, 21).

The book of Numbers also deals with Israel's repeated rebellion against God. Not surprisingly, we find that God was keeping careful track of their numerous revolts against him. The people's rebellion reached its culmination in Numbers 14, when God declared that Israel "disobeyed and tested me ten times" (Numbers 14:22). That God keeps account of sin is a sobering and terrifying reality. Not one of our sins escapes God's notice.

But there is hope. In Numbers, when we read of the people's rebellion, we also read of God's compassion. Moses declared God's own Word: "The LORD is slow to anger, abounding in love and forgiving sin and rebellion" (Numbers 14:18).

*If you, O LORD, kept a record of sins,*
*O Lord, who could stand?*
*But with you there is forgiveness;*
*therefore you are feared.*

*O Israel, put your hope in the* LORD,
    *for with the* LORD *is unfailing love*
    *and with him is full redemption.*
*He himself will redeem Israel*
    *from all their sins.*

            *(Psalm 130:3–4, 7–8)*

*Blessed is he,*
    *whose transgressions are forgiven,*
    *whose sins are covered.*
*Blessed is the man*
    *whose sin the* LORD *does not count*
    *against him.*

            *(Psalm 32:1–2)*

Through faith in Christ our sins are covered. In Jesus Christ, not only are our sins forgiven by God, they are also forgotten. Our sins are completely erased from the record, so that they no longer count against us.

*Praise the* LORD, *O my soul.* . . .
*The* LORD *is compassionate and gracious,*
    *slow to anger, abounding in love.*
*He will not always accuse,*
    *nor will he harbor his anger forever;*
*he does not treat us as our sins deserve*
    *or repay us according to our iniquities.*
*For as high as the heavens are above the earth,*
    *so great is his love for those who fear him;*
*as far as the east is from the west,*
    *so far has he removed our transgressions*
    *from us.* . . .
*Praise the* LORD, *O my soul.*

            *(Psalm 103:1, 8–12, 22)*

As with every other book in the Bible, Numbers brings us to our knees in faith and love, with our grateful and thankful hearts overflowing with praise to our God for his great LOVE towards us.

# GOD'S ARMY

- **Numbers 1–2;**
  **9:1–14**
- **Deuteronomy 8:15**

More than a year had passed since the exodus from Egypt, but the Israelites were still in the wilderness at the foot of Mount Sinai. Why? Why had God kept the Israelites waiting in that "dreadful desert" for such a long time? Why wasn't God leading them swiftly and safely into Canaan, the land he had promised to give them?

The Israelites were still waiting because they were not yet prepared to take possession of the Promised Land. It was by faith that they must conquer kingdoms, and their faith was lacking. Before they could fight by faith, they had to learn how to live by faith. During this time in the desert, God was preparing a people for himself, a people who believed in him. Here are some of the ways God strengthened their faith:

1. At the very beginning of their journey in the wilderness, when Israel was camped by the Red Sea, they witnessed God's miraculous deliverance as he made a path for them through the parted waters. The crossing of the Red Sea was salvation for Israel, but destruction for Egypt. This was Israel's baptism, when "they were all baptized . . . in the sea" (I Corinthians 10:2).

2. Day by day in that vast wasteland, the Israelites were learning to trust God to provide for them all the necessities of life. It was a "thirsty and waterless land," a land where that many people should have starved to death or died of thirst, but daily the LORD provided both food and water for them.

3. In that hostile terrain, the Israelites were learning also to trust God to deliver them from evil. That rocky and remote region was filled with venomous snakes and poisonous scorpions. Bands of robbers and murderers hid in those hills; there were whole armies of enemy soldiers who were cruel, wicked, and bloodthirsty. This was also a land inhabited by evil spirits, where not only jackals howled, but demons shrieked in the swirling sand-storms (Ephesians 6:12). There, too, Israel's great enemy, the devil, was prowling around like a roaring lion, looking for someone—or all of them—to devour. The Israelites needed to learn to trust in God to protect them and defend them from all harm.

4. In the desert the Israelites were learning to believe and obey every word that came from the mouth of God. At Mount Sinai they had been given God's Holy Law, the Ten Commandments, that would teach them how to live. Through that law they were learning how to be God's people, a nation holy to the LORD.

5. In the wilderness, God established his covenant with the nation of Israel.

6. In the desert, at the foot of Mount Sinai, the Israelites were learning how to worship the LORD. "The Tabernacle was set up on the first day of the first month in the second year" (Exodus 40:17). During that month the Israelites had been worshipping the LORD according to his commands, with consecrated priests offering morning and evening sacrifices that were pleasing to the LORD. This was just as God had promised Moses before the exodus, when he said, "I will be with you. . . . When you have brought the people out of Egypt, you will worship God on this mountain" (Exodus 3:12), and that is exactly what Israel was doing.

7. During that same month, the LORD spoke to Moses in the Desert of Sinai. God said, "Have the Israelites celebrate the Passover at the appointed time . . . at twilight on the fourteenth day of this month, in accordance with all its rules and regulations" (Numbers 9:1–3). In observing this sacred ceremony, the Israelites would be celebrating the first anniversary of the exodus. One full year had passed since God brought them out of Egypt, out of

the land of slavery. The LORD had commanded Pharaoh, "Let my people go, so they may celebrate a feast to me in the wilderness" (Exodus 5:1). Now the day of their feast had arrived! At last, in the Desert of Sinai, they would hold that festival to the LORD. The Bible records: "The Israelites did everything, just as the LORD commanded Moses" (Numbers 9:5). They celebrated the Feast of Passover in remembrance of the night when God passed over their houses and spared their sons, the night when God set all of them free. This Feast of Passover was their first commemoration service of this great deliverance.

All these things during the past year had strengthened Israel's faith in God. The thirteen months spent in the wasteland had not been a waste. God had been preparing the hearts of his people to fight by faith, which was of utmost importance, to prepare them for the holy war which lay before them.

Of secondary importance was the organization of Israel's army. Now that God's Tabernacle had been erected and the Passover had been celebrated, the LORD again spoke to Moses. On the first day of the second month of the second year, God said, "Take a census of the whole Israelite community, by their clans and families, listing every man by name, one by one." God commanded Moses and Aaron, "Number all the men in Israel twenty years old or more, men who are able to serve in the army." This was not an ordinary census, where the total population of a place was counted and recorded. This census did not include everybody, because this census was really the organization of an army. Soon God would be giving the command: "Forward march, into the Promised Land!" and the army must be ready in every way.

It was an enormous task to take this census, recording all the names of all those men, but God gave Moses and Aaron people to help them. God said, "One man from each tribe, each the head of his family, is to help you." God himself chose these men, telling Moses their names; they were the leaders of their ancestral tribes, the heads of the clans of Israel. So Moses and Aaron took these twelve men, and they called the whole community together. For each tribe, all the men twenty years old or more who were able to serve in the army were listed by name, one by one, according to the records of their clans and families, just as the LORD commanded Moses.

And so it was that in the shadow of the mountain and in the shelter of the desert, God conscripted men into the army of Israel. Far from the battlefield the soldiers were counted and recorded. It was the first physical preparation God's army was making for war (although there had been thirteen months of spiritual preparation). The troops were being assembled and an army was being rallied as the census was taken on that day at Mount Sinai. Here are the numbers of men listed from each tribe:

| | | |
|---|---|---|
| 1. | Reuben | 46,500 soldiers |
| 2. | Simeon | 59,300 soldiers |
| 3. | Gad | 45,650 soldiers |
| 4. | Judah | 74,600 soldiers |
| 5. | Issachar | 54,400 soldiers |
| 6. | Zebulun | 57,400 soldiers |
| 7. | Ephraim | 40,500 soldiers |
| 8. | Manasseh | 32,200 soldiers |
| 9. | Benjamin | 35,400 soldiers |
| 10. | Dan | 62,700 soldiers |
| 11. | Asher | 41,500 soldiers |
| 12. | Naphtali | 53,400 soldiers |

The total number in Israel's army was 603,550 soldiers.

Twelve tribes were listed, but two names were missing. Which two sons of Jacob were not mentioned in the list? One was the third-born son of Jacob, Levi. Why was his tribe not counted? Because the LORD had said to Moses, "You must not count the tribe of Levi or include them in the census of the other Israelites." Instead of being soldiers in Israel's army, they were to be servants in God's house. They were not to carry the bloody weapons of war, but the holy articles for worship. "The Levites are mine," said the LORD. They would have their own census and they would have their own work. God said,

> *Appoint the Levites to be in charge of the Tabernacle of the Testimony—over all its furnishings and everything belonging to it. They are to carry the Tabernacle and all its furnishings; they are to take care of it and encamp around it. Whenever the Tabernacle is to move, the Levites are to take it down, and whenever the Tabernacle is to be set up, the Levites shall do it. Anyone else who goes near it shall be put to death. . . . The Levites are to be responsible for the care of the Tabernacle of the Testimony.*

> *(Numbers 1:50–53)*

The worship of God was not to cease, even in the midst of war; some men would serve the LORD and the nation by fighting, but the Levites would serve the LORD and the nation by caring for the Tabernacle. The worship of God was the very heart and soul of Israel. It was a great honor, a vital task, and a real duty for the Levites to serve in this way.

There was another name missing from the sons of Jacob. Joseph! Where was the favorite son of Jacob? Where was the tribe of Joseph? Remember that Joseph was given a double inheritance. Joseph's two sons, Ephraim and Manasseh, were each numbered as a full tribe in Israel. With the tribe of Levi missing from the army, there would only have been eleven tribes left, except that Joseph was counted twice in his sons, Ephraim and Manasseh, which made it an even twelve again. God had taken care of every detail in the numbering of his people and the ordering of his army.

God then told Moses how the Israelite army was to camp and to march. The LORD said, "The Israelites are to set up their tents by divisions, each man in his own camp under his own standard. The Levites, however, are to set up their tents around the Tabernacle of the Testimony, so that wrath will not fall on the Israelite community." In the center of Israel's camp was the LORD's Tabernacle. Surrounding the Tabernacle were the tents of the Levites, whose duty it was to guard and care for the house of the LORD. Then the rest of Israel, tribe by tribe, camped around the Tabernacle like spokes radiating from the hub of a wheel. Except for the tribe of Levi, who was camped right next to the Tabernacle, all the other tribes were equally close to the LORD.

Each tribe had its own flag that fluttered proudly in its own section of the camp. We do not know what those tribal banners looked like. Perhaps the flags were different colors with different symbols. Perhaps each flag had a different animal on it, such as a lion on Judah's flag, a donkey on Issachar's flag, a serpent on Dan's flag, a deer on Naphtali's flag or a wolf on Benjamin's flag according to the blessings that Jacob gave his sons before he died (see Genesis 49). Whatever those flags looked like, the LORD commanded, "The Israelites are to camp around the Tent of Meeting, some distance from it, each man under his standard with the banners of his family."

God arranged the tribes into four main divisions, like the four main points on a compass. The LORD also told Moses which position each of the twelve tribes was to take, like the twelve numbers on a clock. There could be no grumbling or quarrelling about who should go first or who should go last, who should camp east or who should camp west—for God assigned to each tribe its own position.

EAST—The LORD said, "On the east, toward the sunrise, the divisions of the camp of Judah are to encamp under their standard . . . His division numbers 74,600." Judah was named first, not only because it was the largest tribe, but also because it was the most blessed tribe, the tribe from which Messiah would come. Two other tribes were assigned to the camp of Judah: The LORD said, "The tribe of Issachar will camp next to them . . . His division numbers 54,400. The tribe of Zebulun will be next . . . His division numbers 57,400." The total number of the eastern camp under Judah's commander was 186,400. It was the strongest camp in Israel's army, with the greatest number of soldiers. When it was time to march, the LORD commanded, "They will set out first."

SOUTH—The LORD said, "On the south will be the divisions of the camp of Reuben under their standard . . . His division numbers 46,500." Although Reuben was not one of the largest of the tribes, Reuben was the oldest, the first-born son of Jacob, and so that tribe was honored by being in command of the southern division. Two other tribes were assigned to the camp of Reuben: The LORD said, "The tribe of Simeon will camp next to them . . . His division numbers 59,300. The tribe of Gad will be next . . . His division numbers 45,650." The total number of the southern camp under Reuben's commander was 151,450. The LORD commanded, "They will set out second."

Next came the tribe of Levi. God commanded, "Then the Tent of Meeting and the camp of the Levites will set out in the middle of the camps." In the center of the marching army came the tribe of Levi, carrying the LORD's Tabernacle. Six tribes marched in front of Levi; six tribes marched behind him.

WEST—The LORD said, "On the west will be the divisions of the camp of Ephraim under their standard . . . His division numbers 40,500." Ephraim was the third smallest tribe, in command of the two smallest tribes. Why was Ephraim picked to be a leader? Ephraim was not the largest or oldest tribe of Israel; no, but Ephraim was the most blessed son of Joseph, who was the best loved son of Jacob, so Ephraim was honored by leading the western division of the army. The descendants of Rachel were appointed a place together by God. The LORD said, "The tribe of Manasseh will be next to them . . . His division numbers 32,200. The tribe of Benjamin will be next . . . His division numbers 35,400." The total number of the smallest camp, the western camp, under Ephraim's commander was 108,100. The LORD commanded, "They will set out third."

NORTH—The LORD said, "On the north will be the divisions of the camp of Dan, under their standard . . . His division numbers 62,700." Dan

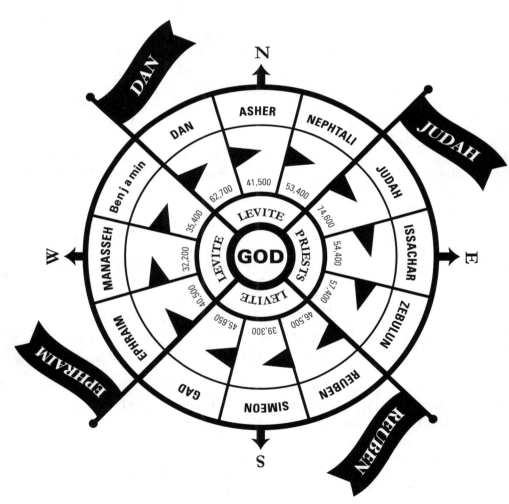

God's arrangement of the tribes as seen in Numbers 2

was last, but not least. Dan was the second largest tribe in Israel, and so he would be in command of the rear guard. The LORD said, "The tribe of Asher will camp next to them . . . His division numbers 41,500. The tribe of Naphtali will be next . . . His division numbers 53,400." The total number of the northern camp, under Dan's commander was 157,600. The LORD commanded, "They will set out last, under their standards."

So the Israelites did everything the LORD commanded Moses. That was the way they camped, and that was the way they marched. Each man had his own place, where he camped and marched under the banner of his tribe, and each tribe had its own assigned place within Israel's army. The men appointed by God to take the census were the same men appointed as officers to lead the troops into battle. Everything and everyone was in place. Israel's army had been put into fighting formation by the Great General of Israel's army—God himself.

The book of Numbers reveals many attributes of our God:

1. He is the LORD of hosts, the LORD of armies. Christ is called "Captain of the Host of the LORD" (KJV) or "Commander of the Army of the LORD" (Joshua 5:14), and Jesus Christ, the Son of God, who gathers his people into a mighty army.

> I looked, and there before me was a white horse! Its rider held a bow, and he was given a crown, and he rode out as a Conqueror bent on conquest . . . I saw heaven standing open and there before me was a white horse, whose rider is called Faithful and True. With justice he judges and makes war . . . His name is the Word of God. The armies of heaven were following him, riding on white horses.
>
> *(Revelation 6:2; 19:11–14)*

2. He is a God who names and numbers. "He counts the number of the stars and calls them each by name" (Psalm 147:4). The LORD took great care to record every soldier, one by one, in the army of Israel because the life of every single person was important to God. Not one of his people can ever be lost, for we are all named and numbered and written in his Book of Life. "Indeed, the very hairs of your head are all numbered, so don't be afraid" (Luke 12:7).

3. He is a faithful God, whose word is true, who fulfills his promises to us. Long ago, when Abraham was an old man with no children at all, God promised to make him into a great nation, with descendants as numerous as the stars in the heavens or the sand on the seashore. At the time of this census in the history of Israel, we can see how God was keeping his word. By then the sons of Abraham were an army, numbering hundreds of thousands of men. One day the number of Abraham's descendants would reach perfection and there would be "a great multitude that no one could count" (Revelation 7:9).

Lesson 2

# GOD'S OWN TRIBE

• **Numbers 3–4; 7–8; 18**

At this time in Israel's history, only Aaron, the high priest, and his remaining two sons, Eleazar and Ithamar, served the LORD as ordained priests. These three men could not possibly do all the work necessary in the religious life of Israel. When it was time to leave Mount Sinai, they could not possibly take care of taking down and setting up God's Tent or transporting the Tabernacle all by themselves. They needed help. So the LORD said to Moses, "Bring the tribe of Levi and present them to Aaron the priest to assist him. They are to perform duties for him and for the whole Israelite community at the Tent of Meeting by doing the work of the Tabernacle . . . Give the Levites to Aaron and his sons." Only Aaron and his sons, however, were appointed by God to serve as priests. Any unauthorized person (even their assistants, the Levites) who approached the sanctuary "must be put to death" (Numbers 3:5–10).

The Levites were a gift to the priests to help them with the work of the Tabernacle. Later God said to Aaron, the high priest,

*Bring your fellow Levites from your ancestral tribe to join you
and assist you when you and your sons [the priests] minister
before the Tent of the Testimony. They [the Levites] are
responsible to you and are to perform all the duties of the
Tent, but they must not go near the furnishings of the
sanctuary or the altar, or both they and you will die. They are
to join you and be responsible for the care of the Tent of
Meeting—all the work at the Tent—and no one else may
come near where you are.*

*You [the priests] are to be responsible for the care of the
sanctuary and altar, so that wrath will not fall upon the
Israelites again. I myself have selected your fellow Levites
from among the Israelites as a gift to you, dedicated to the
LORD, to do the work at the Tent of Meeting. But only you
and your sons may serve as priests in connection with
everything at the altar and inside the curtain. I am giving
you the service of the priesthood as a gift. Anyone else who
comes near the sanctuary must be put to death.*

*(Numbers 18:2–7)*

The Lord also said to Moses, "I have taken the Levites from among the
Israelites in place of the first male offspring of every Israelite woman. The
Levites are mine, for all the firstborn are mine. When I struck down all the
firstborn in Egypt, I set apart for myself every firstborn in Israel . . . They are
to be mine. I am the Lord" (Numbers 3:11–12).

Then God commanded Moses to take another census, just for the tribe
of Levi. In the Desert of Sinai the LORD said, "Count the Levites by their
families and clans. Count every male a month old or more" (Numbers 3:15).
So Moses counted them, as he was commanded by the word of the LORD.
Levi had three sons—Gershon, Kohath, and Merari—whose descendants became the three main clans in the tribe of Levi. The number of all the males
a month old or more in the clan of Gershon was 7,500. The number of all
the males a month old or more in the clan of Kohath was 8,600. The number of all the males a month old or more in the clan of Merari was 6,200.
The total number of Levites counted at the LORD's command was 22,000.

Then the LORD commanded Moses to take another census. God said,
"Count all the firstborn Israelite males who are a month old or more and

make a list of their names. Take the Levites for me in place of all the first-born of the Israelites . . . I am the LORD" (Numbers 3:40–41). So Moses counted all the firstborn males in the other tribes, and the number was almost the same. There were 22,273 firstborn males. It was almost an even trade!

What would happen to the extra 273 men/boys from the other tribes? Would God take them to serve in the Tabernacle along with the Levites? No, the LORD said they could be redeemed or bought back with money, which would then be given to the priests. So Moses collected the redemption money from the extra Israelites who had no Levite to redeem them, and he gave this money to Aaron and his sons.

The LORD then commanded that a census be taken for each of the clans of Levi. This time God said to count all the men from thirty to fifty years of age. They would be the ones who came to serve in the work in the Tent of Meeting.

### The Gershonites

The LORD said to Moses, "Take a census also of the Gershonites by their families and clans. Count all the men thirty to fifty years of age who come to serve in the work at the Tent of Meeting" (Numbers 4:21–22). The number of Gershonite men who were counted in this census was 2,630. The Gershonite clans were to camp on the west, behind the Tabernacle. The Gershonites were responsible for the Tabernacle, for maintaining and transporting all the curtains and all the coverings and everything related to their use. God said, "The Gershonites are to do all that needs to be done with these things. All their service, whether carrying or doing other work, is to be done under the direction of Aaron and his sons. You shall assign to them as their responsibility all they are to carry. This is the service of the Gershonite clans at the Tent of Meeting" (Numbers 4:21–28).

### The Kohathites

The LORD said to Moses and Aaron, "Take a census of the Kohathite branch of the Levites by their clans and families. Count all the men thirty to fifty years of age who come to serve in the work in the Tent of Meeting" (Numbers 4:2–3). The number of Kohathite men who were counted in this census was 2,750. The Kohathite clans were to camp on the south side of the Tabernacle.

The Kohathites were responsible for the care of the sanctuary, including the ark, the table, the lampstand, the altars, and all the articles of the sanctuary used in ministering. God said, "This is the work of the Kohathites in the Tent of Meeting: the care of the most holy things." When Israel's camp was going to move, it was the Kohathites who would carry the most holy things upon their shoulders. However, there was a problem. How could these men come near these most holy things? They were not allowed to touch them or even look at them, not even for a moment, lest they die. Only the priests were allowed in the sanctuary and only the high priest, once a year, was allowed to enter the Most Holy Place, the Holy of Holies. How were they going to carry these things if they were not allowed to look at them or touch them? The LORD said to Moses and Aaron, "See that the Kohathite tribal clans are not cut off from the Levites." So that the Kohathites might live and not die when they came near the most holy things, God commanded the priests to do the following things for them:

a. The priests must cover everything from their sight. The ark, the table, the lampstand, the altars, and all the articles used for ministering in the sanctuary must be wrapped in blue, scarlet or purple cloth and then covered with the hides of sea cows. The Kohathites must not look at the holy things, even for a moment, or they would die. (These coverings would also protect the holy things from damage when they were traveling.)

b. The priests were to insert the poles into the different furnishings or put the different articles on carrying frames, so that the Kohathites would not touch anything. God said, "After Aaron and his sons have finished covering the holy furnishings and all the holy articles, and when the camp is ready to move, the Kohathites are to come and do the carrying. But they must not touch the holy things or they will die." Again and again God commanded the priests: Cover the ark and put the poles in place. Cover the table and puts its poles in place. Cover the lampstand and put it on a carrying frame. Cover the gold altar and put its poles in place. Cover all the articles and put them on a carrying frame. Cover the bronze altar and put its poles in place. The lives of the Kohathites depended upon the priests obeying these commands, for they must not see or touch anything.

c. The Kohathites must take their orders from the priests. They must not take for themselves the honor of carrying a particular holy thing. God said, "Aaron and his sons are to go into the sanctuary and assign to each man his work and what he is to carry" (Numbers 4:1–20).

## The Merarites

The LORD also commanded Moses to take a census of the Merarites by their clans and families. God said, "Count all the men from thirty to fifty years of age, who come to serve in the work at the Tent of Meeting" (Numbers 4:29–30). The number of Merarite men who were counted in this census was 3,200. The Merarite clans were to camp on the north side of the Tabernacle.

The Merarites were appointed to carry and care for the frames of the Tabernacle, its crossbars, posts, bases, pegs and ropes with all its equipment and everything related to their use. God said, "This is the service of the Merarite clans as they work at the Tent of Meeting" (Numbers 4:29–33).

Moses and Aaron and his sons were to camp to the east of the Tabernacle, toward the sunrise, in front of the Tent of Meeting. They were responsible for the care of the sanctuary on behalf of the Israelites. Anyone else who approached the sanctuary was to be put to death.

Thus Moses and Aaron and the leaders of Israel counted the Levites clan by clan according to the LORD's command. All the men from thirty to fifty years of age who came to do the work of serving and carrying the Tent of Meeting numbered a total of 8,580 men. At the LORD's command, each was assigned his work and told what to carry. Thus they were counted, as the LORD commanded Moses.

Even with so many men at work, transporting the LORD's Tabernacle from place to place in the wilderness was a huge undertaking. Thankfully, the leaders of the twelve tribes of Israel (the same ones who took the census and were the captains of the troops) made offerings to the LORD that would help with this work. At the Tabernacle's consecration, when Moses sprinkled everything in it with oil and blood (Leviticus 8:10–11, 15), these men brought as their gifts before the LORD six covered carts and twelve oxen, which they presented before the Tabernacle. The LORD said to Moses, "Accept these [gifts] from them, that they may be used in the work at the Tent of Meeting. Give them to the Levites, as each man's work requires" (Numbers 7:4–5).

So Moses gave two carts and four oxen to the Gershonites, who were to transport the Tabernacle's coverings, and he gave four carts and eight oxen to the Merarites, whose duty it was to transport the heavy posts and beams of the Tabernacle, but Moses did not give the Kohathites anything, because they had to carry the holy things on their own shoulders.

At the consecration of the altar, when it was anointed with blood and oil, these same leaders of the twelve tribes of Israel brought offerings for its dedication and presented them before the altar. The LORD commanded Moses: "Each day one leader is to bring his offering for the dedication of the altar" (Numbers 7:11). These tribal leaders brought their offerings day by day in the marching order of the tribes:

| | |
|---|---|
| Day 1 | The leader of Judah brought his offering. |
| Day 2 | The leader of Issachar brought his offering. |
| Day 3 | The leader of Zebulun brought his offering. |
| Day 4 | The leader of Reuben brought his offering. |
| Day 5 | The leader of Simeon brought his offering. |
| Day 6 | The leader of Gad brought his offering. |
| Day 7 | The leader of Ephraim brought his offering. |
| Day 8 | The leader of Manasseh brought his offering. |
| Day 9 | The leader of Benjamin brought his offering. |
| Day 10 | The leader of Dan brought his offering. |
| Day 11 | The leader of Asher brought his offering. |
| Day 12 | The leader of Naphtali brought his offering. |

Each day the offering was the same: one silver plate and one silver bowl, each filled with fine flour mixed with oil as a grain offering; one gold dish filled with incense; one bull, one ram and one male lamb for a burnt offering; one male goat for a sin offering; and two oxen, five rams, five male goats and five male lambs, to be sacrificed as a fellowship offering. These were the offerings of the Israelite leaders for the dedication of the altar when it was anointed, which was when the priests were consecrated for their sacred service.

The priests, the Tabernacle and everything in it, including the altar, had been consecrated earlier (see Leviticus 8). The priests and the Tabernacle had already been set apart for holy service, but now the Levites themselves must be consecrated for their new work. The LORD said to Moses, "Take the Levites from among the other Israelites and make them ceremonially clean. To purify them, do this:

1. Sprinkle the water of cleansing on them. Have them shave their whole bodies and wash their clothes, and so purify themselves."

2. Then there must be a holy convocation. God said, "Bring the Levites to the front of the Tent of Meeting and assemble the whole Israelite community. You are to bring the Levites before the LORD, and the Israelites are to lay their hands on them. Aaron is to present the Levites before the LORD as a wave offering from the Israelites, so that they may be ready to do the work of the LORD" (Numbers 8:9–11). The Levites were offered to God as "living sacrifices, holy and pleasing to God" (Romans 12:1).

3. But the Levites were not ready yet to begin the work of the LORD. They had only been cleansed with water. To be truly clean in God's sight, they had to be cleansed not only with water, but also with blood! The Levites had to present two young bulls, one as a sin offering and the other as a burnt offering to the LORD. The Levites were to lay their hands on the heads of these two bulls and then the bulls would be sacrificed to make atonement for the Levites. Without the shedding of blood there could be no purification from sin.

God said:

> In this way you are to set the Levites apart from the other Israelites, and the Levites will be mine. After you have purified the Levites [with both water and blood] and presented them as a wave offering, they are to come to do their work at the Tent of Meeting. They are the Israelites who are to be given wholly to me. I have taken them as my own in place of the firstborn, the first male offspring from every Israelite woman. Every firstborn male in Israel, whether man or animal, is mine. When I struck down all the firstborn in Egypt, I set them apart for myself. And I have taken the Levites in place of all the firstborn sons in Israel. Of all the Israelites, I have given the Levites as gifts to Aaron and his sons to do the work at the Tent of Meeting on behalf of the Israelites to make atonement for them, so that no plague will strike the Israelites when they go near the sanctuary.

> (Numbers 8:14–19)

So Moses, Aaron and the whole Israelite community did with the Levites just as the LORD commanded. After that, the Levites came to do their work at the Tent of Meeting, under the supervision of the priests. They were then able to care for God's Tabernacle whenever they were camping or moving. Very soon the Israelites would be traveling again, leaving their campground at the foot of Mount Sinai and pressing forward to the Promised Land. Finally, everything was ready for the journey. God's army was ready and so was God's own tribe of men, the Levites, who would carry and care for the Tabernacle of the LORD.

# GOD'S SPECIAL SERVANTS

• Numbers 6:1–21

While the men of the tribe of Levi were set apart for the Lord's work, either as priests for the people or servants at the Tabernacle, God also provided the opportunity for any man or woman from any tribe in Israel to be his special servant. Any man or woman could make a special vow, a vow of separation to the Lord, and for a certain length of time that person could single-mindedly and whole-heartedly devote himself or herself to the worship and service of God. These people were known as Nazarites (the word means "separated"). These Nazarite men and women separated themselves from the rest of Israel by their vows to lead lives of superlative holiness. All the days of their separation they were "holy unto the Lord" (Numbers 6:8 KJV). Their righteousness was "brighter than snow and whiter than milk" (Lamentations 4:7). Like sparkling rubies or sapphires, the Nazarites were the jewels of Israel and the ornaments of the nation. God was blessing Israel when he raised up Nazarites from among the people (Amos 2:11).

There were three requirements for a Nazarite:

1. A Nazarite must abstain from wine. The LORD instructed Moses to tell the people, "If a man or woman wants to make a special vow, a vow of separation to the LORD as a Nazarite, he must abstain from wine and other fermented drink . . . He must not drink grape juice or eat grapes or raisins. As long as he is a Nazarite, he must not eat anything that comes from the grapevine, not even the seeds or the skin" (Numbers 6:1–4). The Israelites were allowed to drink wine, but they were not to get drunk. However, the Nazarites had to go beyond the ordinary requirements of holiness. Nazarites were not allowed to drink even a sip of wine or taste a single grape, not even one little raisin or one tiny seed! They could not even sprinkle some wine vinegar on their salad. It was a sign that the vows of God were upon them.

In the New Testament we read of a famous Nazarite called John the Baptist who was set apart for God before he was born. An angel of the Lord appeared to his father, a priest, and announced the coming of this son, who had not yet been conceived. About this child the angel said, "He will be a joy and delight to you, and many will rejoice because of his birth, for he will be great in the sight of the Lord. He is never to take wine or other fermented drink, and he will be filled with the Holy Spirit even from his mother's womb. Many of the people of Israel he will bring back to the Lord their God . . . to make ready a people for the Lord" (Luke 1:11–17). John the Baptist drank no wine because he was set apart by God as a Nazarite from birth. His life was one of self-denial. Fine clothes and rich foods were not part of his austere lifestyle. He wore poor, rough clothes and ate plain, wild food. "John wore clothing made of camel's hair . . . and he ate locusts and wild honey" (Mark 1:6). His life was not devoted to his own pleasure, but to God's service. "John the Baptist came neither eating bread nor drinking wine" (Luke 7:33), but he lived in the desert praying and preaching and baptizing. He was a Nazarite indeed!

2. The second requirement for a Nazarite was that he must not cut his hair. The LORD said to Moses, "During the entire period of his vow of separation no razor may be used on his head. He must be holy until the period of his separation is over; he must let the hair of his head grow long" (Numbers 6:5).

In the Old Testament, the most famous Nazarite was a man named Samson from the tribe of Dan. Samson was also set apart by God to be a Nazarite before he was born. Even in his mother's womb, he had to abstain from wine. Not even a trace of alcohol imbibed through the umbilical cord was allowed to reach the tiny Nazarite within her womb. An angel of the Lord appeared to his mother and said, "You are sterile and childless, but you are going to conceive and have a son. Now see to it that you drink no wine or other fermented drink and that you do not eat anything unclean, because you will conceive and give birth to a son. No razor may be used on his head, because the boy is to be a Nazarite, set apart to God from birth, and he will begin the deliverance of Israel" (Judges 13:3–5).

Israel was delivered by the strength of God's Spirit working through Samson, but woven into this history was the story of Samson's hair, which had never been cut because he had been a Nazarite from birth. (Read Judges 13–16 for the amazing account of Samson's life.) The secret of Samson's strength was not his long hair, but what that long hair represented—his separation and consecration to God as a Nazarite.

So we see that not only adults, but also little children (even unborn children still within their mothers' wombs) could be Nazarites. Another little boy who was a Nazarite from birth was Samuel, the son of Hannah, from the tribe of Ephraim. For years Hannah was without any children, which made her very sad. One day, when she was weeping and praying at God's Tabernacle, she made this vow: "O LORD Almighty, if you will only look upon your servant's misery and remember me, and not forget your servant but give her a son, then I will give him to the LORD for all the days of his life, and no razor will ever be used on his head" (I Samuel 1:11). By this vow Hannah promised that her child would be a Nazarite for his whole life. God heard Hannah's prayer and her vow. God gave her a little boy whom she named Samuel ("heard of God"), because she asked the LORD for him. When Samuel was still a very little boy, Hannah took him to God's Tabernacle to present him to the LORD. Hannah said, "I prayed for this child, and the LORD has granted me what I asked of him. So now I give him to the LORD. For his whole life he will be given over to the LORD" (I Samuel 1:27–28). When his mother and father went home, the little boy Samuel stayed at God's Tabernacle and lived there, ministering before the LORD as a servant of the old priest. Samuel wore a tiny priest's robe which his mother made for him, and he worked in the Tabernacle (although he was not a Levite). Samuel even slept in the Tabernacle, for God's house was Samuel's home. Samuel grew up there in the presence of the LORD, and God first spoke to Samuel when he was just a child. The Bible declares that "the LORD was with Samuel as he grew up," and there in the Tabernacle the LORD "revealed himself to Samuel through his word" (1 Samuel 3:19–21). Eventually, all Israel recognized that Samuel was a prophet of the LORD. But it all began when Samuel's mother dedicated him to the LORD, vowing that he would be a Nazarite for his whole life.

3. The third requirement for the Nazarite was that he could not come into contact with any dead body. Just like the priests, he could not attend a funeral, even that of a close relative. God said, "Throughout the period of his separation to the Lord he must not go near a dead body. Even if his own father or mother or brother or sister dies, he must not make himself ceremonially unclean on account of them, because the symbol of his separation to God [his long hair] is on his head" (Numbers 6:6–7). A Nazarite must keep himself or herself pure and undefiled.

This was the law for the Nazarite. The Nazarite had to fulfill these requirements perfectly throughout the time of his or her separation. If a Nazarite accidentally broke one of these requirements, then he was required to begin again the time span that he vowed to set himself apart for God.

When the Nazarite's vow was properly completed, and the period of his separation was accomplished according to all God's commands, then he had to bring offerings to the LORD at the Tent of Meeting. Three lambs were to be sacrificed to the LORD — one for a burnt offering, one for a sin offering, and one for a peace offering (together with the grain and drink offerings). Taking a Nazarite vow and fulfilling its requirements perfectly did not make any person righteous in the sight of God. "There is no one righteous, no, not one," not even a Nazarite. "No one will be declared righteous in God's sight by observing the law," not even the Nazarite laws (Romans 3:10, 20). Even the sins of a Nazarite had to be cleansed by the Old Covenant sacrifices, which pointed to the New Covenant Sacrifice — the final Sacrifice of the Son of God on the cross. Even a Nazarite was cleansed from sin only by the blood of Christ.

There was one final thing a Nazarite was required to do to complete his period of separation and fulfill his vow to God. At the entrance to the Tent of Meeting, the Nazarite shaved off the hair that he had dedicated and burned it in the altar's fire beneath the peace offering. How difficult this final step must have been for the women, whose hair was their glory. The priest would then make wave offerings before the LORD. Then the Nazarite's vow was terminated, and the man or woman could return to a normal life. They were still to obey the Law of God and lead a holy life, but they could enjoy the fruit of the vine or cut their hair to whatever length they wanted or attend the funeral of a friend, for they were no longer under the vows of a Nazarite.

The Nazarite was one more picture for the Israelites, one more preview, one more prophecy, pointing them to the Holy One whom God would one day send to them and to the world. Yes, the Nazarites were a shadowy reflection of the coming Righteous One—even Jesus Christ our Lord. The Nazarites' separation from the common people pointed to Jesus Christ, who was separated from all humanity by his sinlessness. He alone was "set apart from sinners" (Hebrews 7:26). He alone was perfectly pure, blameless and undefiled. Jesus Christ was the only human being whose life was totally devoted to God and completely separated from sin. Christ alone perfectly fulfilled his vows and all God's laws. Jesus was the real Nazarite, the true Nazarite. All the others who came before him were but imperfect reflections.

Should we be Nazarites now, taking those same vows as the saints of old? No. "Now a righteousness from God, apart from the law, has been made known . . . This righteousness from God comes through faith in Jesus Christ to all who believe . . . All have sinned and fall short of the glory of God, and are justified freely by his grace through the redemption that came by Christ Jesus" (Romans 3:21–24). There is only one way to be righteous in God's sight, and that is through faith in Jesus Christ. Every person who believes in him—man or woman, child or adult, Jew or Gentile—should dedicate himself or herself to lead a holy life, not by observing the outward ceremonial laws of the Old Testament, but by leading a life of faith and love.

The New Testament requirements for the people of God are much more stringent than the Nazarite vows. Even our hearts must be pure. We must abstain from all sinful desires which war against our souls (I Peter 2:11). God has "saved us and called us to a holy life" (II Timothy 1:9). "As obedient children, do not conform to the evil desires you had when you lived in ignorance. But just as he who called you is holy, so be holy in all that you do" (I Peter 1:14–15). For the LORD has said, "Be holy, because I am holy" (I Peter 1:16). God calls us to separate ourselves from the sin in ourselves and in this world. In the New Testament God calls all his people to be separate, just as the Nazarites were:

> *"Therefore come out from them*
> > *and be separate," says the Lord.*
> *"Touch no unclean thing,*
> > *and I will receive you."*
> *"I will be a Father to you,*
> > *and you will be my sons and daughters,"*
> > *says the Lord Almighty.*

(II Corinthians 6:17–18)

# FORWARD MARCH!

• Numbers 9:15–10:36

On the twentieth day of the second month of the second year (after the exodus from Egypt), the Israelites set out again on their journey—after a very long delay. They had been camping in the Desert of Sinai at the foot of the mountain for almost a year (see Exodus 19:1–2; Numbers 10:11). Perhaps the people were sad to go. They had been camping there for so long that this place had begun to feel like home, and many amazing things had happened there. On Mount Sinai, God had revealed his Glory to Israel; from Mount Sinai, God had spoken the Ten Commandments to them; on that mountain Moses had met with God, and down its rugged slopes Moses had carried the stone tablets; at Mount Sinai, God had made a covenant with Israel; and in the shadow of that mountain the people had made the Tabernacle and worshipped the LORD, according to all God's laws. Yes, many good and great things had happened at Mount Sinai, but now they would be leaving there, never to return. As they traveled north, towards the Promised Land, Mount Sinai would be far behind them, growing smaller and smaller in the distance. Perhaps the people were scared to go. At Mount Sinai, many blessings had come to them. Why did they have to leave now? How did they know that it really was time to go?

This was how Israel knew it was time to leave Mount Sinai:

1. This was such an important move that God spoke to Moses. The LORD said, "You have stayed long enough at this mountain. Break camp and advance . . . See, I have given you this land. Go in and take possession of the land that the LORD swore he would give to your fathers — to Abraham, Isaac and Jacob — and to their descendants after them" (Deuteronomy 1:6–8). God would not always speak to Moses about when they should leave a place, but this time Israel would set forth at the command of the LORD.

2. God had a very special signal for the Israelites to tell them when it was time to leave and when it was time to rest. Ever since the Tabernacle had been set up, the cloud of God's presence had hovered over it. At night this cloud looked like fire, so God's signal was clearly visible both by day and by night. The Israelites always had to be ready to move, whenever God commanded, whether it was the middle of the day or the middle of the night. Whenever the cloud lifted from above the Tent, that was the signal for the Israelites to set out, and whenever the cloud settled down on the Tent, that was the signal for the Israelites to encamp. When the cloud remained over the Tabernacle a long time, the Israelites were to obey the LORD's command and not set out at all. Sometimes the cloud stayed over the Tabernacle just one night, and when it lifted early the next morning, the Israelites would depart again. Whether the cloud stayed over the Tabernacle for just one day or one month or one year, the Israelites remained in camp and did not set out. But when it lifted, whatever time that was, they had to obey the LORD and break camp.

3. The LORD had commanded Moses to make two trumpets of hammered silver, which Israel's two priests, the sons of Aaron, were to blow as a signal for the camps to set out (later, there would be more trumpets, when there were more priests). At the first blast of the trumpet, Judah's camp on the east was to set out. At the second blast of the trumpet, Reuben's camp on the south was to set out. The third trumpet blast was the signal for Ephraim's camp on the west. The final trumpet blast was for Dan's camp on the north.

So, on the twentieth day of the second month of the second year, at the foot of Mount Sinai, things began to happen. The cloud that covered the Tabernacle of the Testimony lifted. The whole camp of Israel became alive with activity. Hundreds of thousands of tents had to be taken down and packed up, including the LORD's Tabernacle. First, the priests covered the most holy things and prepared them for transport. Then the Levites began taking down the curtains and the coverings; they began lifting the posts and the pegs; and they began loading all these things into the ox carts. Every Levite knew his work assignment. Then suddenly, there was a blast on the trumpet! That was the signal for Judah. Their tribe's flag was lifted high and the whole eastern camp began to move forward. Next came some of the Levites, the ones caring for the Tabernacle in the six ox carts. They went ahead of the rest of their tribe, so that the Tabernacle could be set up by the time the holy things arrived. Then there was a second trumpet blast. The flag of Reuben was lifted up and the whole southern camp began to move. In the middle of Israel's procession came the Ark of the Covenant and the other holy things, being borne on the shoulders of the Levites. The priests sounded the trumpet a third time. Now Ephraim's flag was hoisted on high and the entire western camp began to march. Finally came the last trumpet blast, and the flag of Dan was raised. The soldiers of Dan were the last to march forth since they were the rearguard, protecting the people at the end.

Moses also asked a Midianite who had lived his entire life in that rugged region to be their guide. It was a vast wilderness, a "dreadful desert" filled with all kinds of dangers, but this man knew how to survive in those harsh conditions. The information this man possessed about their environment (such as how to face the weather or where to find the water) would be extremely valuable for Moses as he led this multitude of people on their way. Because Moses asked for human help, it did not mean that he trusted any less in Divine help, it did not mean that he trusted any less in God's extraordinary and supernatural provisions for his people. Moses was a man full of faith, who trusted in the goodness and greatness of God to provide everything they needed. Moses asked this man to join them because he knew he could be of help to Israel.

Who was this man? Moses asked a man he trusted, his brother-in-law, Hobab, the son of Jethro and the brother of his wife, Zipporah. Moses said to Hobab, "We are setting out for the place about which the LORD said, 'I will give it to you.' Come with us and we will treat you well, for the LORD has promised good things to Israel." What assurance Moses had in the Word of God!

But Hobab answered, "No, I will not go; I am going back to my own land and my own people." Moses tried to convince him to go, saying, "Please do not leave us. You know where we should camp in the desert, and you can be our eyes." Yes, this man would see things in that wasteland—all sorts of potential dangers—that the rest of them would not notice. "Please do not leave us," said Moses. "If you come with us, we will share with you whatever good things the LORD gives us." This desert man was wanted; he was needed; and he would be rewarded. How great was Moses' faith in the goodness and faithfulness of his God. If silence meant consent, then Moses persuaded Hobab and he went with Israel to be their guide.

Ultimately, though, the LORD himself was guiding Israel. Moses was wisely enlisting the help of Hobab, but Moses was also humbly trusting in the LORD. By faith, believing the promise of God, Moses could say, "The LORD is with me; I will not be afraid. . . . The LORD is with me; he is my helper. . . . It is better to take refuge in the LORD, than to trust in man" (Psalm 118:6–8), even the most noble or powerful or knowledgeable of men.

Before all the people, God was guiding; behind all the people, God was guarding. Ultimately, it was not the army of Israel that would keep them safe. The people were not to trust in the numbers of their soldiers, but in the mercies of their God. Neither Judah's vanguard nor Dan's rearguard could save them from their enemies. The LORD himself would keep the people safe. Each Israelite who was marching forth by faith could say, O LORD, "You hem me in—behind and before; you have laid your hand upon me" (Psalm 139:5). And at night, when the people stopped to rest, even the smallest child in the poorest tent could pray, "I will lie down and sleep in peace, for you alone, O LORD, make me dwell in safety" (Psalm 4:8).

Moses was also covering the people with the protection of his prayers. Whenever they started or ended a segment of their journey, Moses prayed. Whenever the ark set out, Moses prayed, "Rise up, O LORD! May your enemies be scattered; may your foes flee before you." And whenever the ark came to rest, Moses prayed, "Return, O LORD, to the countless thousands of Israel." Moses was relying on the LORD, not the legions of Israel, to protect them. Moses knew that their strength was not in their numbers, but in God.

Each morning and evening, when sacrifices were offered to the LORD in worship, the priests also prayed for the people and pronounced this blessing upon them:

> The LORD bless you
> and keep you;
> the LORD make his face shine upon you
> and be gracious to you;
> the LORD turn his face toward you
> and give you peace.

> (Numbers 6:24–26)

God promised, "So they will put my name on the Israelites, and I will bless them" (Numbers 6:27).

Thus the Israelites set out from Mount Sinai. On the twentieth day of the second month of the second year they left the Mountain of the LORD and began their journey toward the Promised Land. A year earlier they had arrived there as a band of runaway slaves who had set up their refugee camp in the middle of nowhere. Now they were an organized army. It was an amazing transformation! They were leaving Mount Sinai with God's Law and true worship. They were also leaving with Moses' prayers and the priests' blessings. They were leaving with their own tents, but also with God's Tabernacle. Most importantly, they were leaving with the LORD. Yes, God himself would journey with them. When they set out from Mount Sinai Camp that day, the cloud of the LORD covered them and for those first three days, the Ark of the Covenant of the LORD went before them to find them a place to rest.

The LORD commanded the Israelites: "Advance into the hill country of the Amorites" (Deuteronomy 1:7). By God's command they were pressing forward by faith, marching towards enemy territory. They had to believe that God would watch over their lives. By faith they could say:

> I lift up my eyes to the hills—
> where does my help come from?
> My help comes from the LORD,
> the Maker of heaven and earth.
> He will not let your foot slip—
> he who watches over you will not slumber;

*indeed, he who watches over Israel*
*     will neither slumber nor sleep.*
*The LORD watches over you—*
*     the LORD is your shade at your right hand;*
*the sun will not harm you by day,*
*     nor the moon by night.*
*The LORD will keep you from all harm—*
*     he will watch over your life;*
*the LORD will watch over your coming and going*
*     both now and forevermore.*

*(Psalm 121)*

# GRUMBLING AND COMPLAINING

**· Numbers 11:1–3**

The whole camp of Israel left Mount Sinai and began their journey northward to the Promised Land. Life became harder now as they traveled from place to place in the wilderness. Now every morning (whenever the cloud above the Tabernacle lifted) they had to take down their tents; now every evening (whenever the cloud settled) they had to set them up again, and all day long they marched through a rough and rugged region. However, in spite of all the hardships of their journey, they had many reasons to rejoice:

1. First and foremost, the LORD was with them. Whatever hardships they faced on their journey, they did not face alone, for God was with them. There was not a single hardship that should have caused the praise of God to cease in Israel's camp for even a moment. The resolve of each person's heart should have been: "I will extol the LORD at all times; his praise will always be on my lips" (Psalm 34:1). Any and every difficulty should have been faced with joy in the LORD. "Rejoice in the Lord always. I will say it again: Rejoice! Let your forbearance [or perseverance] be evident to all. The Lord is near" (Philippians 4:4–5). God was near

them. How happy they should have been. God's Tabernacle was set up among their tents in the very center of their campground. "How blessed are the people whose God is the LORD" (Psalm 144:15).

2. Because God was with them they had nothing to fear. "Do not be anxious about anything, but in everything, by prayer and petition, with thanksgiving, present your requests to God" (Philippians 4:6). This should have been a stress-free march and a worry-free journey, marked by joy, thanks, peace and prayer, not fear. God was guiding them and guarding them and giving to them in that wilderness. The people could see for themselves that the LORD was leading them. How comforting it must have been to see the cloud's procession before them by day and the fire's protection over them by night. There was no need to fear being lost in the wilderness, for God was guiding them, and there was no need to fear being killed in the wilderness, for God was guarding them. They also had no reason to worry about what they would eat or what they would drink, no reason to fear starving to death or dying of thirst in the wilderness, for daily they could see (and taste) the provision of the LORD. Every night the LORD sent them bread from heaven and every day they gathered the manna, which was both nutritious and delicious. They had nothing to fear. They only had to live by faith. They only had to rejoice in the LORD and give thanks to God.

3. The Israelites had God's Word to strengthen them and God's Law to govern them. This was their national treasure, "more precious than thousands of pieces of silver and gold" (Psalm 119:72).

4. The Israelites participated in the true worship of the Living God. What a blessing. Daily, both morning and evening, sacrifices were offered to atone for their sins. Although the Son of God had not yet come to save them, nevertheless, the Israelites had the shadowy preview of his perfect and final sacrifice. That perfect sacrifice would be sufficient to secure for them, by faith, the forgiveness of their sins. One of the hardships the Israelites did not have to face on their journey was the unbearable burden of carrying their own sins. The forgiveness of their sins was a reality, and in that, the people should always rejoice. They should always praise the LORD for that great and gracious gift.

5. The people had the Sabbath Day, a holy day set aside for the worship of God. The people had a day of rest, one day in seven when they could be refreshed and restored from the hardships of their journey in the wilderness.

This regular time of rest and relaxation was a gift from God. Even in that barren wasteland the Israelites had regular feast days, holidays, festivals and celebrations, all of which made their life in the desert a full and rich experience.

6. The people had good leaders. They had Moses, who was no ordinary man. He was exceptional! Moses talked with God, as a man talks to his friend. The people also had priests, elders and commanders to lead them through the wilderness. This, too, should have been a great comfort for them and a cause for thanks and praise.

7. The people had each other. They were not like their forefather Jacob, who traveled through the wilderness as a fugitive, completely alone. No, the Israelites had numbers. They were a whole nation of people, protected by their own army of soldiers. They could rejoice that they were traveling with friends, neighbors and relatives. They were God's own people, and so they could help, comfort and encourage one another. This was also a great blessing.

8. The Israelites were free, and they could rejoice in that freedom. They were no longer slaves, for God had delivered them from their terrible bondage in Egypt. No longer did they hear the cracking of whips or the rattling of chains or the cursing of guards. No longer did they face the back-breaking work or heart-rending laws of their masters. Never again would an evil Pharaoh command them to drown their children in the Nile River. God had seen all their misery—all the shame and grief and toil and dread and pain of their slavery—and it was far behind them. God had delivered them from evil and now they were walking through the wilderness as a free people. Now the burdens the people carried were their own belongings, and so the load was not too heavy. Now the work they did was for themselves and their own families and their own people, and so the labor was not too hard. With uplifted heads they could walk through the wilderness; they could even sing and dance in that desert, because God had set them free.

9. When people lose hope, they lose everything. People shrivel up and die if they have no hope. "Where there is no vision, the people perish" (Proverbs 29:18 KJV), but these people had God's revelation, which brought hope and life. They had a future in front of them. They were not destined to wander endlessly through this wilderness. There was a Promised Land

before them, a good land, a land flowing with milk and honey. As Moses testified, "The LORD has promised good things to Israel" (Numbers 10:29), and they had every reason to believe in God's promises, to hope in God's Word, and to rejoice in what lay ahead of them.

Sadly, the Israelites did not count these blessings. They had only been traveling for three days when the hardships of their journey began to bother them. These were just small discomforts and minor difficulties along the way, just "light and momentary afflictions" (II Corinthians 4:17), troubles so slight that they were not even worth mentioning or recording, but the Israelites focused on them and forgot about all the good things God had graciously given to them. Instead of giving thanks to God, they complained. One of the saddest statements recorded in the Bible is this: "The people complained." They did not take their troubles to the LORD; they did not cast their cares upon God, trusting in his LOVE; they did not pour out their hearts to him in prayer, asking for his strength and help. No, they complained.

Did they think God could not hear them? Did they not believe that the LORD was with them? Did they not yet understand that God was dwelling among them? If they did not trust this by faith, could they not see by sight that the LORD's Tabernacle was pitched in the heart of their camp? God was there, and God heard every single word they uttered. Nothing was hidden from the LORD. Whether they murmured silently in their hearts or whispered quietly in their tents or shouted angrily in the camp, God heard all their complaints. Whatever they said and wherever they said it—it was all in the hearing of the LORD.

We are not told what the people said, but it must have been serious. We know that the LORD is slow to wrath and abounding in LOVE, but what God heard that day aroused his anger. Then fire from the LORD burned among them and consumed some of the outskirts of the camp. This was not the first time the people had seen the fire of God's anger. The last time it had consumed those closest to the LORD, the priests Nadab and Abihu, who were inside God's Tabernacle. This time it consumed the outer edges of the camp, the area farthest from the LORD. Distance from God did not mean safety from God. No, the fire of his anger could touch anyone. How terrifying those flames must have been as they surrounded and threatened Israel's whole camp. It may be that no lives were lost in this burning, but those flames were a serious warning to Israel to stop complaining. As a spanking quickly stops a whining child, so this fire quickly stopped the complaining people. Because their lives were in danger, they found something better to do with their voices than grumbling and complaining. Now they cried out for help.

The people cried out to Moses to save them, but what could Moses do? This fire was from the LORD. Dousing the flames with water by the best fire-fighters in the world could not stop the burning of God's wrath. Only the power of prayer could extinguish these flames. Once again Moses raced to the rescue by falling on his knees. He prayed to the LORD, begging for God to forgive their sin, pleading with God to show them mercy. The LORD heard Moses' prayer, and the fire died.

That place on their journey was called "Taberah" or "Burning," because fire from the LORD had burned among them. Taberah would be a memorial to remind them (and us) to fear and praise the LORD. We read in the New Testament: "Do everything without complaining" (Philippians 2:14). "Do not grumble, as some of them did—and were killed by the destroying angel. These things happened to them as examples and were written down as warnings for us" (I Corinthians 10:10).

Just as the Israelites had a choice, so do we. We can use our minds and our mouths for grumbling and complaining or we can use them for praising and rejoicing. We can rise in the morning singing of God's LOVE; we can walk through the day talking of God's blessings; we can rest at night thinking of God's many mercies to us. We can rejoice always and pray without ceasing, thanking God for everything he has done for us (1 Thessalonians 5:16–18). The New Testament commands: "Do everything without complaining or arguing, so that you may become blameless and pure, children of God without fault in a crooked and depraved generation, in which you shine like stars in the universe, as you hold out the word of life" (Philippians 2:14–16). In spite of all the hardships in this life, we must use our voices for praising God, for blessing people, for sharing the good news of eternal life in Jesus Christ. If we do this, we will be children of God, shining as brightly as stars, in a world filled with darkness and weariness and wickedness.

> It is good to praise the LORD
>    and make music to your name, O Most High,
> to proclaim your love in the morning
>    and your faithfulness at night. . .

> *(Psalm 92:1–2)*

# WHINING AND WAILING

- **Numbers 11**
- **Psalm 78:17–31**
- **John 6:25–59**

L ong ago, in the beginning, in the Garden of Eden, after the first man and woman sinned, God said to Adam, "Cursed is the ground because of you; through painful toil you will eat of it all the days of your life . . . By the sweat of your brow you will eat your food, until you return to the ground" (Genesis 3:17–19). That curse has remained upon the earth and its inhabitants to this day. But when the Israelites were in the wilderness, God suspended that curse just for them, just for a time. The Israelites did not work for what they ate. While they slept, God provided for them. Each morning, when they awoke, their daily portion awaited them. "[God] gave a command to the skies above and opened the doors of the heavens. He rained down manna for the people to eat; he gave them the grain of heaven — [and] men ate the bread of angels. [God] sent them all the food they could eat" (Psalm 78:23–25). They ate that food without cost, without work. It was a gift.

When you buy a loaf of bread at the store, do you think about all the work that is wrapped up in that one small plastic bag? First, there is the plowing of the soil and the planting of the seed. Then the crop must be protected from weeds, bugs, frost, drought, wind, hail, blight, etc. If the crop survives, it must be harvested and threshed. Then the grain is hauled to a mill where it is ground into flour. The flour is then bagged and transported to a factory, where it is mixed and baked into bread. Finally, it is cut into slices, packaged in plastic, delivered to a store and arranged on a shelf, where you find it stacked with the other loaves of bread. What a lot of work there is to get a slice of bread onto your plate. When the Israelites were in the wilderness, they did not work for their daily bread. They simply stepped outside their tents, and there it was — covering the ground, ready to gather. It was a miracle, a miracle that happened six days a week.

God provided food for his people, food that was not simply nutritious for their long journey, but also delicious. The manna could be boiled into a thick rich soup or baked into sweet moist cakes. It had a lovely fragrance and flavor. The breads baked from the manna had the taste of spice, honey and oil. The entire population of Israel was in the millions, yet not even the tiniest or poorest child went hungry in that barren region. Not one malnourished child was crying with an empty bowl or an empty belly. There was an abundance of food. Everyone could eat as much as he wanted. Truly the manna was a miracle. It was a daily blessing, for which there should have been daily thanksgiving and constant rejoicing.

### The People Whined and Wailed

But some of the people were not satisfied. Although God had provided as much good food as they could eat, they were not content. They desired something more; they wanted something else. The Bible says that the rabble began to "crave other food." Soon their sinful craving turned into a sinful wailing. Whining would have been bad enough, but they were actually *wailing*. They lamented, "If only we had meat to eat. We remember the fish we ate in Egypt at no cost, also the cucumbers, melons, leeks, onions and garlic. But now we have lost our appetite. We never see anything but this manna!" What untruthful and ungrateful words.

The people lied when they said:

*"If only we had meat to eat."* They did have meat to eat. They had flocks and herds with them. They could have had roast beef or lamb stew any night

of the week, but it would have cost them something. They were shepherds
and herdsmen, whose wealth was counted in their livestock. The problem
for them was that they didn't want to pay for their meat. They wanted meat
without cost. What they were demanding from God was free meat, just as
they ate free bread. Oh greedy, ungrateful people.

The people lied when they said:

*"We remember the fish we ate in Egypt at no cost."* Had they forgotten so
quickly how dearly they paid for their food in Egypt? It had cost them everything. They paid for it with their sweat and blood and tears. They were slaves
in Egypt, living and dying in cruelty and poverty. How dare they say they ate
in Egypt at no cost? What were the few little fish that they found in the river,
compared to the freedom that was stolen from them or the children who were
taken from them? Had they forgotten that the Nile River, which provided
fish for them, had also been the grave that swallowed their drowned children?
The fish they ate in Egypt had been at a very great cost.

The people lied when they said:

*"Now we have lost our appetite."* Not true! Their appetites had grown to
gigantic proportions. It would have been better to lose their appetites completely than to have them raging like this. Their appetites were so strong that
they were whining and wailing at the risk of their very lives.

## The People Rejected God

More was going on than the people simply wanting a change in their diet.
The people were rebelling against God. (This incident marked Israel's sixth
rebellion against the LORD.) They did not just despise the manna; they despised God. The Bible says, "They continued to sin against him, rebelling
in the desert against the Most High. They willfully put God to the test by
demanding the food they craved. They spoke against God." They doubted
that he could provide for them. They said, "Can God spread a table in the
desert . . . Can he supply meat for his people?" (Psalm 78:17–20). "When
the LORD heard them, he was very angry . . . for they did not believe in God
or trust in his deliverance." (Psalm 78:21–22). They were "a stubborn and
rebellious generation, whose hearts were not loyal to God, whose spirits were
not faithful to him" (Psalm 78:8). God declared, "You have rejected the
Lord, who is among you" (Numbers 11:20).

How had the Israelites rejected the LORD?

1. They rejected the LORD by despising his good gift to them—the miraculous manna. In rejecting the gift, they were rejecting the giver of the gift.

2. They rejected the LORD by doubting his goodness, his greatness, and his love. They willfully put God to the test by demanding the food they craved. They did not believe that God was providing what was best for them. But the LORD of love did not give them ordinary bread and water. He did not simply satisfy their physical hunger and thirst. They all ate "spiritual food" and drank "spiritual drink" (I Corinthians 10:3) on that journey. The bread and water he gave them pointed them to their Messiah. The LORD wanted them to feast upon Christ, who accompanied them in the wilderness.

Fifteen hundred years later, Christ taught that he was the "Bread of Life" (John 6:35). He also said, "Whoever drinks the water I give him will never thirst. Indeed, the water I give him will become in him a spring of water welling up to eternal life" (John 4:14). In giving the Israelites bread from heaven and water from the rock, the LORD was teaching them to rely on Christ to sustain their very lives. God could have provided whatever they wanted, but the LORD had a very important reason for giving them just bread and water in the wilderness. The Israelites did not understand it then, but one day, far in the future, Christ would make it plain to them. The bread and water were signs, pointing them to Christ. The Israelites were on a spiritual journey as well as a physical journey. The onions, leeks and garlic that they craved and the melons that they missed had no spiritual significance. The cucumbers that they wanted could not point them to Christ.

3. They rejected the LORD by wishing they were back in Egypt and wailing, "We were better off in Egypt! Why did we ever leave Egypt?" The LORD had delivered them out of cruelty and slavery, but they scorned God's great deliverance. How could they escape God's wrath, neglecting and despising so great a salvation?

4. They rejected the LORD by not believing his promises. Did they want other food? All they had to do was wait, trusting in the promises of God. They could have said to themselves: "This manna is food for our journey. It is only for a short time that God will provide for us in this miraculous way, and then we will never taste this heavenly food again. In the Promised Land we will not eat the 'bread of angels' anymore. Once we are there, we will eat all the ordinary food we want and we will work for it in the ordinary way. In the

Promised Land we will eat food from our own gardens and fruit from our own orchards; there we will eat grain from our own fields, fish from our own seas, and meat from our own farms. Ahead of us lies a land flowing with milk and honey. God has promised us this land, and we believe in God's promise to us." But the Israelites did not say this by faith, looking ahead to the Land of Promise. Instead, they wailed in unbelief, looking back to the land of bondage.

5. They rejected the LORD by rejecting Christ. How could they possibly be guilty of rejecting Christ, when they lived fifteen hundred years before he was even born? In rejecting the manna, they were rejecting the One who was foreshadowed in the manna. In despising the manna, which was the shadow, they were despising the real and true bread from heaven—Jesus Christ, the Son of God, who became flesh and blood for us, sharing in our humanity and dying on the cross to set us free. God gave his people the manna in the wilderness to nourish their bodies in a desolate land, but the manna was also meant to strengthen their faith. That miraculous manna was a shadow, pointing to a greater reality and a greater miracle, which was the true bread from heaven, even Jesus Christ our Lord, whom God sent from heaven to bring life—abundant life and eternal life—to those who were languishing and perishing in the wilderness of this world. "For God so loved the world, that he gave his one and only Son, that whoever believes in him shall not perish, but have eternal life" (John 3:16). Jesus said, "I tell you the truth, it is not Moses who has given you the *bread from heaven*, but it is my Father who gives you the *true bread* from heaven. For the *bread of God* is he who comes down from heaven and gives life to the world." Then Jesus declared, "I am the *bread of life*. He who comes to me will never go hungry, and he who believes in me will never go thirsty. . . . Everyone who looks to the Son and believes in him shall have eternal life, and I will raise him up at the last day." Jesus continued, "I tell you the truth, he who believes has everlasting life. I am the bread of life. Your fathers ate the manna in the desert, yet they died. But here is the bread that comes down from heaven, which a man may eat and not die. I am the *living bread* that came down from heaven. If anyone eats of this bread, he will live forever. This bread is my flesh, which I will give for the life of the world." Then Jesus declared, "I tell you the truth, unless you eat the flesh of the Son of Man and drink his blood, you have no life in you. Whoever eats my flesh and drinks my blood has eternal life, and I will raise him up at the last day. For my flesh is real food and my blood is real drink" (John 6:32–55 italics mine).

What did Jesus mean by these difficult words? Jesus was speaking of his death upon the cross, which would secure for us eternal life. He was speaking of his body, broken for us, and his blood, shed for us. As surely as food and drink are necessary for us to stay alive in this world, the bruising of his body and spilling of his blood was necessary in order for us to stay alive forever. "He was pierced for our transgressions; he was crushed for our iniquities . . . by his wounds we are healed . . . because he poured out his life unto death" (Isaiah 53:5, 12). Just as our bodies cannot survive without food and drink, so our souls cannot survive without Christ and his sacrifice.

But how can we eat his flesh and drink his blood? We feed upon Christ by faith, by believing that Jesus is the Son of God, by believing in his sacrifice for our sins, by believing that he alone can save us from death and grant us life. Jesus explained: "The one who feeds on me will live because of me. This is the bread that came down from heaven. Your forefathers ate manna and died, but he who feeds on this bread will live forever" (John 6:57–58). Thus the manna foreshadowed the true bread that God sent from heaven, "for God so loved the world that he gave his one and only Son, that whoever believes in him should not perish but have eternal life" (John 3:16). In rejecting the manna, the Israelites were rejecting their Messiah.

You see, in despising the manna, these Israelites were despising *everything* that God was giving to them. They were not just whining and wailing about their earthly food and daily bread (which would have been bad enough, especially in their extreme circumstances). They were also reviling God's spiritual blessing for them. Ultimately, they were rejecting God's salvation and the Savior himself. God's own Word declared: "You have rejected the LORD, who is among you"

## Moses Prayed to God

What effect did the Israelites' rebellion have on Moses? When Moses heard the wailing all around him, from every section of the campground, from every family in every tribe in all of Israel, he was greatly distressed. Each man stood at the entrance to his tent, whining and wailing, for no good reason. Moses was in such despair at this latest rebellion that he wanted to quit. He even wanted to die. What should he do? Where could he turn? Moses poured out his heart to God in prayer. He asked the LORD, "Why have you brought this trouble on your servant? What have I done to displease you that you have put the burden of all these people on me? Did I conceive all these people? Did I give them birth? Why do you tell me to carry them in my arms, as a nurse carries an infant, to the land promised on oath to their fore-fathers? Where can I get meat for all these people? They keep wailing to me, 'Give us meat to eat! Give us meat to eat!' I cannot carry all these people by myself; the burden is too heavy for me. If this is how you are going to treat me, put me to death right now . . . and do not let me face my own ruin."

The LORD heard Moses praying. He also heard the people wailing. The LORD answered both the prayers and the wails. Moses said, "Put me to death right now"—but God in mercy answered, "No!" to his request. The Israelites said, "Give us meat to eat, right now," and God in anger answered, "Yes!" to their demand. Far better that God should say "no" in mercy, than "yes" in anger. Oh foolish Israelites, who feared not the anger of the LORD.

### God Answered Moses

The LORD refused Moses' request to remove him, but God did relieve his burden. The LORD instructed Moses: "Bring me seventy of Israel's elders, who are known to you as leaders among the people. Have them come to the Tent of Meeting, that they may stand there with you. I will come down and speak with you there, and I will take of the Spirit that is on you and put the Spirit on them. They will help you carry the burden of the people, so that you will not have to carry it alone." So Moses did as God said.

The seventy elders stood before the Tabernacle, and the LORD came down in the cloud and spoke. God sent the Holy Spirit to these men. When the Spirit rested upon them, they prophesied. They spoke the Word of God, and by that Holy Word and Spirit of Wisdom they would lead God's people. "Man does not live on bread alone, but on every word that comes from the mouth of the LORD" (Deuteronomy 8:3; Matthew 4:4). Through Moses' prayer, Israel was blessed once again, for God sent his Spirit and his Word to them in an abundant, seven-times-ten, number-of-perfection measure.

God was gracious in pouring out his Spirit upon all these leaders of Israel, but one day God would demonstrate an even greater LOVE for Israel. Fifteen hundred years later, God would send his Son from heaven to them. Long before he arrived, God pointed to him through his prophets, saying: "Here is my servant, whom I have chosen, the one I love and in whom I delight; I will put my Spirit on him" (Isaiah 42:1). Again the prophet said: "The

Spirit of the LORD will rest on him—the Spirit of wisdom and understanding, the Spirit of counsel and of power, the Spirit of knowledge and the fear of the LORD" (Isaiah 11:2–3). The One whom God sent from heaven to speak the words of God and the One to whom he gave the Spirit without measure, was Jesus Christ (John 3:31, 34). Jesus himself said: "The Spirit of the Sovereign LORD is on me, because he has anointed me to preach good news" (Isaiah 61:1; Luke 4:18). Christ not only *spoke* the Word of God; Christ *was* the Word of God, full of grace and truth (John 1:14). "God was pleased to have all his fullness dwell in him . . . In Christ all the fullness of the Deity lives in bodily form" (Colossians 1:19; 2:9).

Through faith in Christ, the Holy Spirit was also given to all God's people. When Moses led Israel in the wilderness, he was not jealous or envious that God's Spirit rested on the seventy elders and that they, too, prophesied. No, Moses was delighted. He exclaimed, "I wish that all the LORD's people were prophets and that the LORD would put his Spirit on them all." That wish of Moses was granted in Christ. Moses was the first to speak of it and hope for it, but many years later the LORD spoke of that same desire through another prophet, saying: "I will pour out my Spirit on all people. Your sons and daughters will prophesy . . . Even on my servants, both men and women, I will pour out my Spirit in those days. . . . And everyone who calls on the name of the LORD will be saved. . . . there will be deliverance" (Joel 2:28–29, 32). That prophecy was fulfilled after the crucifixion, resurrection and ascension of Jesus Christ, after he was exalted to the right hand of God, when Jesus received from his Father the promised Holy Spirit whom he poured out upon his disciples so that they, too, would proclaim the gospel, the good news of eternal life in Jesus Christ: "Repent and be baptized, every one of you, in the name of Jesus Christ for the forgiveness of your sins. And you will receive the gift of the Holy Spirit. This promise is for you and your children and for all who are far off—for all whom the Lord our God will call" (Acts 2:38–39).

That was how, fifteen hundred years later, Moses' prayer was ultimately answered, far beyond what he could hope or even imagine.

## God Answered the People

But what about the people's complaint? How did God answer them? For those who cared not for the blessing of God, for those who loved not the bread from heaven or the Word of God, for those who craved other food,

God granted their desires. God said: "Now the LORD will give you meat, and you will eat it. You will not eat it for just one day, or two days, or five, ten or twenty days, but for a whole month—until it comes out of your nostrils and you loathe it—because you have rejected the LORD, who is among you and have wailed before him."

This seemed impossible, even to Moses. How could so many people have meat for a whole month? He said to the LORD, "Would they have enough if flocks and herds were slaughtered for them? Would they have enough if all the fish in the sea were caught for them?" But the LORD answered Moses' incredulous questions with another question: "Is the LORD's arm too short?" God said, "You will now see whether or not what I say will come true for you."

Then a wind went out from the LORD and drove quail in from the sea. The LORD's wind brought millions and millions of quail to Israel's camp. For miles around the camp, for a day's walk in any direction, there was a thick cloud of quail, hovering just above the ground. They were so thick and so close that even the children could catch them. The Bible says, "[God] let loose the east wind from the heavens and led forth the south wind by his power. He rained meat down on them like dust, flying birds like sand on the seashore. He made them come down inside their camp, all around their tents" (Psalm 78:26–28). So the people gathered the meat—armloads and baskets full of quail. They worked day and night and no one gathered less than sixty bushels of birds. What were they going to do with all that meat? The people cut it up and spread it on the ground to dry in the desert sun. They would save the dried meat for their journey. No longer would they have to rely upon God for their daily manna, which they loathed. And right now they could feast upon all this fresh meat.

Quail tastes similar to chicken. Do you like roast chicken? Fried chicken? Grilled chicken? Chicken stew? Chicken soup? Chicken sandwiches? Now Israel could eat quail sandwiches on manna bread, or they could have quail stew with manna dumplings, or they could eat whole roast quail filled with manna stuffing. They could sit before their campfires and roast quail meat skewered on sticks to eat with their manna cakes. This was what their hearts had desired, more than anything else. How happy they were as they gorged themselves on this new food.

But while they feasted, while the aroma of cooked quail wafted on the evening breeze, the anger of the LORD burned against the people, and he struck them with a severe plague. All the people who had craved other food died. God had given them the meat they had craved and they had stuffed themselves with the food, like animals being fattened for the slaughter. "They ate till they had more than enough . . . But before they turned from the food they craved, even while it was still in their mouths, God's anger rose against them. He put to death the sturdiest among them, cutting down the young men of Israel" (Psalm 78:29–31).

Now there was another wailing in the camp, and weeping too, as the people mourned for their dead. Those strong young men, so recently counted in Israel's census, so happily honored in Israel's army, were gone. Graves had to be dug for many of these soldiers, although there had been no battle. They had fallen because they had rejected the LORD. The people named that place "Kibroth Hattaavah," which means "Graves of Craving," because there they buried the people who had craved other food.

Let us take warning from this sad chapter in Israel's history. May none of us ever reject the LORD. May none of us ever rebel against him. May we never neglect or despise the salvation he has provided. We have God's true gospel and God's pure Word; may we never crave anything else or some other way—for it will lead to death. Jesus said, "Whoever believes in the Son has eternal life, but whoever rejects the Son will not see life, for God's wrath remains on him" (John 3:36).

# A HIDEOUS PLAGUE FOR A HIDEOUS SIN

• Numbers 12

The Bible doesn't tell us much about Moses' private life. Moses was a public figure, the head of an entire nation, whose work was the welfare of the whole household of Israel, and the Scriptures focus on that part of Moses' life and work. We often read about Moses at the Tabernacle, where he interceded for all the people in the Tent of God, but we never read about Moses in his own tent, where he found rest from his work, where he ate his manna meals, where he talked with his wife. Moses did have a home and a family, just like any other man in Israel, but we know very little about it.

Long ago, when Moses fled from Egypt, he went to the land of Midian and married a Midianite woman named Zipporah. For forty years Moses lived and worked in Midian with Zipporah's family. Moses liked his Midianite in-laws; he respected them and relied upon them, although they were not Israelites. His wife's father, Jethro, had come to believe in the LORD, the God of Israel. When he heard what God had done for Moses and how the LORD had delivered Israel out of Egypt, he was delighted and professed his faith in God, proclaiming: "Praise be to the LORD, who rescued you . . . Now I know that the LORD is greater than all other gods " (Exodus 18:10–11). Then Jethro brought a burnt offering and other sacrifices to God. Zipporah's father and brother even helped to lead Israel through the wilderness, acting as advisors for Moses (Exodus 18 and Numbers 10:29–32). Moses and Zipporah also had children, at least two sons.

However, it seems that somewhere along the way in the wilderness, Zipporah (Moses' Midianite wife) left or died, for we read that Moses married a Cushite woman. We are not told anything about this woman, not even her name, but it is most likely that Moses, the man of God, married a woman of God. She was not an Israelite, but a foreigner, a Cushite who probably had joined herself to Israel when they left Egypt. She was, however, a woman who believed in the LORD and could say, "Where you go, I will go, and where you stay I will stay. Your people will be my people and your God my God" (Ruth 1:16). God had graciously given to Moses a partner to help him in his difficult life and work. Just as God had given Moses seventy elders to help carry the burden of the nation, so God also had given him a wife, because it was not good for him to be alone in this great task.

But sadly, not everyone approved Moses' new wife. Moses' own sister and brother, Miriam and Aaron, did not like Moses' new wife. Why? They were opposed to the marriage because she was a Cushite. As far as we know, they had accepted Zipporah, who also was not an Israelite, but a Midianite. So why were there problems now with Moses having a Cushite wife? The land of Cush was in Africa, in the region south of Egypt, and the people who lived there were dark-skinned Africans. When the Bible records that Moses married a Cushite, we are being told that Moses married a black woman. Apparently they opposed the marriage because it was inter-racial. Miriam and Aaron despised Moses' new wife because of the color of her skin. Racial prejudice! That was the loathsome and ugly sin that began all the trouble that was to follow.

Sin has a way of spreading like a deadly disease. Miriam and Aaron first despised Moses' dark-skinned wife, but soon they despised Moses himself. Perhaps they were thinking: How could Moses have done such a thing? Should we allow a black woman and her family to influence the nation, the way Zipporah and her family did? Never! Moses has gone too far. He is so proud and willful and arrogant; he thinks he can do anything he pleases. But we, Miriam and Aaron, have power too, and we will stop him.

Very quickly the sin of Moses' sister and brother had spilled from the private sphere of Moses' own tent into the public sphere of Israel's whole camp. Miriam and Aaron were openly talking against Moses. What they were saying was treacherous, ruinous, treasonous. It was affecting the entire nation. What had begun as a family affair was becoming a national concern, for Miriam and Aaron were questioning Moses' authority to lead the people and speak to the people as God's chosen prophet. They were opposing Moses' exalted position and claiming it for themselves. They said, "Has the LORD spoken only through Moses . . . Hasn't he also spoken through us?"

The sin of racial prejudice against Moses' wife was a particularly hideous one, but their sin against Moses was worse:

1. Moses was their own brother. How hurt he must have been by their accusations and insurrections against him. Moses loved his sister, Miriam, who had supported him from his earliest days; she was the one who stood by the Nile River guarding his life when he was just a baby floating in a basket. Moses loved his brother too; Aaron had stood by Moses during some of the hardest days of his life, when he faced Pharaoh in Egypt and commanded that evil king to let God's people go. Miriam and Aaron had been the two people throughout his life on whom Moses had depended, but now his beloved sister and brother had turned against him.

2. It was true that Moses, the younger brother, was the great leader and prophet of Israel, but he had not taken this position for himself. God himself had placed Moses (in fact, had forced Moses) into this position of power (see Exodus 3:11; 4:10, 13). What Miriam and Aaron said about Moses was untrue. God's Word declares: "Moses was a very humble man, more humble than anyone else on the face of the earth."

3. The LORD had chosen Moses as the greatest prophet in the Old Testament, the one who gave God's Law to Israel, and it was through their connection to Moses that both Miriam and Aaron had been exalted to powerful positions in Israel too. The Scriptures state that Miriam was also a prophetess. She, too, spoke God's Word to Israel and led the people in worship (see Exodus 15:20–21). Aaron had been appointed the high priest and he daily brought the whole nation before God's throne of grace. Miriam and Aaron were both named along with Moses as the leaders of God's people. The LORD said to Israel, "I sent Moses to lead you, also Aaron and Miriam"

(Micah 6:4). This brother and sister had been raised up because of Moses, but now they sought to tear him down. They repaid his good to them with evil. How great was their sin against him.

4. Moses was God's greatest prophet, second only to Christ. Moses was a type of Christ, foreshadowing the Son of God. Christ's prophetic ministry was compared to Moses' prophetic ministry (Deuteronomy 18:15) and Christ's faithfulness was compared to Moses' faithfulness. God said that Jesus "was faithful to the one who appointed him, just as Moses was faithful in all God's house" (Hebrews 3:2). Miriam and Aaron should have honored Moses, whom God had so honored, but they maligned him and accused him and opposed him, while seeking to exalt themselves. These were satanic activities. In rebelling against Moses, Miriam and Aaron were rebelling against the LORD. In rejecting Moses, they were ultimately rejecting Christ himself.

Moses must have heard what his sister and brother were saying against him, but he said nothing in his own defense, for Moses was truly a very humble man. Moses did not cry out to God for justice or vengeance. He loved Miriam and Aaron. Moses raised neither voice nor hand against them, even though they were rising up as angry rivals against him. No, Moses remained silent before his accusers. In many situations Moses was quick to defend the honor of God, but when it came to himself, Moses said nothing.

Moses would not defend his own honor, but God would. The LORD heard the accusations that were on Miriam's and Aaron's lips; God knew the rebellion that was in their hearts, and God was quick to vindicate his faithful servant Moses. At once the LORD said to Moses, Aaron and Miriam, "Come out to the Tent of Meeting, all three of you." So the three of them walked out to meet the LORD. Perhaps Miriam and Aaron walked there confidently, their prideful hearts assuring them that at last they would receive the recognition that they deserved. More likely, they walked there nervously, their truthful hearts accusing them of the sins they had committed. As these three stood before the Tabernacle, the LORD came down in a pillar of cloud and stood at the entrance to the Tent. Then God summoned Aaron and Miriam. When both of them had stepped forward, God commanded them to listen to his words:

> When a prophet of the LORD is among you,
> I reveal myself to him in visions,
> I speak to him in dreams.

> But this is not true of my servant Moses;
>  He is faithful in all my house.
> With him I speak face to face,
>  clearly, and not in riddles;
>  he sees the form of the LORD.
> Why then were you not afraid
>  to speak against my servant Moses?

(Numbers 12:6–8)

God did not wait for their answer, nor did he wait to hear their excuses. The LORD judges righteously and they were wrong. Miriam and Aaron should have confessed their sin immediately. They should have begged God for mercy and forgiveness before another moment passed, before the anger of the LORD burned against them, before the LORD departed from them in his wrath. But they were silent. Then God left them and when the cloud lifted from above the Tabernacle, there stood Miriam—with leprosy.

*How just are God's judgments?* Although we do not know the full story in all its details, nothing is hidden from the LORD. Why was Miriam alone singled out for punishment? Possibly, she was the one who instigated all this trouble, with Aaron just following her lead. Probably she was the one first named because she was the one who first sinned. What we do know is this: God judges fairly, showing no favoritism.

*How just are God's judgments?* Miriam, who reviled Moses' Cushite wife because of her black skin, now stood with skin as white as snow. Her skin had a deathly pallor caused by that dreadful disease. She was so sickly pale and ghostly white she could have been a corpse. There she stood, alive, but her flesh was beginning to rot, as if she were already in her grave. All who looked upon Miriam were appalled. She had reviled a black woman because of her skin; now Miriam herself was reviled because of her skin.

*How just are God's judgments?* Miriam's foolishness and wickedness in despising and opposing Moses were now clear for all to see. Was she really a prophet like Moses? Had the LORD really spoken to her, just as he had spoken to Moses? When Moses met with the LORD, he returned with a face full of glory; but when Miriam met with the LORD, she returned with a face full of leprosy. After Moses spoke with God, he veiled his face to hide a fading glory;

but after Miriam spoke with the LORD, she veiled her face to hide a growing horror. How ashamed Miriam should have been, but not because of her face. She should have been ashamed because of her heart and her sin. Now the inner corruption of her heart had been exposed for all to see by this outer corruption of her flesh. The pit of contempt, which Miriam had dug for someone else, she had fallen into herself. *How just are the judgments of the LORD!*

When Aaron turned towards Miriam and saw that she had leprosy, he was horrified at the hideous punishment that had befallen his sister because of their sin. Aaron, who had so recently spoken against Moses, now pleaded with Moses: "Please, my lord, do not hold against us the sin we have so foolishly committed. Do not let her be like a stillborn infant, coming from its mother's womb with its flesh half eaten away." Aaron, the high priest, confessed their sin and asked for pardon. (Perhaps that was why the LORD spared Aaron, so that Miriam would have a high priest to intercede for her healing.) And Moses, who had not raised his voice against them, now raised his voice for them. Moses cried out to the LORD, "O God, please heal her!" The LORD answered Moses' prayer for his sister and the LORD did heal her. However, she still had to remain outside the camp as an unclean person for seven days (according to the laws of purification for skin diseases). Being Moses' sister did not exempt Miriam from God's law or God's wrath. The LORD said, "If her father had spit in her face, would she not have been in disgrace for seven days? Confine her outside the camp for seven days; after that she can be brought back" (Numbers 12:11–14).

So, Miriam was led away in disgrace. She was led from the heart of the nation, from the Tabernacle in the center of Israel's campground, past the tents of the Levites where Miriam's tribe lived, past the tents of the people of Israel, to the outskirts of the camp where all the lepers dwelt in their unclean tents. It was Miriam, not the black Cushite woman, who was segregated from the congregation of Israel. Moses' black wife remained in her rightful place, which was in Moses' tent, pitched in the center of Israel's camp, at the front of the Tent of God. It was Miriam, through her sins of pride and envy and prejudice, who found herself despised and debased—by the very hand and Word of God.

But Moses was exalted. "Moses was faithful as a servant in all God's house" (Hebrews 3:5). Those words of God, first spoken in the Old Testament, then repeated in the New Testament, brought honor and glory to Moses then— and now, even to this very day.

In this account we see God's great LOVE for his people:

1. We see God's LOVE for Moses' Cushite wife. God himself protected her person and her position. God vindicated her, judging the situation righteously, without any prejudice against her. The color of her skin mattered not to the LORD; it was the condition of her heart and life that he took into account. God is just, and judges every person fairly without regard to race, sex, age, wealth or any other like consideration.

2. We see God's LOVE for Miriam. Her leprosy lasted only a short time before God answered her brothers' pleas and healed her. However, more important than the healing of her flesh was the healing of her heart. "The LORD disciplines those he loves, and he punishes everyone he accepts as a son. . . . God disciplines us for our good, that we may share in his holiness. No discipline seems pleasant at the time, but painful. Later on, however, it produces a harvest of righteousness and peace, for those who have been trained by it" (Hebrews 12:6, 10–11). God, in mercy, did not allow Miriam to continue in her sins. He disciplined her because he loved her. One day Miriam would again sing of the goodness and faithfulness of the LORD.

3. We see God's LOVE for Aaron. God mercifully showed Aaron his sin in siding with Miriam against Moses, and Aaron confessed that sin to his brother. Once again Aaron was made aware of his weakness as a high priest: He was not without sin and he himself needed the intercession of a greater High Priest, yet God did not take away his place or his work in Israel.

4. We see God's LOVE for Moses. God dealt mercifully with all Moses' family, with all the people whom Moses loved. And the LORD honored Moses, proclaiming: "My servant Moses—he is faithful in all my house!"

5. We see God's LOVE for Israel. The nation's leading family was not irreparably broken or immediately taken from them. Moses, Aaron and Miriam continued to lead the people through the wilderness to the Promised Land.

> *Herein is love, not that we loved God, but that he loved us,*
> *and sent his Son to be the propitiation for our sins.*
>
> (I John 4:10 KJV, *emphasis added*)

# EYES OF UNBELIEF

• **Numbers 13**
• **Deuteronomy 1:19–33**

When the Israelites were still at Mount Sinai, the LORD said to them there, "You have stayed long enough at this mountain. Break camp and advance into the hill country of the Amorites. Go to all the neighboring peoples in the Arabah, in the mountains, in the western foothills, in the Negev and along the coast, to the land of the Canaanites and to Lebanon, as far as the great river, the Euphrates. See, I have given you this land. Go in and take possession of it. Take possession of the land that the LORD swore he would give to your fathers—to Abraham, Isaac and Jacob—and to their descendants after them" (Deuteronomy 1:6–8).

So the Israelites left Mount Sinai and advanced towards the Promised Land. Their journey would not be easy through that "vast and dreadful desert" (Deuteronomy 1:19), but it would have taken only a few days, except that the people's sin hindered their progress: The Israelites had to fight fires at Taberah (or "Burning") when fire from the LORD burned among them; they had to dig graves at Kibroth Hattaavah (or "Graves of Craving") when the LORD struck them with a severe plague; and they had to wait a week at Hazeroth when Miriam was confined outside the camp. But at last the Israelites proceeded on their journey and arrived at Kadesh Barnea, which was right on the edge of the Promised Land.

Moses must have been very excited. He said to the people, "You have reached the hill country of the Amorites, which the LORD our God is giving to us. See, the LORD your God has given you the land. Go up and take possession of it, as the LORD, the God of your fathers, told you. Do not be afraid. Do not be discouraged" (Deuteronomy 1:20–21). The soldiers of Israel lifted their eyes towards the land, but they could not see beyond the hills to the land God had promised to give to them. They did not want to march blindly into battle. They were not ready to press forward by faith—not yet. First they wanted a peek at the Promised Land. They wanted to see the land they were fighting for and see the people they were fighting against. They did not want to trust their loving LORD and his faithful Word only. They did not want to rely on the power and promise of Almighty God alone.

The soldiers of Israel wanted to send spies into the land, men who would be the eyes for the entire army. They said to Moses, "Let us send men ahead to spy out the land for us and bring back a report about the route we are to take and the towns we will come to" (Deuteronomy 1:22). Wouldn't God show them the right route? Wouldn't God lead them with his cloud by day and his fire by night? Yes, but the idea seemed good to Moses anyway. It wouldn't hurt to have information about the region before they marched in to conquer it. But before Moses gave the order to send spies, he checked with the LORD. God confirmed the plan; the LORD said, "Send some men to explore the land of Canaan, which I am giving to the Israelites. From each ancestral tribe, send one of its leaders." So Moses selected twelve men, one from each of the tribes that made up Israel's army. Then Moses sent the twelve spies to explore the land lying just beyond them. They were to gather two things on their expedition:

1. *The spies were to gather information* about the land and the people. Moses said, "See what the land is like and whether the people who live there are strong or weak, few or many. What kind of land do they live in? Is it good or bad? What kind of towns do they live in? Are they unwalled or fortified? How is the soil? Is it fertile or poor? Are there trees on it or not?"

None of the Israelites, not even Moses, had ever seen the Promised Land. They had many questions about the land, but many of those questions were already answered. Did the Israelites really need to send spies ahead to see if the land was good or bad? Hadn't the LORD already told them it was a good land, a land flowing with milk and honey (see Exodus 3:8)? And did they really need to know about the strength of their enemies? They knew the strength of the LORD. Wasn't that enough?

2. *The spies were to gather food* produced in the land. Moses said, "Do your best to bring back some of the fruit of the land."

So the twelve spies entered the Promised Land. It was a dangerous, but marvelous, mission. These twelve men had been chosen from among hundreds of thousands of soldiers in Israel to be the first ones to venture into this unknown land, which was their homeland by faith. These former slaves must have experienced overflowing joy as they looked at last upon their beautiful and bountiful land. They must have felt overwhelming awe as they stood at last upon the solid, fertile ground which was the very substance of their hopes and dreams. What an amazing privilege they had been given, to be the first ones to walk within the Promised Land.

The twelve spies explored the land for forty days. They traveled all the way to Hebron, the place where Abraham, Isaac and Jacob were buried. Did they go there hoping to find that ancient cemetery of their faithful forefathers? It is doubtful whether they found that field and that cave which Abraham had bought hundreds of years earlier, for there were no relatives left in the land to tend his graveyard. They had been enslaved in Egypt for four hundred years. But Abraham had believed God; he believed that one day God would fulfill his promise by giving that whole land to his descendants, and now, here they were, twelve men representing twelve tribes of hundreds of thousands of his descendants. Right now these men were just exploring the land, but soon the army of Israel would be conquering it. If the twelve spies had found that hallowed sepulcher of their honored ancestors, it would have encouraged them greatly, for it would have reminded them of God's promise to them.

What the spies did find at Hebron discouraged them greatly. The people in that region were a powerful and terrible race of men, the notorious Anakites, whose bodies were like giants and whose spirits were like demons. Their cities were armed fortresses, with walls higher than the Hebrews had ever seen. When some of the spies saw this, fears and doubts began to rise within them. The people living here were the descendants of giants, who had inherited great power. These people had great strength and great wealth in their fortress cities and fertile valleys. What had they, the Israelites, inherited from Abraham, Isaac and Jacob? Nothing! A lost burial plot and some ancient promises, which seemed as old and useless as their ancestors' dry and crumbling bones. How could they possibly conquer these people? Hebron was a great discouragement to the spies.

The time came for the twelve spies to turn around and go back to Israel's camp in the wilderness. On their way home, as they went through a valley of vineyards and fruit groves, they cut a branch bearing a single cluster of large, luscious grapes. It was so large that two men carried it between them on a pole. From the trees they also picked pomegranates and figs to show to the people. They called that place the Valley of Eschol (or "Cluster Valley") because of the large cluster of grapes they cut there.

The spies had been traveling through that fertile farmland for forty days and forty nights, but at last they returned home to the barren wasteland where Israel was camped in the desert. All Israel gathered to hear and see what the spies had to "show-and-tell" about the land. Imagine how happy (and hungry) the people felt when they saw that gigantic cluster of grapes. Fresh fruit! It was almost enough to pull them forward into the Promised Land. They had been living in the desert for over two years, subsisting almost entirely upon manna. Moses knew that they were longing for other food, and perhaps that was one reason he had instructed the spies to bring back some fruit from the Promised Land. It would entice the Israelites to go forward, for just ahead of them lay a land where such fabulous fruits flourished. Also, this was proof—proof they could see with their own eyes—that the land was a good land, just as the LORD had promised them. Perhaps Moses had instructed the spies to get this fruit in order to strengthen the people's faith in God's Word.

Then the spies told Moses and the people about the land. The good news they told first: "We went into the land to which you sent us, and it does flow with milk and honey!" Here is the proof. "Here is its fruit." Then came the bad news: "But the people who live there are powerful, and the cities are fortified and very large. We even saw the descendants of Anak there." Giants! There were giants living in that land!

At once the people began to rebel. They did not want to go forward to fight these giants. There was moaning and weeping, murmuring and whispering, talking and shouting until one of the spies stepped forward and silenced the people. His name was Caleb. He was the man chosen from Israel's leading tribe, the tribe of Judah. The people must listen to him. Caleb said, "We should go up and take possession of the land. We can certainly do it." But ten of the other spies opposed him. They said "We can't attack those people. They are stronger than we are." These ten spies also opposed the LORD. God said it was a good land, but these men spread an evil report about the land they had explored. They lied about it, saying the land devoured anyone entering it. They said, "All the people we saw there are of great size. We saw the giants there . . . We seemed like grasshoppers in our own eyes, and we looked the same to them." They grossly exaggerated the difficulties and greatly discouraged the people (Numbers 13:27–33).

Now the people had a choice. Whose report should they believe? Should they listen to just one man or the other ten? Who was telling the truth? The words of men must always be measured or tested by the Word of God, which is the Word of truth. God said, "It is a good land . . . I have given you this land . . . Go in and take possession of it." The Israelites should listen to the man whose words agreed with God's Word.

Although all twelve spies saw exactly the same things—and not even Caleb contradicted the actual facts, that in the land there were big strong people living in large walled cities—their reports were very different. Ten of the spies looked at the land with eyes of unbelief and said, "We cannot do it." Only two of the spies, Caleb and Joshua, had eyes of faith. These men, because they believed in God and the promises of God, said, "We can certainly do it."

# ISRAEL'S CHOICE

- **Numbers 14**
- **Deuteronomy 1:26–46**
- **Psalm 95**
- **Hebrews 3:7–4:13**

Israel sent twelve spies into the Promised Land. When they returned, the people listened eagerly to the spies' report, but they were soon disheartened. Could they conquer Canaan? Ten of the spies said, "We cannot do it!" Now the people had a choice: Would they trust the Word of the LORD or would they trust the words of these men? Would they go forward by faith, believing God's promises and obeying God's commands, or would they refuse to advance into enemy territory?

That night the people gave their answer. All the people of the community raised their voices together, and, sadly, it was not in a song of praise or a shout of joy or a prayer of faith. It was not even in a cry for help. No, that night the people raised their voices one more time in rebellion against the LORD. Weeping and wailing filled the night, and in the howling darkness terrible thoughts came to their minds and horrible words came from their lips. They said, "The LORD hates us!" What an awful accusation against the LORD of LOVE, who had demonstrated his great LOVE for them times beyond counting. But the people forgot about God's love and said, "The LORD hates us; he brought us out of Egypt . . . to destroy us" (Deuteronomy 1:27). It was a wicked lie, whispered from the pits of hell into the depths of their hearts, and the people chose to believe Satan's evil lie rather than God's holy truth. The people refused to trust in God's LOVE.

When the spies returned to Israel's camp, Moses received the same information that the people did. He, too, must have been disappointed, for he, too, would have been hoping for a favorable report about the land. Now he learned for the first time that Israel's enemies were gigantic men and that Canaan's cities were strong fortresses. Moses heard the same disheartening words from the same ten spies that the people did, but there was a difference: Moses responded with faith. "Faith is being sure of what we hope for and certain of what we do not see" (Hebrews 11:1). Because Moses trusted in God, he was absolutely *certain* that they could conquer Canaan and because Moses believed God's Word, he was positively *sure* that they would win the war. Moses tried to encourage the people: "Do not be terrified. Do not be afraid of them," said Moses. "The LORD your God, who is going before you, will fight for you, before your very eyes, just as he did for you in Egypt and in the desert. There you saw how the LORD your God carried you, as a father carries his child, all the way you went until you reached this place" (Deuteronomy 1:29–31).

Again the Israelites had a choice. They could take the words of Moses to heart. They could say to themselves, "Yes, Moses is right. Look, here we are standing at the edge of the Promised Land. How did we get here? It is a miracle! Only by the mighty power and mercy of God have we arrived at this place. Let us remember how God fought for us in Egypt and in the desert. What God did to our enemies behind us, he will surely do to our enemies before us. Let us trust in the LORD and follow Moses into the Promised Land."

But the people did not think such thoughts or speak such words to themselves. They did not want to believe and advance; they wanted to rebel and retreat. All the Israelites grumbled against Moses, and the whole congregation said, "If only we had died in Egypt! Or in this desert! Why is the LORD bringing us to this land only to let us fall by the sword? Our wives and children will be taken as plunder. Wouldn't it be better for us to go back to Egypt?" Then they actually said to each other, "We should choose a leader and go back to Egypt." This idea was not only wicked; it was stupid. If they made it back to Egypt, if they survived wandering through the wilderness without God, what did they think awaited them in Egypt? It would be sudden slaughter for many of them and certain slavery for the rest of them, the very things that they feared would happen to them if they advanced into Canaan. Their plan was not only rebellious; it was ridiculous.

Moses and Aaron, in utter dismay, fell facedown on the ground in front of the whole Israelite assembly gathered there. What else could they do? What else could they say? They had led these people out of Egypt, through the desert, to the edge of the Promised Land, and now these people were turning back, rejecting their leadership and refusing to follow them any longer. Moses and Aaron had nothing more to say. But two other voices rose above the wicked clamor.

Those two voices belonged to two of the spies, Joshua and Caleb. They were so distressed by the people's response that they stood up and tore their clothes in front of the entire assembly. That got the people's attention. That quieted the mob for a few moments, during which time the two spies spoke to the crowd. Joshua and Caleb testified to the goodness of the land and the goodness of the LORD. These two men, who were eyewitnesses of the Promised Land, said, "The land we passed through and explored is exceedingly good. If the LORD is pleased with us, *He will lead us into that land,* a land flowing with milk and honey, *and He will give it to us.* Only do not rebel against the LORD. And do not be afraid of the people of the land." Why shouldn't they be afraid of them? The other ten spies said that Israel would be devoured by these giants living in the land. But Joshua and Caleb disagreed. No! Not true! They said, "We will swallow them. Their protection is gone, but the LORD is with us! Do not be afraid of them."

What blessed words. The Israelites were given another chance to conquer their fear with faith. They were given another opportunity to go forward, with faithful words to strengthen their fearful hearts. Even now, after a night of weeping and wailing, they could choose to believe and obey the LORD. It was not too late to cast aside their fears, to press forward into the Promised Land, to face their foes and fight the good fight of faith. They could still choose to do what was right.

At that critical moment, in that most crucial decision in Israel's history, what did the people choose? How did they respond to the faithful urging of these two righteous men? This was their response: They began talking about putting Joshua and Caleb to death, although these two good men had done nothing wrong at all. "Stone them!" the people cried. "Put them to death!"

LESSON 9: *Israel's Choice* ——— 67

There was nothing more that could be said. The Israelites had made their choice. They chose not to listen to the two brave spies, Joshua and Caleb, who stood with torn clothes before them. They chose not to listen to their faithful leaders, Moses and Aaron, who lay with their faces on the ground before them. They chose not to listen even to God, whose fiery cloud hovered above them, visibly showing them that the LORD Almighty was with his people. What more could be said or done for these people? They were determined to rebel against the LORD. They were determined to reject all words of wisdom and to slaughter anyone who uttered them. They were plotting murder and planning retreat. Who could stop them? What could so few faithful men do to stop this vast multitude that was roaring and churning with madness and wickedness? Nothing.

But God could stop them. In an instant God could silence that multitude, and he did. The glory of the LORD appeared at the Tent of Meeting to all the Israelites, and they were suddenly quiet. The majesty of Almighty God had come to them—in anger—and no one dared to utter a sound. Now the LORD would speak. With one word, one breath, God could wipe out the entire nation, and that was exactly what God intended to do. The LORD said to Moses, "How long will these people treat me with contempt? How long will they refuse to believe in me, in spite of all the miraculous signs I have performed among them?" How long? God answered his own question with a truly terrifying answer: No longer! The LORD said, "I will strike them down with a plague and destroy them." What about God's promise to Abraham, to make him into a great nation? God would fulfill that promise through Moses, who was also a descendant of Abraham. God said to Moses, "I will make you into a nation greater and stronger than they." God would begin again, making a people for himself through Moses. The LORD had had enough of these rebellious, contemptuous people.

The Israelites had given Moses nothing but trouble too. They had repaid his good to them with grief. They had treated Moses so badly that at times he wanted to quit or to die. Even now, they wanted to get rid of him. They were planning new leaders, and they were plotting vile murders. This was Moses' chance to be rid of these people in an instant and forever. He need not lift a hand or even a finger to accomplish this end. All Moses had to do was—*nothing*—and they would be gone for good.

But Moses did something. He prayed. He lifted his voice in prayer to God, a prayer for these people, not against them. He did not repay evil with evil. Although the people wanted to get rid of him, Moses did not want to get rid of them. Moses, the servant of God, the servant of Israel, put the glory of his God and the welfare of his people before himself. Moses really was a very humble man who could have grasped at the greatness being offered to him. Moses could have become a great nation, but he humbly declined. In this he was like Christ, who loved God and the people more than his own life. Even as he hung on the cross, Christ prayed for his enemies: "Father, forgive them" (Luke 23:34). So Moses pleaded with God to let this nation of people live.

Moses' main argument was that the LORD should display his power before the whole world because that would be to the honor and glory of God. Moses argued with the LORD that destroying Israel would bring dishonor to God's name among the nations. What would the world think about what God had done? What would all the God-hating, idol-worshipping peoples (especially the Egyptians and the Canaanites) say about the LORD? These people knew that the LORD was with Israel. They would think that Israel's God did not have the power to bring them into the Promised Land. Moses argued, "If you put these people to death all at one time, the nations who have heard this report about you will say, 'The LORD was not able to bring these people into the land he promised them on oath, so he slaughtered them in the desert.'"

Moses also argued that God should display his power to the whole world by showing mercy, as well as justice, to Israel. Somehow, God must display both mercy and justice at the same time. God must pardon the people, as well as punish them. Somehow, in this situation, God must display his LOVE. Moses said, "Now, may the LORD's power be displayed, just as you have declared." Moses would "remind" God of God's own word, spoken to him on Mount Sinai: "The LORD is slow to anger, abounding in LOVE, and forgiving sin and rebellion. Yet he does not leave the guilty unpunished; he punishes the children for the sin of the fathers to the third and fourth generation" (Exodus 34:5–7). This was God's Holy Word, which Moses was proclaiming to God himself, as he pleaded for Israel's life. Moses begged the LORD, "In accordance with your great love, forgive the sin of these people, just as you have pardoned them from the time they left Egypt until now" (Numbers 14:19).

Would God listen to Moses? How could God punish them and pardon them at the same time? How could God destroy them for their sin, and so display his justice, while at the same time forgive them for their sin, and so display his mercy? God, in his infinite wisdom, devised a way to kill the Israelites and keep them out of the Promised Land, while at the same time sparing the Israelites and bringing them into the Promised Land. God, the righteous Judge, pronounced this sentence upon the nation of Israel. The LORD answered Moses, "I have forgiven them, as you asked. Nevertheless, as surely as I live and as surely as the glory of the LORD fills the whole earth, not one of the men who saw my glory and the miraculous signs I performed in Egypt and in the desert, but who disobeyed me and tested me ten times[1] — not one of them will ever see the land I promised on oath to their forefathers. No one who has treated me with contempt will ever see it" (Numbers 14:20–23).

The LORD also said,

> "How long will this wicked community grumble against me? I have heard the complaints of these grumbling Israelites. So tell them, 'As surely as I live, declares the LORD, I will do to you the very things I heard you say: In this desert your bodies will fall—every one of you twenty years old or more who was counted in the census and who has grumbled against me. Not one of you will enter the land I swore with uplifted hand to make your home, except Caleb . . . and Joshua . . . As for your children, that you said would be taken as plunder, I will bring them in to enjoy the land that you have rejected. But you—your bodies will fall in this desert. Your children will be shepherds here for forty years, suffering for your unfaithfulness, until the last of your bodies lies in the desert. For forty years—one year for each of the forty days you explored the land—you will suffer for your sins and know what it is like to have me against you.' I, the LORD, have spoken, and will surely do these things to this whole wicked community, which has banded together against me. They will meet their end in this desert. Here they will die."
>
> (Numbers 14:27–35)

The whole army of Israel, all those soldiers counted by name in the census, would die in the desert. How many men were counted in that census?

There were 603,550 soldiers; from that number 603,548 would die in the desert. Only two men would survive to enter the Promised Land, because those two soldiers, Joshua and Caleb, were servants of God; they had a different spirit in them and followed the LORD wholeheartedly.

To die in the desert, that was Israel's punishment. Because the army of Israel refused to obey their Commander-in-Chief, who was the LORD, and because these soldiers refused to go forward and fight, God would send them back to die. These faithless cowards were sentenced to retreat to the desert immediately, where eventually they would die. Their grown-up children would be the ones to possess the exceedingly good land. Only two men, out of all those numbered, would ever have homes and farms in the Promised Land. The rest would wander aimlessly and homelessly in the wilderness for the remainder of their lives. Not even in death would they enter the Promised Land. Their bones would not be carried there for burial. No, that vast, desolate wasteland would become their graveyard. God began the executions immediately. The first men to die in the desert according to God's Word were the ten spies who had incited the rebellion against the LORD. Because they spread a bad report about the Promised Land among the people, they would be the first to perish for their sin. God struck them down, and they died of a plague. Joshua and Caleb were the only spies left alive. It was clear now to the people which spies had told them the truth, for God had silenced the lying lips forever. "O LORD . . . You destroy those who tell lies" (Psalm 5:6).

When Moses told the Israelites everything that God had said, and that the LORD had solemnly sworn: "Not a man of this generation shall see the good land I swore to give your forefathers" (Deuteronomy 1:34–35), and that God had given them new marching orders: "Turn back tomorrow and set out towards the desert," we do not read that the Israelites cheered heartily. No, we read that the Israelites mourned bitterly. But wasn't this what they wanted? Weren't they the ones who said they wanted to retreat? Didn't they say it would be better to die in the desert? Once again God had given them the desires of their hearts and the demands of their lips. Why then did another night carry the sound of weeping and wailing from Israel's camp? Why? The people were crying because they suddenly and finally realized what they had rejected. They had rejected nothing less than the promise of God; their exceedingly good inheritance, the land flowing with milk and honey. Like godless Esau, they had despised their birthright, and now, though they sought to inherit this blessing with tears, they could not regain it. Alas! They realized too late what they had lost forever. God would not change his mind, though there was weeping and wailing throughout the camp all through the night (see Hebrews 12:16–17).

But maybe it wasn't too late. Early the next morning the soldiers of Israel began strapping on their weapons and marching forward into the hills. "We have sinned," they said. "[Now] we will go up to the place the LORD promised." "[Now] we will go up and fight as the LORD our God commanded us" (Deuteronomy 1:41). Yesterday they believed it was impossible to fight for the land. Today they thought it would be easy. But God said, "Do not go up and fight, because I will not be with you. You will be defeated by your enemies." Moses was alarmed. "Why are you disobeying the LORD's command?" he asked. "This will not succeed!" Moses warned. This was the very day they were supposed to "turn around and set out toward the desert" (Deuteronomy 1:40). They were disobeying God again. "Do not go up," said Moses, "because the LORD is not with you. You will be defeated by your enemies . . . Because you have turned away from the LORD, he will not be with you and you will fall by the sword!"

But once again, the Israelites did not listen but rebelled against the Word of the LORD. They ignored Moses' pleadings and warnings; they rejected God's commands. Proudly, recklessly, arrogantly, and presumptuously, they marched toward the high hill country where their enemies were hiding and waiting. The Israelites marched there on their own—without Moses, without the Ark of the LORD's Covenant, without God. Then the Amorites, Amalekites and Canaanites, who lived in that hill country, came down and attacked them. Their enemies swarmed down upon them like swarms of angry bees, and the Israelites were badly beaten.

The soldiers who survived came back and wept before the LORD, but God paid no attention to their weeping. God's ears were deaf to their cries; God's eyes were blind to their tears. They would die in the desert, just as God had declared. The punishment he had promised would surely come to pass; their remorse would not alter God's Word.

The LORD displayed his justice by making the Israelites wander in the wilderness for forty years. By his justice, they suffered defeat and were driven into the desert where they slowly died—one by one by one—until all but two from that generation passed away. But God also displayed his mercy by preserving a people for himself. God kept his Promise to Israel and after forty years he led his people into the Promised Land. Blessed be the name of the LORD.

There are lessons for us to learn from this account in the Bible. "These things happened to them as examples and were written down as warnings for us" (I Corinthians 10:11).

1. *We must continue to believe and obey the Word of God.* The Israelites "were all under the cloud and they all passed through the sea. They were all baptized into Moses in the cloud and in the sea. They all ate the same spiritual food and drank the same spiritual drink . . . Nevertheless, God was not pleased with most of them and their bodies were scattered over the desert . . . So, if you think you are standing firm, be careful that you do not fall " (I Corinthians 10:1–5, 12). We must not harden our hearts, if we want to enter heaven. What does the Holy Spirit say?

> *"Today, if you hear his voice,*
> *do not harden your hearts*
> *as you did in the rebellion,*
> *during the time of testing in the desert,*
> *where your fathers tried and tested me*
> *and for forty years saw what I did.*
> *That is why I was angry with that generation,*
> *and I said, 'Their hearts are always going astray,*
> *and they have not known my ways.'*
> *So I declared on oath in my anger,*
> *'They shall never enter my rest.'"*

> *(Hebrews 3:7–11 quoting Psalm 95:7–11)*

*Who were they who heard and rebelled? Were they not all those Moses led out of Egypt? And with whom was he angry for forty years? Was it not with those who sinned, whose bodies fell in the desert? And to whom did God swear that they would not enter his rest, if not to those who disobeyed? So we see that they were not able to enter, because of their unbelief. Therefore, since the promise of entering his rest still stands, let us be careful that none of you be found to have fallen short of it. For we also have had the gospel preached to us, just as they*

*did; but the message they heard was of no value to them,*
*because those who heard it did not combine it with faith.*
*Now we who have believed enter that rest. . . .*

(Hebrews 3:16–4:3)

We must be careful to continue to believe and obey the Word of God. We must "see to it . . . that none of you has a sinful, unbelieving heart that turns away from the living God." We must be careful "so that none of you may be hardened by sin's deceitfulness. We have come to share in Christ, if we hold firmly till the end the confidence we had at first . . . Let us, therefore, make every effort to enter that rest, so that no one will fall by following their example of disobedience" (Hebrews 3:12–14; 4:11). Instead, we must "imitate those who through faith and patience inherit what has been promised" (Hebrews 6:12). The Israelites' disobedient example teaches us to believe and obey the Word of God.

2. *God did not completely destroy Israel.* The people were spared because of the prayers of Moses. Now we have One who intercedes for us, who is greater than Moses. We have Jesus Christ, the Son of God, who prays continually for us. "He is able to save completely those who come to God through him, because he always lives to intercede for them" (Hebrews 7:25). That is great comfort for us, because we all sin and fail to keep God's commands.

3. *God's justice and mercy were both displayed upon the cross.* How could God punish our sins in justice, but also pardon our sins in mercy? On the cross, Jesus Christ was put to death in our place. "He was pierced for our transgressions, he was crushed for our iniquities. The punishment that brought us peace was upon him" (Isaiah 53:5). "God demonstrates his own love for us in this: While we were still sinners, Christ died for us" (Romans 5:8). Thus God displayed his mercy toward us by saving us from our sins and sparing us from the death we deserved, but God also displayed his justice, by exacting payment for our sins. "Christ died for sins once for all, the righteous for the unrighteous, [the just for the unjust], to bring you to God" (I Peter 3:18). Jesus Christ died for us; he paid the penalty for our sins, and for that great salvation we should worship him forever. "Worthy is the Lamb, who was slain, to receive power and wealth and wisdom and strength and honor and glory and praise" (Revelation 5:12).

## Endnotes

1. This marked another of Israel's rebellions, but which one? I counted it as their eighth rebellion, but God declared it to be their tenth, saying, "They disobeyed me and tested me ten times" (Numbers 14:22). Obviously, I was too lenient in what I reckoned as full-scale rebellions, overlooking two which God clearly counted. Matthew Henry writes: "The Jewish writers reckon this exactly the tenth time that the body of the congregation had provoked God." They count that Israel rebelled:

1. At the Red Sea, pursued by Egypt's army (Exodus 14:10–12).
2. At Marah with the bitter water (Exodus 15:22–25).
3. In the Desert of Sin without food (Exodus 16:2–3).
4. Concerning the manna (Exodus 16:20).
5. Concerning the manna (Exodus 16:27).
6. At Rephidim with no water (Exodus 17:1–4).
7. At Mount Sinai with the golden calf (Exodus 32).
8. At Tarerah with their complaints (Numbers 11:1–3).
9. At Kibroth Hattaavah, with craving other food (Numbers 11).
10. At Kadesh, when they refused to advance (Numbers 14).

I did not count Israel's disobedience concerning the manna as two more rebellions. One could count instead the rebellions of Nadab and Abihu (Leviticus 10) and Miriam and Aaron (Numbers 12) as two other rebellions, in which Israel's leaders rebelled against God. However, when God said that Israel "disobeyed me and tested me ten times," this number might simply represent a fullness of provocation. Regarding this verse Matthew Henry writes, "They had repeated the provocation ten times, that is, very often." John Calvin writes, "God complains that he had been tempted by them ten times, because they had not ceased constantly to provoke him by their frowardness; for it is no fixed or definite number that is intended, but God would merely indicate that they had done so without measure or end." My opinion is that this number of rebellions is both a definite counting of their rebellions (although we are not told which ones God included in that reckoning) as well as a symbolic number indicating not only the constancy of their rebellions but also the fullness of them. One can say that God did view this particular rebellion as climactic and elsewhere it is referred to in Scripture as "The Rebellion" (Hebrews 3:15). It certainly had the most serious consequences for the nation.

# A TRAGIC EXPERIMENT

- **Numbers 16**
- **Deuteronomy 2:7;**
  **8:1–5**
- **Psalm 106:24–26**

The Israelites began their forty years of wandering in the wilderness. They had come to the very edge of the Promised Land, but as God's Word testifies, "They despised the pleasant land; they did not believe [God's] Promise. They grumbled in their tents and did not obey the LORD. So [God] swore to them with uplifted hand that he would make them fall in the desert" (Psalm 106:24–26). One by one, those men did die in the desert, but during that time the LORD continued to bless Israel, for God was still with them. The LORD, in his unfailing LOVE, continued to guide them and guard them and give them everything they needed for *life*. Miraculously, for forty years the bread on the ground did not run out and the clothes on their backs did not wear out. The LORD also continued to speak to Moses. The people were blessed with God's Holy Word and God's righteous laws.

At some point during these forty years, the LORD spoke to Moses and instructed the Israelites to make something that they must wear and see every day to remind them of God's Laws. The LORD said, "Make tassels on the corners of your garments, with a blue cord on each tassel. You will have these tassels to look at and so you will re-member all the commands of the LORD, that you may obey them and not prostitute yourselves by going after the lusts of your own hearts and eyes. Then you will remember to obey all my commands and will be consecrated to your God. I am the LORD your God, who brought you out of Egypt to be your God. I am the LORD your God" (Numbers 15:37–41). Even those lit-tle tassels were a good gift from God. They were a reminder of God's Law, to keep the Israelites from sin.

This time in the desert was for Israel's growth. It was a time to humble Israel and make them learn that most vital lesson — to rely on God and not themselves. God had ordained this time in the desert for Israel's teaching and training and testing. God wanted to know what was in their hearts: Would they believe God's Word? Would they follow God's laws? This time in the desert was a time of discipline. They must not despise the LORD's discipline; they must not resent God's rebuke, "because the LORD disciplines those he loves" (Proverbs 3:11–12), just as a father disciplines the child in whom he delights. This time in the desert was difficult for Israel. It was a punishment, but it was not without God's LOVE. The Israelites were still the most privi-leged people on the face of the earth, for they alone worshipped the true God. The LORD was with them. "Blessed are the people whose God is the LORD" (Psalm 144:15).

We are told very little about those forty years. That generation of people lived in the desert, wandering day after day from place to place (as listed in Numbers 33:1–49), and then they died. On one of those days, during one of those forty years in the desert, there was another great rebellion, known as "Korah's Rebellion" (Jude 11). We are not told exactly when it happened or where it happened, but we are told what happened:

The rebellion began in one man's heart. The man's name was Korah, and what was stirring in his heart was envy. He was growing envious of Moses and Aaron. He was jealous of their positions in Israel and he began think-ing: Why should Moses be the great prophet? Why should Aaron be the high priest? What's so special about them? Why should they be the ones leading Israel? Is it right that only Moses and Aaron enter the Holy Place and hear the voice of God? Are they holier than the rest of the Israelites? Korah wasn't just thinking these things; soon he was speaking with other people, many of whom were feeling the same way. It did not take long for Korah to gather around himself a powerful group of discontented men. Among them were

250 Levites (like himself) who were elders in Israel, all well-known leaders in the community and members of the council. With this kind of support Korah became insolent and arrogant towards Moses and Aaron. Finally, Korah and his 250 followers rose up in outright rebellion. They came as a group to oppose Moses and Aaron and said to them, "You have gone too far! The whole community is holy, every one of them, and the LORD is with them. Why then do you set yourselves above the LORD's assembly?"

What was amazing was that Korah and these 250 rebels were all Levites. What was their complaint? They should have been satisfied — no, *delighted* — with their position in Israel. The Levites had a very special place in the congregation: God had chosen the tribe of Levi. "The Levites are mine," declared the LORD. They had been chosen by God to stand before all the people to lead them in the praises of God. The tents of Levi circled God's Tabernacle and the hands of Levi carried God's Tabernacle. The Levites had been brought close to the holy God, closer than any other tribe in Israel.

But Korah and his followers were not content, because the Levites were not as powerful as the priests. Only the priests were allowed to enter the Holy Place, and only the High Priest was permitted to enter the Most Holy Place. Aside from Moses, anyone else who approached the sanctuary must be put to death. But Korah and his rebels wanted to enter the Tabernacle, for it was there that the LORD spoke to Moses and Aaron. From that sacred meeting place, Moses and Aaron then brought the Word of God to the entire nation of Israel, and that word must be obeyed. How powerful Moses and Aaron were, because they spoke to God in the Tabernacle. What was Korah (or any of the other Levites) compared to them? They may have been leaders and elders in Israel, but compared to Moses and Aaron, they were nothing. The Levites were merely assistants, lowly servants, given to Aaron and his sons to help them in the work of the Tabernacle. Aaron and his sons were in charge, assigning each man's work to the Levites. Even when the Levites carried the most holy things, their hands could not touch, nor their eyes see, these sacred things lest they die. Only the priests could touch and see the holy articles of the Tabernacle. The priests were the ones who covered up these things, so no one else (not even the Levites) could gaze upon them. The Levites may have been close to God, but Moses and Aaron were closer.

That was Korah's complaint. He was dissatisfied with the place that God had given him, although it was a good place. He followed in the sinful footsteps of his father, the devil, who also was not content with his God-appointed position. Korah did not want to be the one assisting in the work; he wanted to be the one assigning the work, like the priests. He wanted to be the one in charge, the one giving orders instead of the one taking orders. Korah wanted to be the one directly speaking to God and thus completely ruling the people. Korah was envious, ambitious, and presumptuous. He wanted the priesthood for himself. He wasn't honest enough, however, to come right out and say that, so he tried to make the priesthood open to everyone, not just to the sons of Aaron. Then Korah could take that powerful position for himself. So Korah, very sneakily and very haughtily and very wickedly said to Moses and Aaron, "You have gone too far! The whole community is holy, every one of them, and the LORD is with them. Why then do you set yourselves above the LORD's assembly?"

When Moses heard this he fell facedown on the ground. These accusations were not true. Moses and Aaron had not set themselves above the LORD's assembly. God had placed them there. They had not made themselves the leaders of Israel; God had done that. Moses and Aaron were simply servants of the LORD. They were only obeying their Master. As Moses said to Korah, "Who is Aaron, that you should grumble against him?" Aaron was just doing his job, as the LORD had commanded him. Moses had not asked to be the great prophet, nor had Aaron asked to be the high priest. God had appointed them to do that work and to take that place. Korah and his followers, by opposing them, were rebelling against God himself. But how could Moses show these rebels and all Israel and even the whole world— that it was God who had chosen them?

Moses would run an experiment. Moses said to Korah and all his followers: "In the morning the LORD will show who belongs to him and who is holy, and he will have that person come near him. The man he chooses, he will cause to come near him. You, Korah, and all of your followers, are to do this: Take censers and tomorrow put fire and incense in them before the LORD. The man the LORD chooses will be the one who is holy." That man would be the one who entered the Tabernacle to offer the incense of worship to God. It would be a contest between the priests and the Levites, between Aaron and Korah.

There must have been many questions about this experiment: Whose incense offering would the LORD accept—Aaron's or Korah's? Which offering would please God? Wouldn't the offering of 250 men be more pleasing to God than the offering of just one man? How would God show who was holy, whose offering was acceptable to him? Everyone's questions would be answered the next day. All of Israel would see the awful results of Moses' experiment. Every generation thereafter would hear of it and the whole world would know of it. God himself would settle this dispute.

Korah and his followers said to Moses and Aaron, "You have gone too far." But Moses warned them, "You Levites have gone too far!" He confronted them with their sin and said: "Now listen, isn't it enough for you that the God of Israel has separated you from the rest of the Israelite community and brought you near himself to do the work at the LORD's Tabernacle and to stand before the community and minister to them? He has brought you and all your fellow Levites near himself, but now you are trying to get the priesthood too. It is against the LORD that you and all your followers have banded together."

Was Korah not afraid? Wasn't he terrified to be part of this experiment? Didn't he remember what had happened to Aaron's own sons, Nadab and Abihu, when they offered incense before the LORD? Because they offered unauthorized fire, contrary to God's command, fire came out from the presence of the LORD and consumed them. They died before the LORD, although they were ordained priests. What would happen to Korah and his followers, whom God had not authorized to offer any incense at all?

Korah and the rebel Levites had a day and a night to think about what they were doing, a time of grace in which they could repent of their sin, turn from their wickedness, and live. The fear of the LORD is the beginning of wisdom, but Korah and his followers were foolish men, who had no fear of God. They were bold in their unbelief. They appeared the next morning before the Tabernacle and stood proudly with censers in their hands. They stood with Moses and Aaron before the LORD and before all the people. This was exactly where they wanted to be, standing in the same powerful position as Moses and Aaron, standing equal to them. Korah and his rebels put fire and incense in their censers to lead the entire nation in worship. Although Moses had not summoned the people to attend this event, the whole assembly of Israel had gathered there, possibly to show their support for Korah, certainly to watch this new kind of worship.

There were two competing sides in Moses' contest:

1. Korah's contingent was an impressive sight. They stood together, all on one side — 250 leaders of Israel with 250 bronze censers, shining in the

morning sun. As they waved their burning incense, clouds of sweet-smelling smoke billowed up to heaven. It was quite a spectacle and no doubt very pleasing to the people. (But was this worship pleasing to God?)

2. On the other side stood Aaron, all by himself, one wrinkled old man, holding his censer in a feeble old arm, with a thin wisp of smoke quickly vanishing into the air. Israel's great high priest did not look so special to the people this morning. (But how did he look in God's sight?)

This then was Moses' experiment. Whom would God choose? Which offering would be impressive to God? Which worship would be acceptable to God? How would God show who was holy? Which "priests" would the LORD permit to enter into his Tabernacle to meet with him?

This was a matter of God's command, not the people's choice. How Israel should worship their God was not an issue to be decided by an opinion poll or a democratic vote. The people—the whole congregation that had crowded around to watch—were impressed by the exciting ceremony produced by this mighty array of new priests. Aaron seemed so insignificant and ineffectual standing opposite them. But how did it seem to God? The LORD's ways are not our ways. He is not influenced by the displays of man's artistic endeavor, arrogant splendor or ignorant fervor. God is pleased with faith, expressed in obedience.

Suddenly, the glory of the LORD appeared to the entire assembly, but it was to Moses and Aaron that the LORD spoke. This in itself showed whom the LORD had chosen to be near him. God did not speak to Korah or to the 250 new priests offering incense or to the whole community. God spoke to Moses and his old priest, Aaron. Now God would reveal his will and declare his choice: The LORD said to Moses and Aaron, "Separate yourselves from this assembly, so I can put an end to them at once." This was not the answer Moses or Aaron had expected. They did not want the entire nation to be destroyed. So Moses and Aaron fell facedown and cried out, "O God, God of the spirits of all mankind, will you be angry with the entire assembly, when only one man sins?" And the LORD listened to Moses and Aaron. This too showed who was holy. The man who is close to God and called by God is the man to whom the LORD listens and answers.

God had already shown who the great prophet and high priest of Israel were. They were the two men with whom God spoke, the two men whose prayers God heard—Moses and Aaron. But God showed his choice in another way too. Fire came out from the LORD and consumed the 250 men who were offering incense, but Aaron's life was spared. God's choice was clear. Aaron alone was able to stand near the Holy God of Israel and live, for our God is a consuming fire.

What a disaster! No less than 250 leaders of Israel died before the LORD that day. In front of the beautiful Tabernacle lay the smoking remains of the men who thought they could succeed in their opposition against God. They couldn't even survive. In an instant their glamorous new ministry became grey ashes in the wind and black cinders on the ground. Their rebellion had come to nothing. They had come to nothing. What they offered now before the LORD and before all the people was not the sweet-smelling aroma of burning incense, but the sickening odor of burning human flesh. That was how these new priests glorified God. All that remained were the 250 bronze censers, still shining in the sun as they lay on the charred ground. The LORD said to Moses, "Take the censers out of the smoldering remains . . . for the censers are holy—the censers of the men who sinned at the cost of their lives. Hammer the censers into sheets to overlay the altar, for they were presented before the LORD and have become holy. Let them be a sign to the Israelites." This would be the task of one of God's real priests. Eleazar, son of Aaron, collected the bronze censers of the men who had been burned up, and he had them hammered out to overlay the altar, just as the LORD directed him to do through Moses. This was to remind the Israelites that no one except a descendant of Aaron could come to burn incense before the LORD, or he would become like Korah and his followers. And it would remind the people of God forever, that they must worship according to God's commands.

It was a tragic experiment that cost the lives of 250 men. There was, however, a holy result to this wicked rebellion. The Word of the LORD prevailed. It prevailed against the evil plots and proud desires of wicked men. The conclusion of the experiment was this: The Sovereign LORD reigns. God will uphold his servants, and he will destroy all impostors and pretenders and deceivers who think they can fool God with their false worship. God will crush all rebellion against him. Even man's foolishness and wickedness will praise the LORD. To God be the glory forever and ever. Amen.

# SOMETHING TOTALLY NEW

- **Numbers 16; 26:5–11**
- **Psalm 106:16–18**
- **John 5:31–47**
- **Jude**

Let us return to that evil uprising called Korah's Rebellion. This rebellion was not confined to the tribe of Levi, but it spread beyond Levi's borders and infected another tribe, the tribe of Reuben. From the beginning stages of this rebellion, Korah was not alone in his wickedness. He had accomplices in high places. There were certain leading men of the tribe of Reuben who also joined wholeheartedly in Korah's rebellion. Their names were Dathan, Abiram and On.

What were the grievances of these Reubenites? Perhaps they were angry because their tribe, Reuben, who was the first-born son of Jacob, was not given a pre-eminent place in Israel. Reuben was neither the spiritual leader nor the military leader of the nation. Those places of honor were given to the tribes of Levi, who led Israel's worship, and Judah, who led Israel's army, not Reuben. Perhaps that was the problem, but the real grievance of these Reubenites was not against the leading tribes of Israel; it was against the leading men of Israel, Moses and Aaron. Why should they lead Israel? Why shouldn't two Reubenite brothers, like Dathan and Abiram, be the leaders? Why should two Levite brothers, like Moses and Aaron, be the ones to lead Israel? So, along with Korah, these two powerful men led in the uprising against God's servants. They challenged the authority of Moses and Aaron. They joined Korah in opposing them and accusing them. Along with Korah they said to Moses and Aaron: "You have gone too far! The whole community is holy, every one of them, and the LORD is with them. Why then do you set yourselves above the LORD's assembly?" Dathan, Abiram and On believed they had as much right as Moses and Aaron to be the leaders of Israel. No, they believed they had more right to be leaders, because they were Reubenites.

Poor Moses! Not only did he have to deal with Korah and the Levites; he also had to deal with these Reubenites at the same time. First, Moses set up his experiment with Korah and the 250 Levites. Then he summoned Dathan and Abiram, but they refused to obey Moses. They weren't going to take orders from him any longer. "We will not come!" they said. But they did send a message to Moses, accusing him of many crimes against the people. They charged Moses with being a cruel tyrant, who lied and robbed and killed the people. They said Moses wanted to make them all his slaves. They said that Moses had deceived the Israelites by promising them a land flowing with milk and honey, but what had Moses done? He had led them out of Egypt, which really was a beautiful and bountiful land, and he had brought them into this barren desert instead. They said Moses had led them here to rule them, to enslave them, to kill them. Dathan and Abiram said, "You have brought us out of a land flowing with milk and honey [Egypt] to kill us in the desert . . . No, we will not come!" They showed they would not obey such a wicked tyrant as Moses.

When Moses received their message he was furious. What they had said was not true. It was the Israelites' own fault that they were not now enjoying the Promised Land, a land flowing with milk and honey. It was because of their sin that they were in this desert, and Moses was here too, suffering because of them. What had Moses gained? He had taken nothing. He had harmed no one. This was when Moses cried out to the LORD against them. Yes, Moses prayed against Korah, Dathan and Abiram. "Do not accept their offering," prayed Moses. "I have not wronged any of them." When Korah and his followers offered their incense, they would do so with Moses' prayers against them. It could only end in disaster.

The following day, Korah and the 250 Levites assembled before the Tabernacle with their censers. Dathan and Abiram stayed home. They refused to meet with Moses. They refused to be part of Moses' experiment. Dathan and Abiram stayed in their tents where they thought they were safe from the wrath of God. If fire came out from the LORD again (as it had with Nadab and Abihu) they would not be burned. So, when Korah had gathered all his followers in opposition to Moses and Aaron at the entrance to the Tent of Meeting, Dathan and Abiram were not with them.

Then the glory of the LORD appeared to the entire assembly, and the LORD said to Moses and Aaron that he was going to destroy all the Israelites. But Moses and Aaron pleaded for Israel's life and cried out in prayer, "O God, God of the spirits of all mankind, will you be angry with the entire assembly when only one man sins?" God heard their prayers and once again the LORD of LOVE extended his mercy to this rebellious people. God would give Israel the chance to choose. Would they follow Korah, Dathan and Abiram or would they follow the LORD their God?

The LORD said to Moses, "Tell the assembly to move away from the tents of Korah, Dathan and Abiram." Moses obeyed the LORD and immediately left the entrance of the Tabernacle, where the contest between Aaron and Korah's 250 Levites was in progress. Moses had more important work to do: He must warn the people; he must save their lives. Moses now went to the tents of Dathan and Abiram. They were there, standing with their families at the entrances to their tents. Moses warned the Israelites: "Move back from the tents of these wicked men! Do not touch anything belonging to them, or you too will be swept away because of all their sins." So the people moved away from the tents of Korah, Dathan and Abiram. Unlike these rebels, the rest of Israel were still willing to obey Moses' commands. When Moses ordered them to move, they moved. The crowd that had gathered in support of these rebels now backed away from their tents; their friends, who had rallied around them, also distanced themselves; and their neighbors, who had camped next to them, also moved away from their tents as quickly as possible. But, sadly, the families of these wicked men did not move. The wives remained standing next to their husbands; the children refused to leave their fathers' sides. As difficult as it was to break a family bond, choosing loyalty to an earthly father instead of loyalty to the Heavenly Father, was a very bad and very wrong choice. What about the little ones who were too young to make their own decision, the babies cradled in their mothers' arms and the toddlers clinging to their fathers' hands? What would happen to them? Their parents made the dreadful decision for them that they too must stand in opposition to God.

Moses gave every person in the assembly time to move away from the tents of Korah, Dathan and Abiram. Then Moses set up another experiment to prove to the people that what these men had said about him was untrue. Moses said, "This is how you will know that the LORD has sent me to do all these things and that it was not my idea: If these men die a natural death and experience only what usually happens to men, then the LORD has not sent me. But if the LORD brings about something totally new . . . then you will know that these men have treated the LORD with contempt."

What was something totally new? In the days of Noah, the wicked world was swept away in a flood. In the days of Abraham, fire and brimstone rained down upon two evil cities, turning their people to piles of ashes and pillars of salt. In their own day, they had seen with their own eyes what God had done to the Egyptians, when they had been killed by hailstones, lightening, sickness and drowning. The Israelites had seen their own people burned by fire, struck by plague and felled by the sword. What could be totally new? Moses pronounced what it would be before it happened: "If the earth opens its mouth and swallows them, with everything that belongs to them, and they go down alive into the grave, then you will know that these men have treated the LORD with contempt."

The words had barely left Moses' lips when the ground under these wicked men split apart and the earth opened its mouth and swallowed them. Everything and everyone they owned was devoured in one great gulp, and they went into a vast grave. They were buried alive! The people could hear them screaming, and then there was silence. Their crying and their breathing were smothered when the earth closed over them again. In a moment they perished and vanished forever.

Panic gripped the Israelites who witnessed this terrifying scene. They began running and screaming, "The earth is going to swallow us too!" Then the other frightening judgment occurred: Fire came out from the LORD and consumed Korah's followers—the 250 men who were offering incense at the Tabernacle. So, all the rebels were devoured at once, some by the earth swallowing them, others by fire consuming them. There was no doubt about whom God had chosen. All the rebels died horrifying deaths, but Moses and Aaron stood there alive.

One could draw many conclusions from the events of that dreadful day, but the main result of those two experiments was this: God himself proved that it was he himself who had appointed Moses as the great prophet and

Aaron as the high priest in Israel. Rebelling against them was rebelling against God. There was a very important lesson to be learned from this rebellion in the desert, because one day, many hundreds of years later, God would send a greater prophet than Moses and a higher priest than Aaron. One day God would send his only begotten and beloved Son, Jesus Christ, our Lord. Would people honor him?

No, many people would rebel against the Son of God. Many people would refuse to accept him or follow him or worship him. Many false prophets and phony priests would arise to challenge his authority and oppose his sovereignty. Many fake Christs would arise and many people would follow these impostors and deceivers. But just as the LORD proved that Moses and Aaron were indeed appointed by him, so, also, God gave overwhelming evidence that Jesus was the Anointed One, the Messiah, the Son of God:

1. God's voice from heaven testified: "This is my Son, whom I love; with him I am well pleased. Listen to him" (Matthew 17:5). Twice God spoke from heaven declaring Jesus to be his beloved Son, once at his baptism and again at the transfiguration.

2. Jesus himself confessed many times to be the Son of God. "The Pharisees challenged him: 'Here you are, appearing as your own witness; your testimony is not valid.' Jesus answered, 'Even if I testify on my own behalf, my testimony is valid, for I know where I came from and where I am going . . . In your own Law it is written that the testimony of two men is valid. I am one who testifies for myself; my other witness is the Father who sent me'" (John 8:13–14, 17).

3. The Holy Spirit gave evidence that Jesus was the Christ. At his baptism "as he was praying, heaven was opened and the Holy Spirit descended on him in bodily form like a dove" (Luke 3:22).

4. The angels from heaven declared Jesus to be the Christ. At his birth an angel of the Lord said about him: "He is Christ the Lord" (Luke 2:11). Then a great company of the heavenly host appeared with the angel, praising God.

5. Jesus said, "If I testify about myself, my testimony is not valid. There is another who testifies in my favor, and I know that his testimony about me is valid." Who was this witness? Jesus was speaking about John the Baptist.

Jesus said, "He has testified to the truth. Not that I accept human testimony; but I mention it that you may be saved. John was a lamp that burned and gave light" (John 5:31–35), a light that revealed that Jesus was the Son of God. John the Baptist said, "I have seen and I testify that this is the Son of God!" John also said, "Look, the Lamb of God, who takes away the sin of the world" (John 1:29).

6. Jesus said, "I have testimony weightier than that of John. For the very work that the Father has given me to finish, and which I am doing, testifies that the Father has sent me" (John 5:36). All the miracles that Jesus performed testified to the fact that he was the Son of God: "The blind receive sight, the lame walk, those who have leprosy are cured, the deaf hear, the dead are raised, and the good news is preached to the poor" (Matthew 11:5). The unbelieving Jews said to Jesus, "How long will you keep us in suspense? If you are the Christ, tell us plainly." Jesus answered, "I did tell you, but you do not believe. The miracles I do in my Father's name speak for me, but [still] you do not believe . . . Why then do you accuse me of blasphemy because I said 'I am God's Son'? Do not believe me unless I do what my Father does. But if I do it, even though you do not believe me, believe the miracles, that you may know and understand that the Father is in me, and I in the Father" (John 10:24–38). Again Jesus said, "At least believe on the evidence of the miracles themselves" (John 14:11). Jesus performed all these miracles so that people would believe in him and be saved from sin and death. Once, Jesus healed a paralyzed man so that people would know "that the Son of Man has authority on earth to forgive sins" (Matthew 9:1–8). The greatest work that Jesus did as evidence that he was the Son of God was dying on the cross and rising from the dead.

7. Jesus also said, "The Scriptures testify about me." Hundreds of years before Christ was born, the prophets of the Old Testament were faithful witnesses to the truth. They spoke of Christ long before his birth or death. Jesus said, "If you believed Moses, you would believe me, for he wrote about me" (John 5:39, 46). Again Jesus said, "How foolish you are, and how slow of heart to believe all that the prophets have spoken! Did not the Christ have to suffer these things and then enter his glory? And beginning with Moses and all the Prophets, he explained to them what was said in all the Scriptures concerning himself" (Luke 24:25–27). Again Jesus said to his disciples, "This is what I told you while I was still with you: Everything must be ful-

filled that is written about me in the Law of Moses, the Prophets and the Psalms. Then Jesus opened their minds so they could understand the Scriptures" (Luke 24:44–45).

8. The New Testament is the recorded testimony of many people declaring that Jesus was the Christ, the Son of God. For example, the apostle John wrote in his epistle that he was a reliable eye-witness of all that happened. He said, "That which was from the beginning, which we have heard, which we have seen with our eyes, which we have looked at and our hands have touched—this we proclaim concerning the Word of life. The life appeared; we have seen it and testify to it, and we proclaim to you the eternal life, which was with the Father and has appeared to us. We proclaim to you what we have seen and heard, so that you also may have fellowship with us. And our fellowship is with the Father and with his Son, Jesus Christ. We write this to make our [your] joy complete" (I John 1:1–4).

In his gospel, the apostle John said that he was "the disciple who testifies to these things and who wrote them down. We know that his testimony is true" (John 21:24). He urged, "These are written that you may believe that Jesus is the Christ, the Son of God, and that by believing you may have life in his name" (John 20:31).

9. Even the heavens declared that Jesus was the Christ. At his birth, wise men saw his star and came to worship him. At his death, even the sun was blotted out as darkness covered the land.

10. Our faith is also evidence. Those who hold to the testimony of Jesus are witnesses to the truth. Believers are living proof that there is a God who saves people from their sins.

God has provided abundant evidence that Jesus is the Son of God. If those who rebelled against Moses and Aaron were not spared, what will happen to those who rebel against the Son of God? How will they escape, if they neglect so great a salvation? How will they escape, if they despise so great a Savior? If those who joined Korah's rebellion received such terrifying punishments—being swallowed by the earth and devoured by fire—what will happen to those who join Satan's rebellion against God's own Son? Woe to them! How terrifying their destruction will be. They will be buried in the pit of blackest darkness; they will be burned in the flames of fiercest fire; they will be consumed in hell forever.

With this in view, we must make sure that we do not have an unbeliev-ing heart and miss the grace of God. We must build ourselves up in our most holy faith. We must pray. We must keep ourselves in God's most wondrous Love, as we wait for the mercy of our Lord Jesus Christ to bring us to eter-nal life. We must show mercy to others (see Jude 20–23).

> *To him who is able to keep you from falling and to present you before his glorious presence without fault and with great joy—to the only God our Savior be glory, majesty, power, and authority, through Jesus Christ our Lord, before all ages, now and forevermore! Amen.*

> *(Jude 24–25)*

# AARON'S CENSER

• Numbers 16:41–50

Korah, Dathan and Abiram, with their families and their followers, were all swept away by the LORD because of their rebellion against Moses and Aaron, whom God had appointed prophet and priest of Israel. Although it was a day filled with terror and horror for the people, and although there should have been sorrow because of the sin and death of many of their leaders, nonetheless, the Israelites should have been solemnly and sincerely thankful that God had vindicated his righteous servants and executed the wicked rebels. On that day the people had seen the awesome works of Almighty God. It was a day in which God glorified himself, and the people should have rejoiced in that dreadful day that the LORD had made. Their response should have been to praise God.

But that is not what happened. The Bible records: "The next day the whole Israelite community grumbled against Moses and Aaron." How could that be possible? How could the Israelites so soon join in the same sin as Korah, Dathan and Abiram? How could they ever rebel against God again, not to mention the very next day? The ashes of the corpses still lay upon the blackened ground; the stench of burned human flesh still hung in the heavy air. The Israelites had not forgotten what had happened, because the evidence of the rebels' folly was all around them.

The Israelites had seen with their own eyes that to rebel against Moses and Aaron was to rebel against God himself, yet they did it anyway. The Israelites joined in the demonic activity of rebelling against God by opposing and accusing God's servants. They charged Moses and Aaron with the crime of murder. They said, "You have killed the LORD's people." It was a lie. Neither Moses nor Aaron had lifted a finger against these men. Although they had lifted their prayers against them, it was the LORD who had killed them. Could Moses or Aaron rip open the earth? Could they breathe forth flames of fire? No, of course not; they were only men.

Clearly these strange deaths had been the work of God, yet the Israelites accused Moses and Aaron of murdering innocent men. "You have killed the LORD's people," they said. It was a lie. These rebels against God had proven that they were not "the LORD's people." These men were not innocent victims, nor were they loyal subjects. They were treacherous men who had instigated a rebellion that endangered the entire nation. These men were guilty of treason; they deserved death, and God, the righteous judge, had executed them for their crimes.

But the Israelites did not have the wisdom to reason righteously or to tremble fearfully before the LORD who dwelled in their midst. The fear of the LORD was the beginning of wisdom, but these Israelites did not fear God. They joined in Korah's rebellion, assembling themselves into an angry mob in opposition to Moses and Aaron. Thousands of Israelites gathered before the Tent of Meeting to oppose God's faithful servants. What would happen to Israel now? Did they think God could not hear or see? Did they think God would not act? Did they think God would not care that they had joined in the rebellion? Did they think nothing would happen? Did they think at all?

Suddenly the cloud covered the Tabernacle and the glory of the LORD appeared. Moses and Aaron went to the entrance of God's Tent to meet with him. The LORD said to Moses, "Get away from this assembly, so I can put an end to them at once." Moses and Aaron fell facedown on the ground. Again Israel's faithful prophet and priest pleaded for the people in prayer, but this time, God's anger had already broken out among the people. Already they were dying because of their sin. Before the Tabernacle stretched the dead, right where they had dropped. A plague had come out from the LORD and was spreading rapidly outwards into the camp. "Hurry!" urged Moses to Aaron. "Take your censer and put incense in it, along with fire from the altar, and hurry to the assembly to make atonement for them. Wrath has come out from the LORD; the plague has started!"

Aaron obeyed immediately. Not fearing for his own life, he walked through the death and disease; he waded past the plague-struck corpses into the chaos of dying, screaming, panicking people. Aaron placed himself between the living and the dead. He stood there, waving his censer, to make atonement for their sin. The sacred smoke wafting from his censer was not to purify the plague-filled air, but to pacify a wrath-filled God. The LORD saw his high priest standing there and the LORD heard his high priest praying there, and the LORD stopped the plague. God accepted the offering of incense made to him by Israel's high priest. However, 14,700 people died of the plague that day.

Would there ever again be a question that Aaron was the high priest whom God had appointed? The censers of the 250 self-appointed "priests" had brought only death. Their offerings of incense could not even save themselves. However, Aaron's censer had brought life. It was Aaron's censer that had stopped the plague, saving hundreds of thousands of people from death.

In this ministry of life, Aaron foreshadowed God's Great High Priest, Jesus Christ, who would save his people from their sins. Christ himself would stand in the breach between the living and the dead; he would hang on the cross between heaven and hell to reconcile a holy God to sinful men. God's furious wrath was poured out on Christ instead of on us.

> *Surely he took up our infirmities and carried our sorrows,*
> *yet we considered him stricken by God, smitten by him*
> *and afflicted. But he was pierced for our transgressions;*
> *he was crushed for our iniquities; the punishment that*
> *brought us peace was upon him; and by his wounds we*
> *are healed. We all, like sheep, have gone astray, each of*
> *us has turned to his own way; and the LORD has laid on*
> *him the iniquity of us all . . . for the transgression of my*
> *people he was stricken . . . He bore the sin of many, and*
> *made intercession for the transgressors.*
>
> *(Isaiah 53:4–6, 8, 12)*

Jesus, our Great High Priest, now lives forever and "He is able to save completely those who come to God through him, because he always lives to intercede for them" (Hebrews 7:25). "There is one Mediator between God and men, the man Christ Jesus" (I Timothy 2:5). "We have peace with God through our Lord Jesus Christ" (Romans 5:1).

# AARON'S STAFF

• Numbers 17

Korah's Rebellion was one of the blackest times in Israel's early history. It was the rebellion of the nation against Aaron as God's high priest. The leading men of two of Israel's tribes wanted the priesthood for themselves. These leaders of the Levites and the Reubenites lusted after the power and the honor that was bestowed upon the high priest. Their sin led to the death of over 15,000 people in Israel. God, who did not desire the death of any man, was concerned that such a rebellion might happen again. Perhaps there were other leaders from other tribes, men who still were envious of Aaron's position. God, who knew the secrets in the hearts of all men, wanted to prevent another disaster in the future. This opposition to Aaron as the high priest must come to an end. God had already demonstrated with proof upon proof that Aaron alone was appointed by him to be the high priest. These people had seen with their own eyes what God would do to those who opposed his appointed priest. These people had seen the earth devour the offenders; they had seen fire consume the pretenders; they had seen a plague destroy the grumblers, but now God would provide one more proof, an enduring piece of evidence, that it was Aaron alone (and his sons after him) whom God had called to be priests.

The LORD said to Moses, "Speak to the Israelites and get twelve staffs from them, one from the leader of each of their ancestral tribes. Write the name of each man on his staff. On the staff of Levi write Aaron's name." God instructed that these staffs should be placed in the Tabernacle overnight, in the Holy of Holies, before the Ark of the Covenant, which was God's throne on earth. The LORD would show all Israel clearly, visibly, undoubtedly and miraculously that he had chosen Aaron as his priest. How would God show this? The LORD said, "The staff belonging to the man I choose will sprout." These staffs were made of old, dry, hard, dead wood. There was not a drop of life-giving sap left in them. It was not natural or possible for such brittle wood to sprout, any more than it would be for buried bones to dance. Such an occurrence would be supernatural.

The LORD also told Moses why he was going to do this. He said, "I will rid myself of the constant grumbling against you by the Israelites." This would not be a miracle of wrath, but a miracle of grace, a miracle to prevent sin, rather than a miracle to punish sin. This was an act of LOVE, designed by the LORD to protect his people from their own deadly sin of rebellion. If the people could be kept from falling again into this fatal sin, what a great blessing it would be, not only for Moses and Aaron, but also for the whole nation. This miracle would be for the good of man, as well as for the glory of God.

So, Moses did as the LORD commanded. He collected the twelve staffs, each with a name written upon it. There was one staff for each tribe, and Aaron's staff was among them. Then Moses placed all of them in the Tabernacle before the LORD.

That night, as everyone in Israel went to sleep in their own tents; they must have been wondering and dreaming about what was happening in the LORD's Tent. The faithful were convinced that Aaron's staff was sprouting in the presence of the LORD. The skeptics were suspicious that Moses might be creeping about in the dark, switching Aaron's old brown staff with a live green branch. The envious were anxious that the staff belonging to them or their tribe be chosen. Everyone in Israel (according to what was in his heart) had his own thoughts and hopes about what was occurring in the Tabernacle that night.

The next morning, Moses entered the Tabernacle and there he saw an amazing sight. Aaron's staff had not only sprouted; it had budded and blossomed and produced almonds. Then Moses brought out all the staffs from the LORD's presence and showed them to the Israelites. There were eleven staffs as dry and dead as they had been for years, and there was another staff bearing Aaron's name, which was bursting with life. Aaron's staff was covered with fresh green leaves, full round buds, pretty fragrant blossoms and ripe brown nuts. Everyone in Israel must have been amazed. The faithful were rewarded, for God had provided a sign beyond anything they had expected or imagined. The skeptics were silenced, for not even a branch growing on a living tree could produce leaves, buds, blooms and fruit, all at the same time and in a single night. It would take an entire season for a branch to produce each of these things in its turn. Yes, this was a miracle. Moses could not have found such a branch growing anywhere. The envious and arrogant were humbled, for all the staves bearing their names produced nothing, not so much as a little green sprout of life.

Eleven of the staffs were returned to their owners, but Aaron's staff was to be kept forever in the Most Holy Place (or the Holy of Holies) as a sign to the rebellious. God said, "This will put an end to their grumbling against me, so that they will not die!" God had performed this miracle (and was now preserving it throughout their generations) so that the Israelites would not die. It was an act of God's grace, a miracle of God's LOVE to a rebellious people. This was a sign for them to stop their rebellion, which brought only death. It was a sign to lead them from death to life. This staff was a perfect symbol of that life from death, since it had been transformed from an old, dry, dead stick to a fresh, green, live branch. Aaron's staff was a sign of *life*. God's people could entrust themselves to this LORD of *life*, who could do to them what he had done to Aaron's staff—raise them from death to life. It was an amazing miracle and an amazing symbol, which should have led the people to entrust their souls to such a God. He was the LORD of *life* and love.

But the Israelites missed the LORD's benediction upon them. They missed the meaning of the sign; they missed the message of his *life* and his LOVE. Although the LORD himself declared that he had done this "so that they will not die," the Israelites contradicted God, wailing, "We will die! We are lost, we are all lost! Anyone who even comes near the Tabernacle of the LORD will die. Are we all going to die?" Somehow the Israelites missed the grace of God in this miracle. Aaron's staff was a sign of life for them. It was because they had a high priest (not any high priest, but the one whom God had chosen) that they could draw close to God and not die. It was because they had such a high priest interceding for them that they could live. The ministry of their high priest brought them life.

Aaron's staff was also a sign of life for them, because it pointed to Christ. Jesus was the Branch, in whom was life; that tender green shoot out of dry dead ground, whom the prophets foretold was coming. Jesus was "the Branch of the LORD . . . beautiful and glorious" (Isaiah 4:2). Jesus was the Righteous Branch: "The days are coming," declares the LORD, "when I will raise up to David a righteous Branch, a King who will reign wisely and do what is just and right in the land. In his days Judah will be saved and Israel will live in safety. This is the name by which he will be called: The LORD Our Righteousness" (Jeremiah 23:5–6). God said, "Listen . . . I am going to bring my servant, the Branch . . . This is what the LORD Almighty says: 'Here is the man whose name is the Branch, and he will branch out from his place and build the temple of the LORD. . . . He will be clothed with majesty and will sit and rule on his throne. And he will be a priest on his throne'" (Zechariah 3:8; 6:12–13). Jesus Christ alone fulfilled that prophesy; he became both our Holy Priest and Righteous King.

Jesus is the life-giving branch or vine and we are the little green off-shoots, deriving life from him. Jesus declared,

> I am the true vine . . . Remain in me and I will remain in you. No branch can bear fruit by itself; it must remain in the vine. Neither can you bear fruit unless you remain in me. I am the vine; you are the branches. If a man remains in me and I in him, he will bear much fruit; apart from me you can do nothing. If anyone does not remain in me, he is like a branch that is thrown away and withers; such branches are picked up, thrown into the fire and burned. If you remain in me and my words remain in you, ask whatever you wish and it will be given to you. This is to my Father's glory, that you bear much fruit, showing yourselves to be my disciples . . . You did not choose me, but I chose you and appointed you to go and bear fruit—fruit that will last."

(John 15:1, 4–8, 16)

Jesus also said,

> I am the resurrection and the life. He who believes in me will live, even though he dies; and whoever lives and believes in me will never die.

(John 11:25–26)

The Israelites cried, "We will all die. We are all lost," but "God so loved the world that he gave his one and only Son, that whoever believes in him shall not perish, but have eternal life" (John 3:16). We must trust in that love and believe in God's Son.

# THE MISSING MIRACLE OF MERIBAH

- **Numbers 20:1–13; 27:14**
- **Exodus 17:1–7**
- **Deuteronomy 32:48–52**
- **Psalms 103; 106:32–33**

Israel's punishment of wandering in the wilderness was nearing its end. For almost forty years they had traveled back and forth from here to there, pitching their tents in this place and that place, coming and going, backwards and forwards and around in circles, but never arriving anywhere, and never reaching their destination—the Promised Land. It was a journey that went on and on and on, but those years of wandering were drawing to a close. They were approaching the thirty-ninth year (see Deuteronomy 2:14). Only a few more months were left. Once again the Israelites found themselves on the edge of the Promised Land.

It should have been a happy time, camping there so close to the end of their journey, but something very sad happened. Miriam died and was buried. She was a very old woman, more than one hundred years old. Her ancient eyes, which had grown dim in the desert, never saw the Promised Land. Her death must have brought sorrow to the whole nation, for Miriam had led Israel for many years along with her two brothers (see Micah 6:4). Miriam was a "prophetess" (see Exodus 15:20–21), proclaiming the

Word of the LORD and singing the praises of God before all the people. But, like the rest of Israel, Miriam had sinned. She, too, had rebelled against God by speaking against Moses (see Numbers 12). Alas, Miriam did not enter the Promised Land. Her body was buried where she had lived the last forty years of her life — in the wilderness.

At this time, when the Israelites were nearing the end of their journey, God gave them a test, the same test that they had faced at the beginning of their journey. There was no water for the people to drink. How would Israel face this trial? How would they respond to this crisis? Had they learned from their past mistakes? Had they repented of their former sins? The Israelites had seen God provide for them for almost forty years in the wilderness. Would they now believe in God, trusting his mercy and power to supply this most basic and vital need for water? Would they now turn to God in prayer, humbly asking their God for help? No, it is sad to say that Israel still did not trust in God's LOVE or God's might. The people did not score any better on the re-test than they had on the first test. They gave the same answer. They responded in exactly the same way, without faith. Their answer was still wrong.

The people gathered together, not for prayer, but to oppose Moses and Aaron. There was quarreling again. The people quarreled with Moses and Aaron, saying, "If only we had died when our brothers fell dead before the LORD! Why did you bring the LORD's community into this desert, that we and our livestock should die here? Why did you bring us up out of Egypt to this terrible place? It has no grain; nor does it have figs, grapevines or pomegranates. *And there is no water to drink!*"

Such stupid wicked words! Did they really wish that they had died in Korah's Rebellion? Would they really have preferred to die one of those gruesome deaths rather than face this present hardship? Had they forgotten how terrifying it was to see the earth open its mouth and swallow men alive? Had they forgotten how frightening it was to watch flames of holy fire devour living men? Also, it seems they had forgotten how cruel their bondage was in Egypt. Did they really wish that they were slaves again, being whipped and maimed and killed for no reason, being forced to drown their own children in the Nile River? Was Egypt really where the people preferred to be? I don't think so. They were lying. They were deceiving themselves, as well as opposing and accusing God's servants. Amazingly, the Israelites also complained that this desert did not have figs, grapes or pomegranates, the very fruits that the spies had brought back from the Promised Land. Of course they didn't have those blessings. They had rejected them by refusing to enter the land where those fruits flourished. The Israelites also complained that they had no grain. Not true! They had the "grain of heaven," and they ate the "bread of angels" (Psalm 78:24–25). Again the Israelites were complaining about the manna. They expressed their faithlessness and thanklessness by rebelling against God and quarreling with his servants one more time.

What could Moses and Aaron do? What could they say? They were old men now, too old to be dealing with such stupidity and iniquity. Moses was 120 years old. Aaron was 123 years old. They were weary of all this foolishness and wickedness. For forty years they had led the Israelites, urging them to live a life of faith, and still these people rebelled against God. Twice now they had led the Israelites to the borders of the Promised Land, but still these people refused to trust in God. What more could Moses and Aaron do? In their distress they did as they had done for forty years: They sought the LORD's help. They left the raging madness and churning chaos of the people. They refused to take part in this quarrel. Instead they went to a place of peace, refuge, sanity and sanctuary. They went to God's Tent to be with the LORD. There they fell facedown in prayer before God, just as they had done many times in these last forty years. And the glory of the LORD appeared to them, to comfort them and strengthen them in their distress. God had not abandoned his faithful servants in this crisis. He was still there, just as he had promised Moses long ago: "I will be with you" (Exodus 3:12). He was still there helping Moses and Aaron with the task of leading these people, just as he had promised so long ago: "I will help both of you" (Exodus 4:15). Every step of the way on this long journey God had told Moses and Aaron what to do and what to say. This step was no different. Just because the journey was almost over didn't mean that God was going to abandon them now. No, the LORD would tell them exactly what to do.

God was merciful to the people too. He knew that the people were weary and thirsty, that they had been traveling for a very long time. As a father has compassion on his children, so the LORD had compassion on the children of Israel. "The LORD is compassionate and gracious, slow to anger, abounding in love. He will not always accuse, nor will he harbor his anger forever; he does not treat us as our sins deserve or repay us according to our iniquities" (Psalm 103:8–10). This time God did not threaten to destroy the people; he simply and kindly told Moses how he would provide them with water. The LORD said to Moses, "Take the staff, and you and your brother Aaron gather the assembly together. Speak to that rock before their eyes and it will pour out its water. You will bring water out of the rock for the community, so they and their livestock can drink" (Numbers 20:8).

But Moses was furious with the people. Why was God dealing with them so gently, so patiently, so leniently? They deserved God's wrath, not God's grace. Nevertheless, Moses did as God commanded him: He took the staff from the LORD's presence and gathered the assembly together in front of the rock, but in his heart Moses was still fuming with anger against these people, and it was about to explode.

It is important to understand the place and the work that Moses and Aaron had. They were God's representatives to the people, speaking God's Word and showing God's works to them. It was very, very important for Moses and Aaron to say and do exactly what God commanded them because they mediated between God and the people. The people would not know who God was unless Moses and Aaron accurately represented him. Grace and LOVE were what Moses and Aaron must bring to the people that day, for God had not come to them in wrath. The LORD had in mind a gentle miracle for the people this time—a hard rock yielding to a mere word. The LORD had in mind a different miracle, but one no less amazing: God wanted the people to see that even the rocks and the streams obey his Word. God wanted the people to see that by the Word of the LORD they had *life*, even streams of living water. God wanted the people to see his great LOVE for them. God had spoken to Moses softly and graciously, but when Moses spoke to the people, it was loudly and angrily. "Rash words came from Moses' lips" (Psalm 106:33). He yelled, "Listen, you rebels, must we bring you water out of this rock?" Moses was so angry that he raised his arm and smashed the rock with his staff twice. Perhaps nothing happened the first time, but with the second blow, water gushed out, so that all the people and animals drank. They had water, but they did not have the real gift that God intended for them that day, the miracle of a rock listening to the LORD.

This incident in the Bible does not have a happy ending. The cold clear water that gushed from the rock, the smiles on the people as they wet their dry lips and eased their parched throats and splashed their hot faces, the slurping of the thirsty animals, these were not the joyful sights and sounds that ended this day's events, because the water, which was God's good gift, was brought forth in great sin. The people sinned, and so did Moses and Aaron. "By the waters of Meribah they angered the LORD, and trouble came to Moses because of them; for they rebelled against the Spirit of God" (Psalm 106:32–33).

Now the LORD was angry with his servants too. God said to Moses and Aaron, "Because you did not trust in me enough to honor me as holy in the sight of the Israelites, you will not bring this community into the land I give them." God is just. Moses was not spared because he was God's friend and Aaron was not spared because he was God's priest. They both received punishment for their sin. Neither one of them would enter the Promised Land.

What exactly was the sin of Moses and Aaron, that they received such severe punishment?

1. They did not do as the LORD commanded. They disobeyed God. The LORD said, "Both of you disobeyed my command" (Numbers 27:14). God had told them to "speak to that rock," but they said not a single word to the rock. Instead, Moses spoke to the people and then he struck the rock. Does this seem like a small, insignificant sin, a little mistake that God should have overlooked? Was it a small and insignificant thing that God had chosen Moses and Aaron to work his wonders and perform his miracles before all the people? This very great honor was given to Moses and Aaron. To whom much was given, much would be required. What God required was obedience, exact and complete obedience. Carelessness in following God's instructions in the working of a miracle was indeed a grievous sin. Were God's miracles so common that careful attention was not necessary?

Almost forty years earlier God had brought forth water from a rock for Israel (see Exodus 17:1–7). On that occasion, God had commanded Moses to strike the rock, but this was to be something new, a different miracle, a wonder never seen on the earth. When has a man ever spoken to a rock, and the rock listened to him? When has a nation ever been given precious water simply by a word? But that unique miracle never happened, because of Moses' and Aaron's disobedience. It would forever be the miracle missing from the earth, because they had not obeyed God. Moses repeated what he had done the first time. Instead of speaking to the rock, he struck the rock twice—a double disobedience.

2. The Bible says, "Be angry, but do not sin" (Psalm 4:4). Moses allowed his anger to lead to sin. The Bible says, "Everyone should be quick to listen, slow to speak and slow to become angry, for man's anger does not bring about the righteous life that God desires" (James 1:19–20). The Bible says, "Do

not grieve the Holy Spirit of God . . . Get rid of all bitterness, rage and anger"
(Ephesians 4:30–31). The Bible says, "Refrain from anger and turn from
wrath. Do not fret; it leads only to evil" (Psalm 37:8). Again and again God
warns about anger, but Moses went before the people to perform God's miracle—*angry*! It could only end in disaster.

Moses, of course, had reasons why he was angry. Israel was so close to
the Promised Land and so close to the end of their wilderness wanderings.
How could they have failed this test and sinned against the LORD again? Perhaps Moses was worried that the Israelites might be turned back again because of their sin. Moses himself was weary of the wandering, and now he
was angry too. How long must he put up with these provoking people? Just
a little longer, Moses! You are being tried and tested by these people. Don't
fail now! But Moses did fail. Moses, "the meekest man on the face of the
earth," acted neither humbly nor gently, but lashed out in anger. He responded to the seething feeling of an unholy fury inside him, instead of re-
sponding to the clear command of a holy God. Moses' anger boiled over
with rash, harsh words: He yelled at the Israelites, "You rebels!" His anger
boiled over with reckless, faithless actions: Twice he smashed the rock with
his rod. Moses did not control his anger. He was the leader of Israel and "an
elder must be self-controlled . . . not violent, but gentle" (I Timothy 3:2–3).
"Since an elder is entrusted with God's work, he must be blameless . . . not
quick-tempered . . . He must be . . . self-controlled" (Titus 1:7–8). Moses'
uncontrolled anger in the work of God was indeed a serious sin.

3. In this situation, Moses and Aaron did not believe God. In some way,
they doubted the Word of the LORD. God said, "Both of you broke faith with
me" (Deuteronomy 32:51). "You did not trust in me enough." Although
Moses was faithful in all God's house, there was only one man born in the
whole world whose faith was perfect. It was not Moses. It was in this test that
we see the faith of Moses failing. Perhaps Moses and Aaron doubted whether
a mere word would bring forth water; perhaps in their minds they questioned
it, though God had promised it. Unbelief is a very serious sin.

4. Moses and Aaron did not honor God. Three times the LORD declared
that they did not honor him as holy. God said, "You did not trust in me
enough to honor me as holy." God said, "Both of you disobeyed my command to honor me as holy" (Numbers 27:14). God said again, "You did not
uphold my holiness" (Deuteronomy 32:51). How did they dishonor God?

How did they not uphold God's holiness? Moses and Aaron performed this work of God angrily, carelessly, faithlessly, disobediently. Was that honoring to God? Was that showing awe and fear before the God who is *Holy, Holy, Holy?* The LORD's command to speak to the rock that day was a perfect command, issuing from the perfection of his goodness, his justice, his righteousness, and his holiness. How could Moses and Aaron dare to tamper with that command, as if they could improve upon God's perfection? Obviously, Moses and Aaron thought something was missing, that God's miracle needed improving, because they changed it. But the Word of the LORD is right and true and good. Everything God says, everything God does, is holy and perfect. In this situation, Moses and Aaron doubted the rightness and goodness of God's command, and so they did not uphold the absolute holiness of Almighty God.

5. Moses and Aaron were the spiritual leaders in Israel and thus the seriousness of their sin was aggravated by the exaltedness of their positions. What they did—doubting God and disobeying God—was not done privately, which would have been bad enough; what they did was done publicly. Moses and Aaron were to be examples of faith, but they disobeyed God before all the people, "in the sight of the Israelites." This was another reason why God was dealing with their sin so severely. What they did affected not only themselves, but also the whole community. For such serious sin there would be a severe sentence. Moses and Aaron would not lead the Israelites into the Promised Land. They, too, would die and be buried outside those blessed borders. God is just. "Shall not the Judge of all the earth do right" (Genesis 18:25)? Would it be fair for God to punish the people for such sins, but not their leaders? God is just in all his judgments. He is fair to all who live. God is not partial to any person. The great prophet and the high priest of Israel would be measured with the same standard of justice as everyone else. Like the rest, they would not enter the Promised Land because of their rebellion.

The place where this happened was named Meribah, or Quarrelling, because here the Israelites quarreled with the LORD. It could have been named Meribah II, because it was the second place where the Israelites lacked water and quarreled with God. Meribah was a sad place, a continual reminder of sin. Meribah was also the place of the missing miracle, the one that never occurred because of the disobedience of Moses and Aaron. But the final word on Meribah was not a sorrowful one. It was there that God "showed himself holy among them." God was glorified even in this. Moses and Aaron did not honor God as holy, but God displayed his righteousness and his holiness in his judgment of them. Although the lips and the hands of God's own servants did not praise him, God glorified himself. Even the wrath of man shall praise the LORD. To him be the glory forever and ever. Amen.

# GRIEF UPON GRIEF

• **Numbers 20:14–29; 33:37–39**
• **Deuteronomy 2:1–8**

Although the Israelites were near the Promised Land now and although their time of punishment was coming to an end, many difficult and dangerous days lay directly before them. The final stages of their forty-year journey through the wilderness would not be happy or easy. The sin residing in the darkness of their own hearts would ensnare them and impede them; the nations bordering the fertile land of Canaan would harass them and hinder them; the demons plotting in the nether realms of hell would assail them and assault them. However, the Israelites had the love of the LORD. God's grace was greater than the deceitfulness of their sin, the wickedness of the world or the viciousness of the devil. Nothing could stop the promise of God from being fulfilled. "I will be their God and they shall be my people." In spite of all the troubles ahead of them, and all the sorrows behind them, how blessed were these people who could say they had the LORD to be their God.

The Israelites were camped south of the land of Canaan at Kadesh, the place where they had been almost forty years earlier when they had been defeated by the Canaanites and the Amalekites who lived in the hill country of that region. The Israelites did not want to attack Canaan along this southern border again. Rather, they wanted to travel east through the country of Edom and eventually attack the Canaanites along their eastern border. From where they were now camped, the quickest and easiest way to the eastern boundary of the Promised Land was through the country of Edom, but would the Edomites let the Israelites pass through their land? God had warned the Israelites that they must not fight their way into the land of the Edomites, for he would not give them any of their land. The LORD said, "You are about to pass through the territory of your brothers the descendants of Esau, who live in Seir. They will be afraid of you, but be very careful. Do not provoke them to war, for I will not give you any of their land, not even enough to put your foot on" (Deuteronomy 2:4–5). God had given this land to Esau and his descendants, the Edomites, as their own. The LORD himself commanded the Israelites that they must not go to war with them.

So Moses sent a messenger to the king of Edom, politely asking permission for the Israelites to use the main road through his country. After forty years of wandering in the rugged wilderness, Moses now hoped to get his people to the Promised Land along a well-traveled highway. Moses thought the Edomites would agree to this for many reasons:

1. They were part of the same family. The Israelites were the descendants of Jacob; the Edomites were the descendants of Esau. Jacob and Esau were twin brothers, the sons of Isaac and the grandsons of Abraham. God called the Israelites and the Edomites "brothers." Moses hoped that, because they were brothers, the Edomites would let them pass through their land.

2. The Israelites had suffered greatly. Moses hoped that the Edomites would have pity on this nation of escaped slaves. They were refugees who had been wandering in a wasteland for so long. Surely the Edomites, for pity's sake, would show kindness to these poor people, who for four hundred years had been oppressed by the Egyptians.

3. The Israelites had been delivered by the LORD. Moses hoped that the Edomites would consider that fact. God was with them. The LORD would surely bless the Edomites for showing kindness to the Israelites. Long ago their same forefather, Isaac, had blessed Israel with these words: "May those who curse you be cursed and those who bless you be blessed" (Genesis 27:29).

4. The LORD himself had told Moses that the Edomites were afraid of them. Israel had a terrifying reputation. All the nations of that region had heard what Israel's God had done to the Egyptians, how the LORD had destroyed their land and drowned their army. Because the Israelites had Almighty God fighting for them, Moses hoped that Edom would want to avoid war by letting the people peacefully pass through their land.

5. Moses also assured the Edomites that they would not harm anything. When Moses sent his message pleading, "Please let us pass through your country," he promised that the Israelites would not trample their fields or their crops, nor would they take any food from their farms or drink any water from their wells. (God provided all their food and water.) Moses promised, "We will travel along the king's highway and not turn to the right or to the left until we have passed through your territory." The only thing Israel wanted was the use of their road for a short time.

Surely the Edomites would help them. Because the Israelites were not a strange people (but members of the same family) and because they were not an arrogant people (but victims of cruel oppression) and because they were not a cursed race (but a people blessed of the LORD) and because they were not helpless or defenseless (but were protected by an army and by God himself) and also, because they were not asking for very much, surely the Edomites would want to help them. But the Edomites sent this message in reply: "You may not pass through here. If you try, we will march out and attack you with the sword."

The Israelites answered: "We will go along the main road, and if we or our livestock drink any of your water, we will pay for it. We only want to pass through on foot—nothing else." This was not only an opportunity for the Edomites to show kindness; it was also an opportunity for them to make money. The Israelites would be like tourists, leaving a trail of gold and silver behind them as they passed through the land. Most countries want to attract tourists, because it is a multi-million dollar way to make a country rich. But the Edomites were not interested in any kind of benefits for themselves, either spiritual or material. They answered: "You may not pass through!"

Why? Why were the Edomites unwilling to help the Israelites? They were afraid of them. Israel posed a very real threat to Edom. The Edomites had hoped that these homeless people would die in the desert, but they hadn't. The Israelites were alive and well, camped right beside them, already knocking on their doors and begging for favors. Edom was afraid that this great multitude of people would over-run their country, ruin it and conquer it. They were unwilling to help because of their fear, and because of their hate. This hatred went back several centuries to the time of their forefathers. Perhaps the Edomites were suspicious of the Israelites. Hadn't Jacob tricked Esau—twice? Hadn't Jacob stolen Esau's birthright and blessing? Perhaps the Edomites were envious of the Israelites. Hadn't God chosen Jacob, the younger brother, instead of Esau, the older brother, before they were even born? For those two reasons alone—their suspicions and jealousies from the past—the Edomites hated the Israelites. They still hoped that they would all die in the desert. So they would not lift a finger or move an inch to help God's people.

What the Edomites did move was their army. What they did lift were their swords. They lined up their large and powerful army along the border of their country, ready to attack if the Israelites came closer. But the Israelites just turned away from them, because God had warned them not to fight with the Edomites. Thankfully, there was not a war, but where should they go now?

How discouraged they must have been. Again the Israelites were turning back, this time not because of their own sin, but because of the Edomites' wickedness. Now they would have to go all the way around the Edomites' territory. Why hadn't God opened these doors for them? Surely the God of Israel, who could open a path through the sea, who could even open the jaws of the earth, surely he could have opened the hearts of the Edomites, so that Israel could pass through their land. But God did not open the road through Edom for his people. It remained closed to them, barred by the Edomite army, barred by the Word of God. It was a very real disappointment to the people. It was also a test of their faith. Would they continue to trust in the goodness and greatness of God? Would they believe that "God causes all things to work together for good to those who love God, to those who are called according to his purpose" (Romans 8:28, NAS)? It seems that the Israelites passed the test, because this time they continued on their journey, without complaining or rebelling about this hardship.

As they traveled through the rugged mountain region, the Israelites had to face another disappointment. At Mount Hor, near the border of Edom, the LORD said it was Aaron's time to die. God said to Moses, "Aaron will be gathered to his people. He will not enter the land I give the Israelites, because both of you rebelled against my command at the waters of Meribah."

Aaron, who had led these people from the beginning of the journey, would not live to reach its end. Aaron would not lead the Israelites into the Promised Land. His tired feet would never touch that sacred soil; his weary eyes would never gaze upon that blessed land.

It was a sad and severe punishment, yet God was merciful to Aaron: He would be "gathered to his people," not "cut off from his people." He would not be executed for his sin; the earth would not devour him, nor would fire consume him. Aaron's death would be natural and honorable. He would die peacefully and faithfully. His last act on the face of the earth would be one of obedience to the command of God. The LORD commanded Aaron to walk up Mount Hor with his brother Moses and his son Eleazar. So Aaron, with the last of his strength and the last of his breath, climbed the mountain because God had commanded him to do so. Aaron walked up to a mountaintop, as if his last steps upon this earth were leading him homeward to heaven. Aaron would not die alone. He would be with family, his beloved brother and one of his sons. He would die in the hands of God's servants, the spiritual leaders of Israel—Moses, God's prophet, and Eleazar, God's next high priest. When Aaron walked up Mount Hor, it was in the sight of all the people. He was surrounded by the people of God, not only the great crowd of witnesses below the mountain, but also the great cloud of witnesses above the mountain. Aaron would be surrounded by the saints both in heaven and on earth. God had declared, "Aaron will be gathered to his people." Aaron would join his forefathers—Abraham, Isaac and Jacob—and all the faithful who went before him. Aaron would not see Canaan, but he would see heaven. Aaron's good works would not save him, nor would his bad works damn him; Aaron would enter heaven by the grace of God. It is by grace that we are saved, through faith—and this not from ourselves, it is the gift of God. Aaron would die in faith, which was a most precious gift from the LORD.

Also, before he died, God would show Aaron something of great comfort to him: As God commanded, Moses removed Aaron's high-priest garments and put them on his son Eleazar. What a blessing for Aaron. Before his old eyes closed for the last time, he saw his son standing in the high priest's robe that glistened with gold and jewels. Aaron was allowed to see his son standing as the high priest in his place. Aaron's work would not die with him, but it would be carried on by his son. Now Aaron could rest in peace.

So Aaron died there on top of the mountain. The Israelites had watched three men climb slowly up the side of Mount Hor, but only two men came back down to them. Aaron was not with them. They would never again see his dear old face on this earth. Aaron, their high priest for so many years, was dead. He died on the first day of the fifth month of the fortieth year after the Israelites came out of Egypt. Aaron was 123 years old when he died on Mount Hor. The entire house of Israel mourned for him for thirty days.

Although there was another high priest to take his place, the death of Aaron was a great shock and loss and grief to the people. In these last stages of their journey, they were experiencing grief upon grief, one after another. First Miriam died. Now Aaron was gone too. All these years Aaron had stood before them, ministering to them and interceding for them, but now Aaron stood no more. His body lay on top of the mountain, while the people continued on their journey, leaving his remains behind them. Now, not only their feet were weary, but their hearts were heavy, too, as they trudged towards the Promised Land without Aaron.

One day God would give his people another high priest, a better high priest, one who would never leave them nor forsake them, one who would live forever to make intercession for them. That high priest was Jesus Christ, the Son of God, to whom be the glory forever and ever.

# A TASTE OF VICTORY

• **Numbers 21:1–3;**
**33:40**
• **Joshua 12**
• **Ephesians 6:10–18**

As the Israelites drew closer to the Promised Land, the way grew harder. As long as they stayed in the desert, no one cared. Let them live there. Let them die there. They were a threat to no one as long as they were just wandering around in the wilderness. But as soon as the Israelites came close to entering the land of their hopes and their dreams—the Land of God's Promise—then all eyes were upon them, the evil eyes of demons as well as the wicked eyes of humans. The forces of hell would use the nations on earth in an attempt to keep the Israelites out of the Promised Land. The seed of the serpent would be active in resisting the people of God, setting up one barrier after another, one kind of roadblock or obstacle after another, to stop the Israelites from entering the Promised Land.

Why? What interest did Satan have in keeping these people from entering and settling in the land of Canaan? Satan knew that God had a great purpose and a great promise in bringing these people into this land. Oh yes, Satan knew the Word of God very well. Satan knew it was from these people that a Child would be born, the Promised Seed who would crush the serpent's head, destroy the devil's work, and conquer Satan's evil empire. Satan knew it was from these people that a Son would be given, who would save the world from sin and death. Satan knew that salvation was of the Jews and that through them, through one of Abraham's descendants, all peoples on earth would be blessed, while he would be crushed. Satan suspected that all these promises concerning the Christ were somehow connected to Israel entering the Promised Land—and he was right in that suspicion.

Hundreds of years in the future, in a little town in that land, the Promised Child would be born. There, in that land, those who dwelt in darkness and the shadow of death would see a great light as they beheld the Promised Son, the Light of the World. It would be there, as he walked throughout the Promised Land, that the Christ would begin to crush the serpent by resisting the devil, preaching the gospel, driving out demons, healing the sick, forgiving sins, and even raising the dead. And it would be there, in the Promised Land, that a cross would be set up with the Savior nailed upon it, as he gave up his life as a ransom for his people. In the Promised Land Jesus' body would be broken and there his blood would be poured out for the remission of sins. There the Savior would die and there he would be raised to life again. It would all happen in the Promised Land. That would be the place of the devil's defeat, for there God's curse upon that ancient serpent would be fulfilled, just as the LORD had promised Satan, "He will crush your head." There, in the Promised Land, Christ would triumph over God's great enemy.

Did Satan and the hordes of hell have a preview of all these events? No, they only felt slight tremors and heard vague rumors; they only caught glimpses of their impending destruction. They saw only what God slowly unveiled over the centuries. They had only bits and pieces of God's great plan, the little clues that God chose to reveal to his prophets on earth. It was like a giant jigsaw puzzle. Even the prophets, who were given the visions and the revelations, did not understand how it all fit together. They tried very hard to figure it out. The Bible says: "Concerning this salvation, the prophets who spoke . . . searched intently and with the greatest of care, trying to find out" (I Peter 1:10), trying to solve the mystery of God's salvation, trying to pinpoint the exact time and the precise way in which the Christ would suffer to save his people, but it remained hidden from them. God gave them a window into the future, and they were straining their eyes to see clearly all that would happen, but the glass was darkened and the scenes were all in shadows. Even the angels in heaven longed to look into these things, but God kept it veiled from them too. You can be sure also that the demons desperately desired to spy on the battle plans of God, but the LORD kept it a secret, locked within the counsel chambers of the Holy Trinity, leaking only enough information over the ages to secure the salvation of his people and the destruction of his enemy. Christ's victory over the devil would happen in the Promised Land. There the great revival would begin and from there it would spread to the whole world. "No!" screamed the hordes of hell. Canaan belonged to them. The whole world belonged to them. This was their dominion of darkness and wickedness. The Israelites must not be allowed to penetrate that dark domain with the light of God's truth and life. All the demons of hell would fight against this invasion. The Israelites must not enter the Promised Land, for it spelled only one word for the devil and his demons: *Doom!* Every step closer for the Israelites was a step closer to the devil's destruction. Israel must not enter the Promised Land and Israel must not give birth to the Promised Savior.

Did the Israelites know whom they were really fighting and why? Did they know that their fight was not against flesh and blood, but against the corrupted angels and demonic rulers, "against the powers of this dark world and against the spiritual forces of evil in the heavenly realms" (Ephesians 6:12)? Did they know that they were trying to crash through the gates of hell and that their only battering ram was the Word of God and the power of prayer? Did they know that the only way they could conquer kingdoms and overcome the enemy was through faith? Did they know that there was a "war in heaven" (Revelation 12:7) being fought on earth, and that their entry into the Promised Land was crucial in winning that war? On one side of the battle line was the plan of God and on the other side were the schemes of the devil. Did Israel know that they were caught in the middle of this cosmic clash? Did Israel know that, because God's great purpose involved them they would be the target of all Satan's fiery arrows? Did they know how ferociously and unceasingly the Evil One would challenge their entry into the Promised Land and their survival in it? The Israelites had turned back in fear almost forty years earlier because of the gigantic soldiers their spies had seen in the Canaanite armies. Imagine their terror if they could see, in the realms unseen, all the demonic warriors of the satanic legions now blocking their way to the Promised Land.

While demonic spies were watching Israel's progress from those invisible spheres, there were other spies, human ones, who watched all Israel's activities from their hiding places in the hills. Many years earlier, Israel had sent spies along this route through the Negev into the land of Canaan. Now these Canaanites were spying on them. The Canaanites knew that Israel wanted their land, and that Israel didn't just want it; Israel had claimed it as its own. Israel actually believed that God had given it to them. Yes, reports had reached the surrounding nations about the God of Israel and what he promised to do for his people.

At this time, there was a certain evil Canaanite king, the king of Arad, who thought he could fight against the Word of God and win. After all, hadn't his soldiers beaten back the Israelite army forty years earlier? This Canaanite king decided not to wait for Israel to initiate the attack, like the last time. As soon as he heard that Israel was traveling in his vicinity again, he marched out with his army and attacked them by surprise, as they were walking along the road. Some of the Israelites were captured in this ambush.

In their distress, the Israelites did what was right. They turned to God for help. They prayed, making this vow to the LORD: "If you will deliver these people into our hands, we will totally destroy their cities." The LORD listened to Israel's plea. When the Israelites attacked, God gave them success. Then the Israelites did as they had vowed: They completely destroyed these people and all their towns. So the place was named Hormah, which means "*destruction.*"

It was a great victory for Israel, because it was their first victory. This king was the first of many Canaanite kings to be killed, and these cities were the first of many Canaanite cities to be conquered. It was the Israelites' first taste of victory and it was the Canaanites' first taste of defeat. Hormah (or Destruction) was a warning to the evil-practicing, God-hating, idol-worshipping Canaanites of what was going to happen to them all very soon. God was about to execute his righteous judgment on all their wickedness. Hormah/Destruction was also a warning to the whole world: God keeps his promise; God fulfils his Word. Do not fight against the LORD, for unless you repent, you will all likewise perish.

After the victory at Hormah, Israel turned back towards the Red Sea. They had not been planning to enter Canaan this way, nor had they been planning to attack from the south. Had the king of Arad waited, he would have been the last of the Canaanite kings to fall, instead of the first. Israel would not have attacked him at this time, for God was leading his people into the Promised Land by another way, a way where many glorious victories awaited them.

# SERPENTS

The Israelites had defeated the Canaanites, but now God's people were traveling again. That first taste of triumph soon faded away, as day after day they trudged through that rugged region. Once again the Israelites had a long journey ahead of them as they headed south towards the Red Sea to go around Edom. They were not going towards the Promised Land, where they had just experienced the excitement of their first victory; no, they were going away from it. They were not marching forward into battle, but backwards, away from all their hopes of having a homeland at last.

Why was God leading them this way? Didn't he know how weary they were? The Israelites had been wandering in this wilderness for almost forty years. Some of the people had lived this way for their entire lives. Now it felt as if this journey would never ever end, that they would be forced to march around and around and around in this dreadful desert until there was no one left. It felt as if this long-distance detour around Edom would kill them all. And so the people became very discouraged.

In their discouragement, the Israelites did not turn towards God; they turned away from him. They did not look back, recalling how God had delivered them from Egypt. Nor did they look forward, relying on God to bring them to Canaan. They did not look at their situation by faith at all. No, they only looked with their eyes and saw the vast, bleak, wild, harsh desert all around them for miles and miles, and they despaired. Even in that despair they could have acted in faith. They could have thanked God for his past deliverances, for his present conveniences and his future assurances. In their despair they could have cried out to the LORD for peace and patience and perseverance. They could have cried out, "LORD, I believe. Help my unbelief." But the Israelites neither implored the LORD for help nor honored him with thanks. They chose instead to sin.

The Israelites spoke against God and against Moses. They wailed their old refrain: "Why have you brought us up out of Egypt to die in this desert?" What they said was untrue. God loved them, and they should have trusted in that LOVE. God brought them here to give them life, and life abundantly. He had given them what was good; he had given them himself. Had they again forgotten why they had been set free? The LORD had said, "Let my people go, that they may worship me." Now they were free, free to worship God, and they must do that, even here, even in this desert. That was their whole purpose in life. Their chief end was to glorify God and enjoy him forever. But instead of loving God and blessing God and praising God, the Israelites were doubting him and hating him and cursing him. They cried, "There is no bread! There is no water! And we detest this miserable food!" It was true that this wasteland was not rippling with wheat or flowing with streams, yet, by God's grace, the Israelites had been given so much more. Their bread and water were spiritual food and drink, given to nourish both body and soul. They ate, not bread from earth as other peoples; they ate bread from heaven. God gave them food for angels, but the Israelites despised it, as if it were slop for pigs.

What now would God do with these ungrateful people? The LORD gave them what the land produced and what their hearts produced—poison. That rocky region was crawling with venomous snakes and scorpions. For forty years God had guarded his people from these poisonous serpents, but now God let them loose. They slithered out of holes in the ground and slid out of cracks in the rocks. The snakes slithered and slid right into Israel's campground and around their tents. These venomous vipers sank their fangs into the flesh of the people, and many Israelites died because of them.

The snakes served God's purpose and brought the people's rebellion to an immediate halt. Now the people were turning to God for help. They came to Moses and confessed their sin, saying, "We sinned when we spoke against the LORD and against you. Pray that the LORD will take the snakes away from us." So Moses prayed for the people.

But the LORD did not take the snakes away. God did not make the snakes vanish into thin air, nor did God call them back into the crevices of the rocks—not yet. God had another answer to their prayers and another purpose for their hearts. The LORD would require the Israelites to trust in him with the snakes still slithering all around them; God would require the people to believe in him even when they were bitten. This was what God said to Moses: "Make a snake and put it on a pole; anyone who is bitten can look at it and live." So Moses did as the LORD commanded. He made a snake out of bronze and put it on a pole and lifted it up before the people. So anyone who was bitten by a snake would live, but only if he trusted God's Word and looked to the bronze serpent. Anyone injected with the viper's venom was spared from death, but only if he believed God's Word and obeyed God's Word. It was a matter of faith. God was clearly showing the people that they must live by faith.

After this time of testing, the Israelites took that bronze snake with them wherever they went. They brought it with them into the Promised Land, and later in their history they even worshipped it, as if that metal snake were some kind of god. Because the Israelites turned it into an idol, good King Hezekiah smashed it to pieces. The Israelites had not understood. It wasn't because the bronze snake was magical or powerful in itself that the people were healed. It was because God healed those who believed in him by obeying him. There were probably people who reviled God's way, who rejected God's cure, people who said, "What a stupid thing to do. What foolishness. How can looking at a bronze snake help or heal anyone? How can looking at a fake snake save someone who is dying from a real snake?" So some people must have mocked God's Word. Such people were unbelievers, who refused the grace of God and the gift of life. Because they refused to look at the bronze snake, they died in the desert in their disobedience, but all who believed the Word of the LORD were granted life.

Did you know that we all have been bitten by a poisonous snake? Every one of us has been wounded by the fangs of "that ancient serpent called the devil or Satan, who leads the whole world astray" (Revelation 12:9). Every one of us has been injected with his poison of sin before we were even born. As God's Word says and as we must all confess, "Surely I was sinful at birth, sinful from the time my mother conceived me" (Psalm 51:5). We are all born with the serpent's poison within us. We are born dead in our sins and we live our lives dying, because that poison has deeply and thoroughly infected us. That is why the Son of God said, "You must be born again."

Almost two thousand years ago a man came to Jesus in the middle of the night, and that was when Jesus said that a person must be born again. Jesus said, "I tell you the truth, no one can see the kingdom of God unless he is born again . . . I tell you the truth, no one can enter the kingdom of God unless he is born of water and the Spirit. Flesh gives birth to flesh, but the Spirit gives birth to spirit. You must not be surprised at my saying, you must be born again" (John 3:3, 5–7). Then Jesus said an amazing thing:

> Just as Moses lifted up the snake in the wilderness, so the Son of Man must be lifted up, that everyone who believes in him, may have eternal life. For God so loved the world, that he gave his one and only Son, that whoever believes in him shall not perish, but have eternal life. For God did not send his Son into the world to condemn the world, but to save the world through him. Whoever believes in him is not condemned, but whoever does not believe stands condemned already, because he has not believed in the name of God's one and only Son.

> (John 3:14–18)

What happened in the wilderness with the Israelites was written in God's Word for the whole world's instruction. God caused all this to happen, so that there would be a very clear picture pointing to the only way of salvation. Just as the Israelites were dying as a judgment upon their sins, so all people are dying as a judgment upon their sins. Just as the Israelites were bitten by venomous serpents, so the whole human race has been poisoned by "that ancient serpent, called the devil, or Satan, who leads the whole world astray" (Revelation 12:9). Just as God gave the Israelites a bronze snake on a pole to look at in faith to heal them and save them from death, so God gave all people Jesus Christ on the cross to look at in faith to heal them and save them from death. Just as Moses lifted up the bronze serpent in the wilderness, so the Son of Man was lifted up on the cross. Jesus knew that he would be crucified, and he prophesied: "'Now is the time for judgment on this world; now the prince of this world [the devil] will be driven out. But I, when I am lifted up from the earth, will draw all men to myself.' Jesus said this to show the kind of death he was going to die" (John 12:31–32). But God's Word promises: *"Everyone who looks to the son and believes in him shall have eternal life"* (John 6:40).

People mock the gospel and scoff at these words. They say: "How ridiculous! How can looking to the cross and believing in Christ save anyone from dying? What foolishness!" They do not believe God's Word; they reject God's grace; they refuse the gift of life, and so they perish. God has given only one cure for sin, and that is faith in Christ. They must look to Christ upon the cross in order to be saved. "The message of the cross is foolishness to those who are perishing, but to us who are being saved, it is the power of God" (I Corinthians 1:18).

# WAR AND PEACE BY THE WORD OF THE LORD

- **Numbers 21:10–35**
- **Deuteronomy 2:1—3:20**
- **Genesis 19:36–38**
- **Psalms 135–136**

B ecause the Edomites would not let them pass through their territory, the Israelites were forced to travel south towards the Red Sea, which was away from the Promised Land. Then God said, "You have made your way around this hill country long enough; now turn north." Finally, they were headed in the right direction again. The problem was, the land of the Edomites still lay ahead of them. But now the LORD said, "You are about to pass through the territory of your brothers, the descendants of Esau, who live in Seir. They will be afraid of you, but be very careful. Do not provoke them to war, for I will not give you any of their land, not even enough to put your foot on. I have given Esau the hill country of Seir as his own. You are to pay them in silver for the food you eat and the water you drink." Moses reminded the Israelites that for forty years God had provided food and water for them without cost, so they must not grumble now about paying the Edomites. Moses said, "The LORD your God has blessed you . . . These forty years the LORD your God has been with you, and you have not lacked anything" (Deuteronomy 2:7). They must not be tempted to steal from these people or fight with these people, because God had promised the Israelites Canaan, not Edom.

The western Edomites had not allowed Israel passage through their country. Would these eastern Edomites have a different response? Yes, for the news of Israel's victory had reached them. They had heard about Hormah and the total destruction of the Canaanites there, and these Edomites were terrified. Now they were afraid to fight against the Israelites, so this time they granted Israel permission to pass through their territory.

How the people must have cheered. The LORD had opened the door for Israel to pass through Edom. How happy the Israelites must have been to leave that "vast and dreadful desert, that waterless wasteland inhabited by venomous snakes and scorpions" (Deuteronomy 8:15) and enter a region where rivers flowed and people dwelled. As the Israelites walk along the Arabah Road, passing beautiful fields and farms and towns, they must be careful not to sin, not to covet this land which did not belong to them. The Israelites must be careful to obey God and not begin a war with these people. The Israelites could not just steal any land that pleased them or kill anyone who owned them. No! God forbade such wickedness. There were only certain nations whose evil had reached its fullness that God had marked for destruction. Woe to Israel if they did not follow God's commands carefully and travel through this land peacefully. So, although their army was strong enough to conquer the Edomites, the Israelites did not harm anyone or take anything. Both nations benefited from their time together: Israel had an easy journey and Edom had some easy money, and God's name was honored among the heathen because of the good conduct of his people.

The Israelites continued to travel north until they reached the northern border of Edom, which was bounded by the Zered River. The Israelites camped there in the valley. On the other side was another country, the land of Moab. The Moabites were the descendants of Lot, Abraham's nephew. God said, "Do not harass the Moabites or provoke them to war, for I will not give you any part of their land. I have given Ar to the descendants of Lot as a possession" (Deuteronomy 2:9). God had promised the Israelites Canaan, not Moab. The Israelites could not take any of this land either, the land that stretched before them on the other side of the Zered Valley.

It was here, when they were camped in the Zered Valley, that the last of the disobedient soldiers died. By then, that entire generation of fighting men had perished from the camp, just as the LORD had sworn to them. The LORD's hand was against them until he had completely eliminated them from Israel's camp. From that original army, only Joshua and Caleb were still alive. Now Israel had a new army, and how different it was. These soldiers wanted to fight. They had been marching and training and waiting for war for thirty-eight long years. They had been disciplined by God in the desert in order to conquer kingdoms by faith. These soldiers eagerly awaited the command to go forward and fight for the Promised Land. In fact, this army had to be restrained by the Word of the LORD, lest they fight too soon. At last, however, they received their marching orders; the LORD said, "Now get up and cross the Zered Valley" (Deuteronomy 2:13). So the Israelites marched forward, crossing the border into the land of Moab.

There was no bloodshed in that country either, because God, the Commander-in-Chief of Israel's army, had forbidden them to go to war against the Moabites. The Moabites did not help the Israelites on their way (see Deuteronomy 23:4). They did not come out to meet them with bread or water, nor did they have a word of greeting or blessing for the Israelites, but at least the Moabites did not stand in their way. At one point during their sojourn in Moab, the Israelites were without water. The Moabites refused to give or sell any water to Israel, an incident that could have sparked a war, but the Israelites were faithful to God's command. Although their need for water was vital, the Israelites did not fight the Moabites. At that time the LORD said, "Gather the people together and I will give them water." The Israelites were not dependent upon Moab; they were dependent upon God. They prayed for water and they praised the LORD who promised them water. The elders and rulers of the people took their staves and poked the ground in faith, and the LORD caused fresh water to bubble up from the dry earth. Then Israel sang a song about the well that sprang up for them in Moab, the well that their nobles had dug with their staves. It was important for the people to see that God used not only the staff of Moses to perform miracles, but the staves of the other elders as well, for Moses would not be with them much longer.

The Israelites continued to travel north until they reached the northern border of Moab, which was bounded by the Arnon River. To the north of Moab, on the other side of the Arnon Gorge, lay two other countries: the land of the Ammonites was on the northeast; the land of the Amorites was on the northwest. The Ammonites were also descended from Lot, so the LORD said to the Israelites, "When you come to the Ammonites, do not harass them or provoke them to war, for I will not give you possession of any land belonging to the Ammonites. I have given it as a possession to the descendants of Lot" (Deuteronomy 2:19). God had promised the Israelites the land of the Canaanites, not the land of Ammonites. For the third time the army of Israel was restrained by the Word of the LORD.

What about the land to the northwest, the land of the Amorites? The Amorites were Canaanites, descendants of Canaan (see Genesis 10:15–16). Long ago God promised to give the land of the Amorites to Abraham's descendants (see Genesis 15:18–21). God also promised Moses that he would bring the people into the land of the Canaanites and Amorites (see Exodus 3:17). God promised the Israelites, "My angel will go ahead of you and bring you into the land of the Amorites" (Exodus 23:23).

The Amorites were a race of tall, strong, brave, fierce people, who were also extremely wicked. They had a mighty king, named King Sihon, who ruled the country from his fortress-city of Heshbon. Mighty Sihon and his powerful army had swallowed up great chunks of the Moabites' territory. These Amorite warriors were sure of themselves, proud of their strength and skill in war. They were not afraid of the Israelites or the promises of God, but they should have been afraid. The Amorites did not know it, but the day of their destruction was upon them. The LORD had waited for centuries, until "the sin of the Amorites" had "reached its full measure" (Genesis 15:16). Now God would execute his righteous judgment upon them. Now the holy God of heaven would extinguish their evil from the earth, which he had patiently endured for so many years. The Amorites would have one last opportunity to repent—before they were swept away by the justice of Almighty God.

This was their last chance: Moses sent a message to King Sihon in the capital city of Heshbon in the land of the Amorites. It was a message offering him peace. It was a message offering him grace. Moses said, "Let us pass through your country. We will stay on the main road; we will not turn aside to the right or to the left. Sell us food to eat and water to drink for their price in silver. Only let us pass through on foot—as the Edomites and Moabites did for us—until we cross the Jordan River into the land the LORD our God is giving us" (Deuteronomy 2:27–29). King Sihon had every reason to believe this message. He had seen that the Israelites marched peacefully through two other countries. However, mighty Sihon, king of Heshbon, refused to let the Israelites pass through the land of the Amorites. King Sihon refused

Israel's offer of peace and so the Amorites' time of grace came to an end. The day of their destruction had come upon them. This time the Word of the LORD would not restrain the army of Israel; this time it would send them forth to war.

King Sihon mustered his entire army and began marching his troops south. The LORD of hosts had already ordered his troops to march north to meet them in battle. God said, "Set out now and cross the Arnon Gorge," for God had promised his army victory. The LORD said, "See, I have given into your hand Sihon the Amorite, King of Heshbon, and his country. Begin to take possession of it and engage him in battle. This very day I will begin to put the terror and the fear of you on all the nations under heaven. They will hear reports of you and will tremble and be in anguish because of you" (Deuteronomy 2:24–25). When King Sihon refused Moses' offer of peace, it was the sign that God was bringing about Israel's victory. "See," said God, "I have begun to deliver Sihon and his country over to you. Now begin to conquer and possess his land" (Deuteronomy 2:31). For the LORD had made Sihon stubborn and obstinate in order to bring about the destruction of this evil nation.

God did not destroy these wicked people by sweeping them away with a flood, as he did to the whole world in the days of Noah. God did not destroy these wicked cities by raining down fire from heaven, as he did to Sodom and Gomorrah in the days of Abraham. God did not bring judgment upon them or their gods with ten destructive plagues, as he did to Egypt in the days of Moses. No, this time God swept away the wicked with the swords of men. The Amorites were completely destroyed by the Israelites. Mighty King Sihon fell by the sword. All his sons and all his soldiers fell by the sword. All his people fell by the sword. City after fortified city was captured; not one of them was strong enough to withstand the onslaught of Israel's sword. The LORD gave the entire country of the Amorites to Israel.

The Israelites took all the land of the Amorites, from the Arnon River in the south to the Jabbok River in the north, but they did not touch the land to the east, the land of the Ammonites. The Ammonites' border was fortified, not only by the walls they had built, but by the Word of the·LORD. The Israelites did not encroach upon any of the Ammonites' land, in accordance with the command of the LORD their God. The Israelites obeyed the Word of the LORD to fight, and they obeyed the Word of the LORD not to fight, for God was the Commander of Israel's army.

Israel now possessed land for the first time. All the country and the cities of the Amorites belonged to them. To the south, across the Arnon Valley, lay the land of Moab, which they would not invade. To the east, beyond the fortified border, lay the land of Ammon, which they also would not invade. To the west, across the Jordan River, lay the land of Canaan. Soon the Israelites would cross that river border and invade that wicked land. But first Israel would keep marching north. Beyond the Jabbok River lay the land of Bashan.

Bashan was ruled by another Amorite king, a wicked giant of a man named Og. (To remember his name, just think of Og the Ogre!) Og was a huge hulk of a man, so big that he had trouble finding a bed that would hold his grotesque body. King Og had a bed of iron made for himself, it was more than thirteen feet long and six feet wide. This giant ogre marched out with his massive army to do battle with the Israelites. The LORD said to Moses, "Do not be afraid of him, for I have handed him over to you with his whole army and his whole land. Do to him what you did to King Sihon" (Deuteronomy 3:2). So the Israelites struck down these Amorites also. Mighty Og, King of Bashan, fell by the sword. All his army and all his people fell by the sword. There were sixty cities in that region, fortified with high walls and barricaded with strong gates, but all these cities fell by the sword. There were also a great many unwalled villages; they, too, fell by the sword. Men, women and children were all put to death by the Israelites, by the command of God. It was a sweeping judgment, which left no survivors. The sin of the Amorites had reached its full measure, and God was executing his righteous judgment and his holy anger upon this nation.

If there had been even one righteous person in one of those sixty cities, that person would have been spared. We know that is how God works from other accounts in the Bible: God found one righteous man in the city of Sodom—righteous Lot—and God rescued that man and his family from the destruction (see Genesis 18 and 19). God would find one righteous woman in the city of Jericho, faithful Rahab. God would rescue that woman and her entire family from the destruction there, too (see Joshua 2 and 6:15–25). But in these Amorite cities not one man or woman was spared. There was not one faithful person among all those inhabitants of all those cities. The sin of the Amorites had indeed reached its full measure. There was not one righteous person among them all, no not one.

For the first time in their history, the Israelites had a country to call their own. It was the land of the Amorites and it extended all the way from the

Arnon Gorge in the south to Mount Hermon in the north. God had given it, and they had taken it. The Israelites had erased from the face of the earth the two kings of the Amorites, mighty Sihon and wicked Og, along with all their people. Now the Israelites would live in their towns and work on their land. The houses were already built, the fields were already ploughed, the groves were already planted. They had been homeless for so long that it was hard for the Israelites to believe they actually owned this beautiful and bountiful land. Moses divided up this land and gave it to three of the tribes as their inheritance, where they would eventually settle. But before any of the tribes could rest, all of the tribes must fight for the land to the west, the land across the Jordan River, the land of Canaan, the Land of Promise.

Israel would sing of these great victories forever:

> *Praise the LORD.*
> *Praise the name of the LORD;*
> > *praise him you servants of the LORD . . .*
>
> *Praise the LORD, for the LORD is good;*
> > *sing praise to his name, for that is pleasant.*
>
> *I know that the LORD is great,*
> > *that our Lord is greater than all gods.*
>
> *The LORD does whatever pleases him.*
>
> *He struck down many nations*
> > *and killed mighty kings—*
> *Sihon, King of the Amorites,*
> > *Og, King of Bashan*
> > *and all the kings of Canaan—*
> *And he gave their land as an inheritance,*
> > *an inheritance to his people Israel . . .*
>
> *Praise the LORD.*
>
> > *(Psalm 135:1, 3, 5, 6a, 10–12, 21)*
>
> *Give thanks to the LORD, for he is good.*
> > *His LOVE endures forever.*
> *Give thanks to the God of gods.*
> > *His LOVE endures forever.*

*Give thanks to the* LORD *of lords;*
> His LOVE endures forever.
*Who struck down great kings,*
> His LOVE endures forever.
*And killed mighty kings—*
> His LOVE endures forever.
*Sihon, King of the Amorites*
> His LOVE endures forever.
*and Og, King of Bashan—*
> His LOVE endures forever.
*and gave their land as an inheritance,*
> His LOVE endures forever.
*an inheritance to his servant Israel;*
> His LOVE endures forever.

(Psalm 136:1–3, 17–22)

The defeat of these kings was a sign of God's great LOVE for his people.

# A FALSE PROPHET AND
# A WICKED KING

Israel returned from their northern conquests and camped on the eastern side of the Jordan River. Opposite them on the west, across that river border, lay the land of Canaan and the city of Jericho. The Israelites could look from their tents now and see the Promised Land. They were so close. Only a shimmering ribbon of water lay between them and their dreams, or so they thought.

What the Israelites could not see were the hosts of hell, the legions of Satan lined up along the riverbank against them. The Amorites, Israel's flesh-and-blood enemies, had been destroyed, but their great enemy, that evil spirit, Satan, was still prowling around like a roaring lion, seeking to devour them. He was not conquered, nor had he surrendered. Not at all! The devil still had many schemes in his attempt to destroy God's people and God's promise. There would be many more demonic assaults upon the Israelites before they ever crossed the Jordan River.

Many eyes of creatures both visible and invisible, in heaven and on earth, were watching the movements of the Israelites. Where God's people journeyed was of vital interest, not only to angels and demons, but to earthly kings and countries as well. The king of Moab, King Balak, saw all that Israel had done to the Amorites. Yes, he watched as Israel conquered kingdom after kingdom beyond his northern border, and he was horrified because these people could easily conquer his kingdom too. Then King Balak watched as the countless thousands of Israel returned south, marching towards his country again. Was Moab safe? Would Israel attack him this time? King Balak watched as Israel camped beside Moab's border. Israel was now Moab's next-door neighbor to the north. From the highest hills in his country, King Balak could see the tents of Israel in the distance. Israel was a great nation (as God had promised) and Moab was terrified of their vast numbers. Yes, the Moabites were filled with dread because of the Israelites.

King Balak wanted to drive Israel away—far, far away from his country—because he feared that, in spite of their promise of peace with Moab, Israel would soon declare war on them. No, King Balak did not trust Israel, but he also was afraid to attack them. He knew what had happened to the mighty kings, Sihon and Og, who were mightier men than he was. He knew what had happened to their armies and their cities, which were larger and stronger than his own were. King Balak was wise enough to see that Israel was too powerful for him to destroy, but he was not wise enough to see that he should bless Israel and befriend Israel. When they had passed through his country, King Balak should have welcomed these people with bread and water, and helped them on their way. Balak had not done those good deeds, but it was not too late. He could still bless these people, now that he saw how blessed they were of God. Long ago the LORD had promised Abraham: "I will make you into a great nation and I will bless you." God also promised: "I will bless those who bless you, and whoever curses you I will curse" (Genesis 12:2–3). Moab could have had the blessing of God by blessing Israel, but instead, King Balak devised a wicked scheme in an attempt to destroy the people of God.

The first part of King Balak's wicked plan was to make his army larger and stronger. He formed an alliance with a neighboring country called Midian. The Midianites also had been watching the journeys and the victories of Israel. They, too, were worried and wondered: "Who's next?" The Moabite rulers said to the Midianite rulers, "This horde is going to lick up everything around us, as an ox licks up the grass of the field." The Moabites and Midianites were both afraid that they would be devoured by Israel, so they joined forces against them. Together they had a better chance of destroying Israel.

But King Balak was still afraid. He was wise enough to know that someone was blessing Israel, but he was not wise enough to know that he should likewise bless Israel. Instead, King Balak decided to hire a prophet to change Israel's blessing into a curse. That was the second part of King Balak's wicked plan, to pay a prophet to put a curse on Israel. King Balak knew just the man to do it.

In a land far away there lived a famous prophet, named Balaam. Balaam claimed to be a prophet of God, who communed with the LORD, but really, Balaam was a sorcerer, whose dreadful power was demonic. Balaam boasted that he was a prophet "whose eye sees clearly . . . who hears the words of God . . . who has knowledge from the Most High . . . who sees a vision from the Almighty" (Numbers 24:15–16), but really, Balaam was a false prophet, a fraud who only pretended to know God and God's Word. True prophets of the LORD were carried along by the Holy Spirit, but this godless man was carried away by his own corrupt and evil desires. He was a "slave of depravity," who mouthed "empty, boastful words" (II Peter 2:18–19). Nonetheless, Balaam had an international reputation for being a prophet of God who could pronounce terrible curses that produced terrible results. Offer him enough money, and Balaam would travel great distances to do his dark, dirty, demonic work.

This was the man that wicked King Balak wanted, so he sent messengers with money and with the urgent request that the great prophet Balaam come to him immediately to put a curse upon his enemy Israel. The elders of Moab and Midian had to travel a long way to find the prophet and to deliver this message from the king: "A people has come out of Egypt. They cover the face of the land and they have settled next to me. Now come and put a curse on these people, because they are too powerful for me. Perhaps then I will be able to defeat them and drive them out of the country. For I know that those you bless are blessed and those you curse are cursed." How wrong King Balak was. God alone had such power to bless or curse. However, the prophet must have been quite flattered when he heard these words from the king. Balaam answered Balak's messengers by saying that he would have to ask God before he could go. Remember, Balaam pretended to be a servant of God, so he said to the messengers, "Spend the night here and I will bring you back the answer the LORD gives me."

That night an amazing thing happened. The LORD actually did come and speak to Balaam. God said, *"Do not go with them."* God warned, *"You must not put a curse on those people, because they are blessed."* How very disappointed Balaam must have been. Even hearing the voice of God (no doubt for the first time in his life) did not make up for this disappointment, because it was not the Word of the LORD that this "prophet" loved and treasured; it was the glint of gold and the jingle of silver that he loved and treasured above all else. Balaam earned his living by cursing people, and he was very upset that God was stopping him this time. Balaam really wanted to go to Moab and curse Israel, because Balaam really wanted the gold and silver that would be his pay. Although he pretended to be a prophet of God, Balaam was a wicked man, a lover of money and greedy for gain. He was an idolater, who worshipped worldly wealth.

What Balaam had to say the next morning was very difficult for him. He told King Balak's messengers: "Go back to your own country, for the LORD has refused to let me go with you." He made it clear that he wanted to go, but God wouldn't let him go, at least, not now. He did not say why. Balaam was supposed to be a prophet, who revealed the Word of the LORD, but he very carefully hid the truth of God's Word. The LORD's command was clear: *"You must not put a curse on those people,"* but Balaam did not tell this to the King of Moab, because he didn't want him to forsake his plan or pursue it with someone else. No, Balaam was still hoping that he would have an opportunity to do this wicked work and get his filthy pay. Balaam also did not want to repeat to King Balak what God had said about Israel: *"They are blessed!"* Oh no, that would not sound good to the king of Moab. Balaam would lose this client for sure and the job would go to someone else if he repeated those words. He must be careful that King Balak did not get the wrong idea and think that he, Balaam, was pro-Israel, desiring to do good to Israel. So, Balaam was very careful to conceal what God had told him. In that way the prophet Balaam hoped to keep the door open for further negotiations with King Balak.

It worked. When the messengers returned to King Balak, they simply said, "Balaam refused to come with us." The king understood this prophet very well. His answer wasn't, "No!" His answer was: "Make another offer." The king understood that, for the right price, this prophet certainly would come to him. So Balak made Balaam another offer. This time the king sent a whole procession of princes to the prophet. They were more numerous and more distinguished than the first messengers, and their offer was much more enticing. This was the message from King Balak to Prophet Balaam:

"Do not let anything keep you from coming to me, because I will reward you handsomely and do whatever you say. Come and put a curse on these people for me."

Balaam wanted to go so badly; he wanted to curse Israel so terribly, because he wanted to be rewarded so handsomely, but he also did not want to appear to be too greedy. After all, he was supposed to be a righteous man and a servant of God. So Balaam answered piously, pretending to be holy: "Even if Balak gave me his palace filled with silver and gold, I could not do anything great or small, to go beyond the command of the LORD my God." If what was in Balaam's heart matched what was on his lips, he would have been a godly man indeed. But Balaam had no intention of letting all this silver and gold slip away. Very quickly Balaam added these words, "Now stay here tonight . . . and I will find out what else the LORD will tell me."

Balaam already knew what God had to say. God's word to him was: *"You must not put a curse on those people, because they are blessed"* but Balaam hoped that God would change his mind. Perhaps that night Balaam begged God to let him go, but whether he voiced his pleas or not, God knew the desire of Balaam's heart. God was not fooled by Balaam's false claims. One peek into Balaam's heart made it clear that money was the master whom Balaam served and loved, not God. "No one can serve two masters. Either he will hate the one and love the other, or he will be devoted to one and despise the other. You cannot serve both God and Money" (Matthew 6:24). Although Balaam claimed to be a servant and prophet of God, Balaam served and loved money. He loved money more than the people of God, more than the promises of God, more than the praises of God. Balaam had another god that ruled his life, and that god's name was Money. The LORD knew that Balaam was a devoted servant of money, so that night God allowed Balaam to run after his beloved master. The LORD said to Balaam, "Go with them, but do only what I tell you." So God gave Balaam the desire of his heart, but it was not for Balaam's good. The LORD was letting Balaam go, but the LORD was very, very angry with this wicked, money-loving man, who spoke lies and pronounced curses while pretending to be a servant of the Most High God.

Balaam, however, was delighted. It seemed to Balaam that God was changing his mind about cursing these people; at least, this was the first step in that direction. Balaam could hardly wait to get going. The prophet was itching to earn that payment promised to him by the king. When Balaam awoke, he did not pause to ponder the wisdom of this pursuit. He just began running—no, racing—after his rich reward. Very early in the morning, Balaam saddled up his donkey and hurried off towards Moab. Woe to Balaam! This "prophet" was rushing after money into the biggest mistake of his life.

Because Balaam was in a hurry to get to Moab and start earning his wages of wickedness, he urged his little donkey to go faster, faster, but it was going to be a slow journey for Balaam. The way of the sinner is hard. God was very angry when he went. The LORD himself would block Balaam's way and thwart Balaam's work, and in so doing, God would glorify himself.

Because this false prophet set out to curse Israel, because he set out to oppose Israel, the Angel of the LORD stood in the road to oppose him. Who was this angel? The Angel of the LORD refers to the pre-incarnate Son of God. This was the "angel" whom God had promised the Israelites, saying, "I am sending an angel ahead of you to guard you along the way and to bring you to the place I have prepared. . . . I will be an enemy to your enemies and I will oppose those who oppose you. My angel will go ahead of you to bring you into the land" (Exodus 23:20–23). The Angel of the LORD, the Son of God, was the invisible guard who had led Israel on their journey through the wilderness. This "angel" had been there the whole way, but we first see him here, standing in the middle of the road with a drawn sword in his hand to kill Balaam.

Balaam, who claimed to see clearly, saw nothing. Balaam would have galloped right into that flashing sword and collapsed right there on that dusty road, except that his little donkey saw the danger. (The eyes of an ass saw more than Balaam did!) The little donkey saw the Angel of the LORD and veered off the road into a field. But Balaam, who was rushing for profit, was furious at this delay. He had no time to lose. Why was his stupid beast acting this way? Balaam didn't wait for an answer. Balaam beat his poor little donkey to get her back on the road again, and then they continued on their journey.

After awhile, they came to a narrow part in the road with stone walls on both sides. A second time the Angel of the LORD stood in the middle of the road, blocking their way. Again, Balaam saw nothing. But the little donkey saw the Angel and the sword, so she pressed up against the wall, crushing Balaam's foot against it. Again, Balaam was furious, not knowing that she crushed his foot to save his life. He beat her again and again to make her go forward and probably cursed her, too, shouting what a stubborn and stupid creature she was.

Then the Angel of the LORD moved some distance ahead and for the third time stood in the middle of the road. This time it was in a narrow place, where there was no room to turn at all. When the donkey saw him, she did the only thing she could do. She lay down under Balaam, refusing to take another step forward. Balaam was beside himself with rage. He took his staff and struck her with it, again and again, but still she wouldn't move. Then the LORD opened the donkey's mouth and she spoke to Balaam. "What have I done to you to make you beat me these three times?" Balaam was in such a state of uncontrolled rage that even a talking animal did not shock him into his senses. He screamed at her, "You have made a fool of me! If I had a sword in my hand, I would kill you right now." The poor little donkey tried to reason with her master and restrain the prophet's madness. She said, "Am I not your own donkey, which you have always ridden, to this very day? Have I been in the habit of doing this to you?" Balaam had to admit that this was the only time she had behaved like this. Then the LORD opened Balaam's eyes and he saw the Angel of the LORD standing in the road with his sword drawn. How quickly now Balaam's anger turned to terror. He did now what his donkey was already doing; he knelt down on the ground. In his fear, Balaam bowed low with his face to the ground.

Then the Angel of the LORD spoke to Balaam. "Why have you beaten your donkey these three times? I have come here to oppose you because your way is perverse (KJV), your path is a reckless one before me. The donkey saw me and turned away from me these three times. If she had not turned away, I would certainly have killed you by now, but I would have spared her."

Balaam said to the Angel of the LORD, "I have sinned. I did not realize you were standing in the road to oppose me. Now if you are displeased, I will go back." Could Balaam offer to do anything else and continue to live? What other choice did he have? Balaam had not forsaken his sin; he had been stopped at sword-point.

The LORD allowed Balaam to continue on his way, because the LORD was going to use Balaam exactly how he pleased. The LORD was going to glorify himself and benefit his people through Balaam, whether he wanted to be used in this way or not. What Balak and Balaam meant for evil, God meant for good. Their wicked plan could not succeed. The Angel of the LORD said to Balaam, "Go with these men, but speak only what I tell you."

So Balaam went on his journey, a little less eagerly and a little more soberly, but still with the hidden hope of making his money and receiving his reward. It was a false hope. Balaam's talking donkey should have taught him that God was Sovereign, controlling everything, even the tongues of his creatures. If the LORD could cause a dumb animal to speak, he could also make an evil man to bless and force a false prophet with lying lips to tell the truth.

Balaam, the famous prophet, should have been greatly humbled. A brute beast had seen the Angel, when his own eyes had seen nothing. Also, he had been rebuked by a donkey. God used a lowly little animal to confront his wickedness and restrain his madness. This should have humbled Balaam, but he was a proud, wicked man, filled with greed and lust, and hell-bent on doing evil. As Balaam traveled along the road to Moab to meet Balak, he might have been thinking: "We will triumph with our tongues. We own our lips. Who is our master?" (Psalm 12:4). God was about to show this evil man who was the Master. God was about to show this proud prophet, who had acquired such power and honor and riches through his wicked words, that God was the one who owned his lips. It was God's Word alone that would triumph.

# A SIGN OF GOD'S LOVE

- Numbers 23–24
- Deuteronomy 23:3–6
- Joshua 24:9–10

When King Balak heard that the famous prophet, Balaam, was on his way, he rode out to meet him. So eager was the king to meet this powerful prophet that he went to the edge of his territory and waited at a town on the border of Moab. King Balak was impatient for the prophet to arrive and begin his wicked work of pronouncing curses upon Israel. At last the king was told that Balaam was in sight, trotting along the road on his little donkey. Why had it taken him so long to get here? Didn't he know how important this work was? Didn't he know how much money was waiting for him? The king rode out to meet him and asked, "Did I not send you an urgent summons? Why didn't you come to me? Am I really not able to reward you?" Balaam did not tell the king what had happened on the way. He just said, "Well, I have come to you now." Balaam did warn King Balak, however, that this job was not going to be easy. Balaam had just seen the Angel of the Lord and the flashing of his fearful sword. With this memory still vivid in his mind, the prophet now had a question for the king: "Can I say just anything?" No, he told the king that he must speak only what God put in his mouth. What Balaam fervently hoped was that God would put curses on his lips.

As Balaam had been riding along the road to Moab, he had been thinking and plotting. God was angry with him. How could he please God, so that God would let him curse Israel? Balaam knew that Israel's God required sacrifices. Perhaps they could buy God's favor by offering him bulls and rams upon an altar, the way the Israelites did. Perhaps they could bribe God. Perhaps they could get him to break his promise and curse his people. Balaam thought he knew the way: Would it not be by offering the God of Israel the blood of bulls and rams? This was Balaam's new scheme. He hoped it would work, so that he could earn his wages of wickedness.

The next morning, King Balak took Balaam up to a high and holy place in Moab, a place dedicated to Baal, a god of Moab. From this holy height the prophet could see some of the Israelites, and so, thought the king, he could pronounce his deadly curses directly upon his enemies. King Balak also thought that from this sacred site God might be pleased to hear their prayers and bless their plans. In order to sway God to their side, Balaam ordered that not one altar, but seven altars, be built. "Build me seven altars here, and prepare seven bulls and seven rams for me." Balaam was not taking any chances. He did not want to meet that angel with the sword again. Then Balak and Balaam offered their perfect sacrifice to God, seven bulls and seven rams on seven altars. Yes, that money-mad prophet and that curse-crazy king together went from altar to altar to altar, offering their sacrifices to God. With them, they hoped to turn God's Word against the Israelites.

Do you think God was pleased with their offerings? No! They were an abomination to the LORD. The Bible says, "The sacrifice of the wicked is detestable—how much more so when brought with evil intent!" (Proverbs 21:27). God knew what was in the hearts of these wicked men, and it wasn't faith in him or love for him, not at all. Their sacrifices were showing contempt for God. Balaam and Balak were not offering these sacrifices to praise God, but to use God and to bribe God and to trick God. The LORD was not fooled by their outward display of devotion. God knew what Balaam's purpose was: It was not to honor God with sacrifices of righteousness, but to enrich himself with wages of wickedness. God also knew what Balak's purpose was: It was not to bless the God of heaven, but to curse his people on earth. Oh no, God was not fooled. God was not impressed by their many altars, their perfect number of altars, built on this high and holy hill.

At this time in the world's history, there was only one altar on earth where sacrifices could be made that would please God, and that was on the bronze altar at God's Tabernacle in the camp of Israel. Not even a faithful Israelite could build an altar or offer a sacrifice wherever or whenever he pleased. Moses himself would be breaking God's Law if he had built these altars on this mountain without special permission from God. The LORD had ordained that sacrifices were to be made by appointed people at appointed times in the appointed place and for appointed reasons according to all the laws of the LORD. If Balaam and Balak really wanted to worship the LORD in spirit and in truth, then they must believe and obey the God of Israel. It was not impossible. One day there would be another Moabite who joined with Israel saying, "Your people will be my people and your God will be my God" (Ruth 1:16). That woman from Moab found favor with the God of Israel because of her faith. She loved God and she loved the people of God. How different she was from Balaam and Balak, who stood upon that hill trying to manipulate God into doing what they wanted, which was to curse the people of God. They were so arrogant in their wickedness that they really thought they could convince God to forsake his people and forget his promise, just by sacrificing a few animals. How little they knew God. They did not know that the LORD's Word endures forever and the LORD's Love lasts for a thousand generations.

Balaam, however, was confident that these offerings would please God. He said to the king, "Stay here beside your offering, while I go aside. Perhaps the LORD will come to meet with me. Whatever he reveals to me, I will tell you." So Balaam went off alone to a barren height, not to pray, not to seek God or to search for truth, but to begin his wicked work. There, with his sinful sorceries and dark divinations, Balaam hoped to concoct an evil and powerful incantation to pronounce upon the people below him, but Balaam was stopped in the middle of his wicked work. The LORD did come and meet with Balaam. The prophet was quick to point out why God should be pleased with him. "I have prepared seven altars and on each altar I have offered a bull and a ram." Balaam hoped that these offerings would be enough to buy God's favor and so let him put a horrible curse upon Israel. The LORD did put a message in the prophet's mouth and sent him back to the king with it.

King Balak had been waiting a long time for this moment. He had gathered all the princes of Moab so that they could hear this great prophet speak

God's Word against the people camped below them. How their ears itched to hear those horrible curses poured out upon their enemies. While Israel camped peacefully in the plain below them, the prophet would secretly shoot his words like poisoned arrows upon them, and they would be cursed. It would be the beginning of Israel's destruction, when God's Word was turned against them.

The rulers were all there, waiting to witness this crucial moment in their history, but when Balaam opened his mouth, what poured out were words of blessing upon Israel.

## Balaam's First Oracle

Balaam said that King Balak of Moab had brought him all the way from his country in the eastern mountains and said to him, "Come, curse Jacob for me! Come, denounce Israel!" But the prophet said, "How can I curse those whom God has not cursed? How can I denounce those whom the LORD has not denounced? From the rocky peaks I see them; from the heights I view them." What did the prophet perceive? A people blessed of God:

1. A distinct people: The Israelites were blessed in that they were distinct from all the other nations. They were a people set apart for God. Balaam said, "I see a people who live apart and do not consider themselves one of the nations."

2. A numerous people: The Israelites were blessed because of their numbers. God had promised to make the Israelites like the stars in the sky, like the sand on the seashore, like the dust of the earth. Balaam said, "Who can count the dust of Jacob or number the fourth part of Israel?"

3. A victorious people: The Israelites were blessed because their end was not destruction. They had victory, even over death. Balaam said, "Let me die the death of the righteous and may my end be like theirs!"

King Balak must have been surprised, then enraged. "What have you done to me?" he cried. "I brought you here to curse my enemies, but you have done nothing but bless them!" Balaam couldn't help it. It wasn't his fault. God made him do it. "Must I not speak what the LORD puts in my mouth?" he asked. This was not what the prophet had planned or wanted or intended to say either. The words that tumbled out of his mouth had shocked him too. He desperately wanted to curse Israel, but God himself was the one who had blocked the curses.

Balak and Balaam were not quitters. Perhaps they needed a better place, a bigger bribe. Both of them were ready to try again. "Come with me to another place where you can see them," said Balak, "and from there you can curse them for me." Balaam was more than willing, for he was still hoping to earn his handsome reward. They went to the new place and again built seven altars and sacrificed seven bulls and seven rams on them. Perhaps the LORD would be pleased with them this time. Perhaps the LORD would change his mind. Balaam certainly hoped so. Once again Balaam went off by himself and resorted to his black magic to cast his evil spell. But the LORD met with Balaam again and put another message in his mouth. The king and the princes of Moab were waiting for his return. "What did the LORD say?" asked Balak with some apprehension.

Balaam opened his mouth, and again words of blessing poured out upon Israel.

### Balaam's Second Oracle

The prophet commanded the king to arise and listen to the Word of the LORD. His plot to curse Israel could not succeed because:

1. God is unchangeable: The prophet said, "God is not a man, that he should lie, nor a son of man, that he should change his mind. Does he speak, and then not act? Does he promise, and not fulfill?"

2. God is all-powerful: The prophet said that no person, no nation, no weapon, no magic could succeed against Israel, because God was with them. "I have received a command to bless," said Balaam. "He has blessed, and I cannot change it . . . The LORD their God is with them . . . There is no sorcery against Jacob, no divination against Israel." There was no power, not even the dark demonic powers, strong enough to conquer Israel, because their God was with them. O blessed people, whose God is the LORD. Balaam prophesied, "It will now be said of Jacob and of Israel: See what God has done!"

3. God is merciful: The Israelites could depend upon God's LOVE and mercy and forgiveness. The prophet said, "He has not looked on Jacob's

offences or on the wrongs found in Israel." Blessed indeed are the people whose sin the LORD does not count against them. "He has not beheld iniquity in Jacob, neither has he seen perverseness in Israel" (KJV). So great was the cleansing of their sin, that it was not even seen. Israel had been freed of all the sorrows connected with sin. The prophet said, "No misfortune is seen in Jacob, no misery observed in Israel." How blessed were these people.

As Balaam looked out over Israel's camp as they lay resting by the Jordan River and waiting to enter the land of Canaan, he was reminded of a crouching lion, waiting to pounce upon its prey. Balaam prophesied that the Israelites would devour all their enemies. "The people rise like a lioness; they rouse themselves like a lion that does not rest till he devours his prey and drinks the blood of his victims."

"Shut up!" screamed King Balak. That was exactly what he feared, being devoured by Israel. The rulers of Moab must have shuddered in terror and in anger. What was Balaam doing? How could this prophet, who was being paid by them, say such things? It would be better if he said nothing at all, than to say this. "Neither curse them at all, nor bless them at all!" shrieked the king. Balaam was also upset. He was sorry, truly sorry, that this was what had come out of his mouth. He knew there would be no reward from the king for words as damaging to Moab as these ones were, but Balaam could not help what he spoke. God was controlling his speech. "I must do whatever the LORD says," he apologized.

Neither of these wicked men were willing to give up. They would try a third time. Perhaps this third time would be the perfect time. This might be the magic number of altars. Balak took Balaam to another high place in Moab. "Perhaps it will please God to let you curse them for me from there," said Balak. Again they built seven altars. In total they had built twenty-one altars (three times seven altars)—a perfect number. Surely God would be pleased this time to grant them their desire. Again they offered seven bulls and seven rams. So many offerings must please the LORD.

This time Balaam did not resort to sorcery. It hadn't produced favorable results so far. Instead, he just turned his face towards the desert, towards Israel. When he saw the tents of Israel, encamped tribe by tribe in their God-centered, God-ordered formation, the Spirit of God came upon him and he uttered these words.

## Balaam's Third Oracle

"How beautiful are your tents, O Jacob, your dwelling places, O Israel!" The prophet compared their beauty to fruitful valleys and lovely gardens, fragrant spices and graceful trees, all flourishing beside rivers of flowing water. Israel would grow and spread, like well-watered seeds, springing up and sprouting everywhere. By the Spirit of God Balaam prophesied that Israel's King would be greater than the greatest king on earth and their kingdom would be exalted. "They devour hostile nations," warned Balaam. "May those who bless you be blessed and those who curse you be cursed!"

Again Israel had been blessed, and this time Moab had been cursed. The plan of the wicked king had backfired. The pit that Balak had dug for Israel, he had fallen into himself. The curses of God had fallen on him, not his enemies. King Balak was furious. His anger burned against Balaam. He struck his hands together and shouted at him, "I summoned you to curse my enemies, but you have blessed them these three times. Now leave at once and go home! I said I would reward you handsomely, but the LORD has kept you from being rewarded." The prophet pleaded that he had not cheated the king but had warned him from the beginning that he could not go beyond the command of the LORD. Balaam said, "I am going back to my people now," but first he had a few more words to say. "Let me warn you," said Balaam, "what this people [Israel] will do to your people [Moab] in days to come."

## Balaam's Fourth Oracle

Balaam then proclaimed a puzzle or a riddle, saying:

> I see him, but not now;
> > I behold him, but not near.
> A star will come out of Jacob;
> > a scepter will rise out of Israel.
> He will crush the foreheads of Moab . . .
> Seir, his enemy, will be conquered,
> > but Israel will grow strong.
> A ruler will come out of Jacob. . . .

(Numbers 24:17–19)

Can you solve the puzzle? Can you answer the riddle? Balaam, by the Spirit of God, saw someone "not now" and "not near," someone coming in the distant future, a king arising in Israel, a ruler who would destroy Moab. Who was it that he saw? Hundreds of years later King David would arise and shatter Moab's strength, but there was another king, a greater king, who was foreseen and foretold as well. This king was seen from a great distance, from fifteen hundred years away. This king was the Son of David, the promised Messiah, the Savior from sin and death, the seed of the woman who would crush the head of the serpent, Satan. This king was the Conqueror who would destroy all his enemies. Jesus was the star, the "Bright Morning Star" (Revelation 22:16), shining out of Jacob. Jesus was the king rising out of Israel; the scepter of his kingdom was a "scepter of righteousness" (Hebrews 1:8 KJV). This was a prophesy about Jesus Christ our Lord.

And so, Balaam's last words were greater than his first words. God's final blessing (through the mouth of this miserable man) was the greatest blessing he could give to his beloved Israel, the blessing of Messiah. God confirmed his greatest promise to Israel and revealed again his greatest plan for Israel—the coming of Christ. Nothing could break that promise or stop that plan. Neither a powerful prophet nor a mighty monarch, neither the legions of hell nor the armies on earth, could stand in the way of God's great purpose. The Christ would come! The Christ would conquer! Satan and all his servants would be destroyed—forever.

Balaam got up and returned home and Balak also went on his way. They had not been able to curse Israel. Their plan had not prevailed to turn God against Israel. As Moses later told the Israelites, "The LORD your God . . . turned the curse into a blessing for you, *because the* LORD *your God loves you*" (Deuteronomy 23:5). Joshua also told the people that God refused to put a curse on them. "He blessed you again and again, and delivered you" (Joshua 24:10). Yes, God had delivered his people again. God rescued them from the armies of Balak and from the sorceries of Balaam. No weapon formed on earth, no intrigue hatched in hell, could ever harm Israel, because the LOVE of the LORD was protecting them forever.

# ONE LAST TRY

As Balaam rode back to his own land, he could have considered himself blessed because, although the king of Moab had not paid him, the King of kings had spared him and used him. Balaam could have rejoiced because he had witnessed the workings of Almighty God:

1. On the road to Moab, Balaam had seen the Angel of the LORD.
2. Many times Balaam had heard the Voice of the LORD.
3. He also had heard a most amazing thing, which no other man on earth had ever heard: A donkey, a dumb beast, had spoken to him with the voice of a man.
4. Several times Balaam had heard the message of the LORD coming from his own lips. For the first time in his life Balaam was a true prophet; the LORD had used his false lips to proclaim God's Holy Word.
5. The Spirit of God had come upon Balaam (Numbers 24:2) and he had prophesied the good news of Christ in those great words of hope: "A star will come out of

Jacob; a scepter will rise out of Israel." God had chosen Balaam to an-
nounce the coming of the Great King.

6.  Balaam's fame would spread to all peoples. His words would reach the
    ends of the earth and his name would touch the end of time.

7.  For the first time in a long wicked while, Balaam's mouth had poured
    out blessings and he had been used for good. In spite of himself, Balaam
    had glorified God.

Balaam had every reason to rejoice. From that day forward Balaam could
have led a different life, by repenting of his wicked ways. Balaam could have
spent the rest of his days on earth serving and praising the only living God.

But Balaam did not choose to do that. As he trotted along on his little
donkey, it was not joy and thanks that filled his heart. No, grief filled his
heart, but not a grief that was sorrow for his sin. Balaam was sad because he
was riding home without the music he loved best—the jingling of gold and
silver in his saddlebags. Money was the only thing that made Balaam happy,
and on this mission he had not been given so much as a copper coin.

As Balaam rode along that day, mile after miserable mile, he began to
think—and when Balaam thought it was to plot and to scheme about how
to get rich. Balaam did not give up easily. He was a very persistent man as
well as a very wicked man. Every thought of his heart inclined only to evil
all the time. Balaam now had a new plan. It was so simple. Why hadn't he
thought of it sooner? If Balaam and Balak could not entice God to turn away
from Israel, perhaps they could entice Israel to turn away from God. They
had failed in their attempts to influence God. He had proved to be "the
LORD . . . abounding in love and faithfulness" (Exodus 34:6). But what about
the people's love for God? Would Israel's love and faithfulness towards God
prove to be so strong? Balaam suspected that it could be easily shaken.

Balaam was excited. If there was a way to get God to curse Israel, then
there was also a way for him to get his money. He only hoped that it was not
too late to receive his reward. Quickly he spun his donkey around and galloped off towards Moab. This time no angel hindered his speedy return.
When he found the king he told him his plan: "Ensnare the Israelites in sin.
Entice them to do evil. Then the LORD will curse them. Israel's God is a jealous God. If you get the people of Israel to bow down to the gods of Moab,
then the LORD will not only curse them for you; perhaps he will even destroy them!" Balak liked Balaam's plan, but how could they accomplish it?

How could they get the Israelites to bow down to their idols? Balaam had been thinking about this question, too, and he knew exactly how it could be done. So the king listened carefully and then followed all the wicked prophet's instructions:

The king of Moab gathered together an extraordinary army to send against Israel. He chose the most beautiful women from Moab and Midian to send down into the camp of Israel. They came armed with charming smiles, enchanting eyes, alluring lips, enticing speech. These beautiful women welcomed the Israelites and invited them to a great celebration to their gods. The men of Israel were totally captivated by the women's beauty, and so they went, like animals being led to the slaughter.

Beware, oh men of Israel. It is a trap! These women are not friends, but foes, seducing you in order to destroy you. Beware, oh sons of Israel. "For the lips of an adulteress drip honey and her speech is smoother than oil, but in the end she is bitter as gall, sharp as a double-edged sword. Her feet go down to death. Her steps lead straight to the grave" (Proverbs 5:3–5). Remember the Law of the LORD, oh Israel. God's laws will keep you from the immoral woman. "Do not lust in your heart after her beauty or let her captivate you with her eyes . . . for the adulteress preys upon your very life" (Proverbs 6:25–26). Remember the commands of God, oh Israel. "They will keep you from the adulteress, from the wayward wife with her seductive words. . . . Do not let your heart turn to her ways or stray into her paths. Many are the victims she has brought down. Her slain are a mighty throng. Her house is a highway to the grave, leading down to the chambers of death" (Proverbs 7:5, 25–27).

But thousands of men in Israel ignored the warning of God's Word. They were not careful to keep the Law of the LORD: *You shall not commit adultery.* They joined in the great celebration of eating and drinking, singing and dancing . . . but the meat had been offered to idols and the songs glorified false gods. The Israelites were not careful to keep the Law of the LORD: *You shall have no other gods before me . . . you shall not bow down to them or worship them.* Soon the Israelites were drunk with wine and wild with lust. They indulged in sexual sin with these women—and worse. They bowed down before their gods. The Israelites joined in the worship of Baal, the god of Moab, and so they yoked themselves to lifeless gods. They broke God's covenant and they disobeyed God's commandments. They were involved in adultery and idolatry. They committed these sins with God's promises before their very eyes. The Promised Land was within their sight, within their grasp. What would happen to them now? Would they again be turned away and driven back into the desert, or this time would they be destroyed? Either option would please King Balak. To be rid of the Israelites, one way or another, was exactly what he wanted.

We read in the Bible that the LORD's anger burned against Israel. "They provoked the LORD to anger by their wicked deeds and a plague broke out among them" (Psalm 106:29). Israelites were dying by the thousands. How Balaam and Balak must have cheered. This time their plan was working. God was not cursing the soldiers of Israel; he was killing them. The mad prophet and the wicked king were certain that victory was theirs at last.

But they were wrong. Not every man in Israel had lost his head to a harlot. Not every man in Israel had bowed his knee to an idol. There were still faithful men in Israel who loved the LORD their God, who obeyed his law and worshipped him only. One such man turned God's anger away from Israel. His name was Phinehas. He was a priest, the son of Eleazar, the grandson of Aaron. This was what happened:

He and the faithful ones in Israel were at the entrance to the Tent of Meeting, weeping and praying because of Israel's sin. While they were there, grieving before the LORD, an Israelite man (named Zimri) brought a Midianite woman (named Cozbi) right into Israel's camp. In fact, Zimri brought Cozbi right into his own tent to commit adultery with her. Zimri, who was a leader in Israel, wasn't ashamed of his sin. He didn't even try to hide it. Rather, openly and brazenly, he paraded his sin before the eyes of all the people. He was proud of it, boasting in it and daring the elders of Israel to do something about it. Although God had ordered the execution of all the leaders who were involved in this sin, Zimri was not concerned. Who dared to stop him? He was a powerful man in Israel, and the woman was the daughter of a chief in Midian. Lay hands on either one of them, and the elders faced strife in Israel or war with Midian. Zimri was quite certain that none of Israel's elders would dare to risk being embroiled in such conflicts.

But Zimri was wrong. Phinehas the priest dared. Phinehas the priest obeyed the command of the LORD: "Take all the leaders of these people, kill them and expose them in broad daylight before the LORD, so that the LORD's fierce anger may turn away from Israel." Phinehas the priest obeyed the command of Moses: "You must put to death those of your men who have joined in worshipping the Baal." Phinehas the priest dared to punish this evil-doer, no matter how powerful or popular he was, because Phinehas the priest was zealous for the honor of God. By faith, Phinehas the priest stood up. By faith, Phinehas the priest left the grieving congregation, took a spear in his hand and followed Zimri and Cozbi into the tent. By faith, Phinehas the priest put them to death. Phinehas drove his spear through both of them where they lay in their sin. He drove his spear right through the man into the woman's body.

Many people have judged Phinehas, condemning what he did as a dreadful deed, accusing him of viciously murdering a man and a woman inside their tent. But how does God judge what he did?

1. The plague against the Israelites immediately stopped, which was proof of God's approval. God's Word affirms that, because "Phinehas stood up and intervened, and the plague was checked" (Psalm 106:30). God's fierce anger was turned away from the nation because of what Phinehas did. Although 24,000 people died in the plague, the entire nation was not destroyed.
2. God considered what Phinehas did and judged it as a righteous deed and an act of faith. "This was credited to him as righteousness" (Psalm 106:31).
3. Phinehas (along with the other judges in Israel) had been ordered to execute such law-breakers. Phinehas had been given the "sword of the state" to punish these evil-doers. He had not taken the law into his own hands.
4. The LORD said to Moses, "Phinehas, the son of Eleazar, the son of Aaron the priest, has turned my anger away from the Israelites, for he was as zealous as I am for my honor among them, so that in my zeal I did not put an end to them." According to God's own Word, Phinehas was zealous for God's honor.
5. The LORD made a covenant of peace with Phinehas. God said, "He and his descendants will have a covenant of a lasting priesthood, because he was zealous for the honor of his God and made atonement for the Israelites."

But Balaam and Balak were not entirely disappointed. Although God had not destroyed the entire nation, still, thousands of soldiers in Israel had been put to death by the hand of Israel's own God. Yes, 24,000 Israelite men had died because of their adultery and idolatry. Balaam had succeeded in his plot, but only for a brief season. His victory would not last long.

# BALAAM RECEIVES HIS REWARD

Balaam, by the teaching of his evil doctrines, brought disaster on Israel. Balaam was the one "who taught Balak to entice the Israelites to sin by eating food sacrificed to idols and by committing sexual immorality" (Revelation 2:14). Thus God destroyed 24,000 Israelite men in the plague of Peor because they allowed themselves to be led into the sins of adultery and idolatry. King Balak must have given the prophet Balaam a very handsome reward indeed for such useful, powerful, and effectual teaching. At last the wicked prophet would be happy, because he was going home laden with silver and gold.

But Balaam would not live long to enjoy his wages of wickedness. God would strike him down, not with the sword of an angel, but with the sword of a man. One of the soldiers of Israel would put the evil prophet to death. Balaam's heart would cease to beat; his mind would cease to plot; his lips would cease to curse. The gold and the silver that he had earned with the blood of Israel would be worthless; he could not buy himself another moment of life, much less eternal life. No, what Balaam would earn with his filthy, blood-stained, sin-cursed money was everlasting death, torment, and damnation. Did Balaam think that God would let him escape? This was what happened:

The Word of the LORD went out against Israel's enemies. The LORD said to Moses, "Treat the Midianites as enemies and kill them, because they treated you as enemies when they deceived you." The Midianites were descendants of Abraham from the wife of his old age, Keturah (Genesis 25:2). Because they were relatives, Israel had intended to leave the Midianites alone. In fact, Moses had been married to a Midianite. But now God commanded Israel to go to war against Midian. Because the Midianites had deceived them and seduced them into committing hideous sins, and because 24,000 Israelites had died in the resulting plague, God now said to Moses, "Take vengeance on the Midianites for the Israelites!" This would be Moses' last battle. "After that," God said, "you will be gathered to your people."

For the last time before he finally rested in peace, Moses was involved in war. He called the people to arms. "Arm some of your men to go to war against the Midianites and to carry out the LORD's vengeance on them. Send into battle a thousand men from each of the tribes of Israel." So 12,000 men went into battle, along with Phinehas the priest, who had proved himself to be a man who could fight by faith. Phinehas the priest would finish the work that he had begun. The Israelites fought against Midian, as the LORD commanded. They burned their cities and killed their soldiers. Among their victims were five Midianite kings, probably those same "elders of Midian" who had joined with Moab in their early attempts to curse Israel (Numbers 22:4).

During this war the Israelites also killed a wicked and famous prophet who was found there with the Midianites. It was Balaam himself. What was he doing in the midst of this battle? Hadn't he gone home? Didn't he know the outcome of this war? This "prophet," who claimed to foresee the future, who proudly boasted in himself and arrogantly advertised himself as one "whose eyes see clearly . . . who hears the words of God . . . who has knowledge from the Most High . . . who sees a vision from the Almighty . . . whose eyes are opened" (Numbers 24:3–4, 15–16), this same mighty man, could he not see his own violent death, his own everlasting doom? No, this man was always blinded by the glint of gold, and now he had been plunged into the "blackest darkness . . . reserved forever" for him (Jude 13). It seems that the LORD trapped Balaam in this war, perhaps enticing him there with Midian's offer of more money. In whatever way he was caught, at last this evil man received his just reward, not from an earthly king, but from heaven's only king, the LORD himself. Balaam was killed in the battle by one of the soldiers he had been forced to bless. Balaam not only lost his life, but he also lost all his beloved wealth; it all went to the ones he had so desperately wanted to curse — the Israelites. If he had listened to the Word of God, which came forth from his own mouth, he would not have been found with Israel's enemies, for he would have known that those who cursed Israel were themselves cursed.

As well as the five kings from Midian and the one false prophet from a foreign land, all the other men of Midian were put to death. However, the Israelite soldiers did not put to death the Midianite women. Perhaps they were still captivated by their beauty or perhaps they were just moved by human pity. Whatever their reasons, they allowed the women to live. When the soldiers returned to Moses, with the Midianite women and children as captives, Moses was very angry. These were the very women who had enticed the Israelites to sin. "Have you allowed all the women to live?" asked Moses. "They were the ones who followed Balaam's advice and were the means of turning the Israelites away from the LORD . . . so that a plague struck the LORD's people." These women were the ones guilty of ensnaring the Israelites in both adultery and idolatry. Should they be allowed to live? God had executed Israel's men for their part in this same sin, and 24,000 of them had died. God's law was clear and fair: "Both the adulterer and the adulteress must be put to death" (Leviticus 20:10). Both the men and the women involved in sexual sin must pay for it with their lives. Men and women, Jews and Gentiles, they were all treated equally under the Law of the LORD. Then Moses gave this hard command for the Israelite soldiers to obey: "Kill every woman who has slept with a man." Among all the captives, only the young maidens were spared.

In this war, the Israelites plundered the Midianites, taking captive not only some of their people, but also all of their flocks and herds. Hundreds of thousands of animals (including sheep, goats, cattle, donkeys, etc.) were taken as plunder. As well, there were articles of gold, silver, bronze, iron, tin, lead, wood, leather and wool. What should be done with all these valuable things, all these spoils from the war?

First of all, everything must be purified. War is a dirty business and death is its ugly outcome. Both the people and the plunder involved in this war were contaminated, and so, before they could enter Israel's camp, they must be cleansed. Moses commanded, "All of you, who have killed anyone . . . must stay outside the camp seven days. . . . You must purify yourselves and your captives." Even a soldier who had not killed anyone, but had only touched a dead body on the battlefield, even he must remain outside the camp and purify himself. Eleazar the priest said that all the plunder must be purified too, with fire and/or water. He told the soldiers who had gone into battle the requirement of the Law of the LORD: "Gold, silver, bronze, iron, tin, lead and anything else that can withstand fire must be put through the fire, and then it will be clean. But it must also be purified with the water of cleansing." How could the things made of combustible material, such as wool or wood, be purified? Eleazar said that whatever could not withstand fire could be cleansed with water only.

Next, the plunder was to be counted. The LORD said to Moses, "You and Eleazar the priest and the family heads of the community are to count all the people and the animals that were captured." They counted 675,000 sheep, 72,000 cattle and 61,000 donkeys (one of which may have been Balaam's donkey). They also counted 32,000 young Midianite maidens, who had been captured in the war and whose lives had been spared.

Finally, the spoils of war must be divided. Moses divided up this wealth among the whole congregation, for the LORD said, "Divide the spoils between the soldiers who took part in the battle and the rest of the community." The soldiers who had fought received the largest share, but the whole nation benefited from the war. Even the Levites, who were not part of the army at all, received a portion of the plunder. The plunder was split right down the middle into halves:

1. Half of the plunder went to the few thousand soldiers who actually fought in the war. From their half share, a tribute to the LORD was set apart, which went to Eleazar the priest. The fighting soldiers received 337,500 sheep, 36,000 cattle, 30,500 donkeys and 16,000 people. The LORD's tribute was one out of every five hundred people or animals counted.
2. The other half of the plunder went to the rest of the community, to the reserve soldiers, who had not been called up for active service during this war. From their half share, a larger tribute to the LORD was set apart which went to the Levites who were responsible for the care of the LORD's Tabernacle. The worship of God must continue, whether Israel was at peace or at war. The whole community received the same number as the fighting soldiers—337,500 sheep, 36,000 cattle, 30,500 donkeys and 16,000 people. The LORD's tribute was one out of every fifty people or animals counted.

Then the officers in Israel's army counted something else. The commanders of thousands and the commanders of hundreds all came to Moses and said, "Your servants have counted the soldiers under our command, and not one is missing." That was amazing. Israel had fought in a war and not lost a single man. How could that be possible? The officers were truly thankful to the LORD for this miraculous protection. Because of God's great LOVE for them (and because of their own sin in this campaign) they wanted to bring an offering to the LORD to make atonement for themselves. They gave as a gift to God all the gold articles that each of them had acquired in the war. There were gold earrings; there were gold necklaces and chains; there were gold bracelets and bangles; there were even gold diadems and crowns, for they had killed five kings. When it was all counted and weighed, it amounted to 16,750 shekels or 420 pounds of pure gold. These commanders did not keep any of this valuable jewelry for themselves, but gave all their gold to God.

How different these men were from Balaam, who was so greedy for gold. These officers in Israel's army loved God more than they loved earthly treasures, but Balaam loved his ill-gotten gold more than anything else in the whole world. It was a love that cost him his life. How ironic that all Balaam's filthy gold was first purified by fire and water, then offered to God, where it eventually made its way into the treasury of the LORD. And Balaam's little donkey, his little talking donkey who three times saw the Angel of the LORD, perhaps she wound up in a far better place than her master. She probably was taken captive and lived the rest of her donkey's life, happily hee-hawing in the camp of Israel, where she served the people of God.

Moses and Eleazar accepted the officers' gifts of gold and brought them into the Tent of Meeting as a memorial for the Israelites before the LORD. These faithful commanders were both humble and thankful. They wanted neither medals nor memorials for themselves. They wanted the memory of this victory to go to God. They wanted all the glory and honor, as well as all the wealth of gold, to go to God. They wanted the LORD's name to be remembered throughout the generations, because of his great LOVE, mercy, and faithfulness to Israel during this war. Hallelujah!

# PREPARING FOR THE CONQUEST OF CANAAN

- **Numbers 26; 27:12–23; 28–29; 33–35**
- **Deuteronomy 3:21–29**

D o you remember how the book of Numbers began? It began with a census of Israel's army. All the men who were at least twenty years old and able to fight were counted. One by one, the name of every man from every family in every tribe of Israel (except Levi) was listed. Thousands upon thousands of names were recorded. When Israel's army left Mount Sinai, it numbered 603,550 soldiers. These enlisted men marched to the border of the Promised Land, but refused to go in and take it because they were afraid. They did not believe God; they did not obey God, and so they were sentenced to forty years of wandering in that horrible howling wilderness. Because of their rebellion, they forfeited the blessings of the Promised Land. Instead of settling in a green farmland flowing with milk and honey, they were consigned to wander in a bare wasteland crawling with snakes and scorpions. Instead of building houses in their own towns and plowing land on their own farms and planting crops in their own fields and picking fruit from their own trees, the Israelites spent forty years just waiting; waiting until all the men who had refused to follow God had died in the desert. It would be their children who would taste the rich creamy milk and sweet golden honey of the Promised Land.

Those children had now grown up, and once again the army of Israel was camped on the edge of the Promised Land. They were camped on the eastern side of the Jordan River; on the other side were the kingdoms of Canaan that they must conquer by faith. While they were there, God commanded Moses to take another census, once again counting all the men who were old enough to be in Israel's army. Once again every man's name and family and tribe were recorded. There were 601,730 names on this new list, and they were all new names. With the exception of Joshua and Caleb, all the soldiers on the old list had died in the desert—just as the LORD had sworn. This second census was proof for everyone that what God says, he does. The Israelites could trust in the Word of the LORD.

There was another very important reason for this second census. The LORD said to Moses, "The land is to be allotted to them as an inheritance based on the number of names. To a larger group give a larger inheritance and to a smaller group a smaller one. Each is to receive its inheritance according to the number of those listed." It was on the basis of this second census that the land of Canaan was to be divided for the Israelites' inheritance.

What would happen to the tribe of Levi, which was not part of Israel's army and therefore not numbered with them? The names of the Levites were not counted in the census or recorded on the army list. What then would happen to their tribal inheritance? Would they not receive any territory in the Promised Land? Moses said, "The LORD set apart the tribe of Levi to carry the ark of the covenant of the LORD, to stand before the LORD to minister and to pronounce blessings in his name . . . That is why the Levites have no share or inheritance among their brothers. The LORD is their inheritance" (Deuteronomy 10:8–9). However, the LORD did not forget his servants, the Levites. When the land was divided among the tribes, there would not be a region named Levi, but instead, the Levites would be scattered throughout the land in special cities set aside for them. The LORD said to Moses, "Command the Israelites to give the Levites towns to live in from the inheritance the Israelites will possess. And give them pasturelands around the towns" (see Numbers 35:1–5).

It was important for the nation that there were Levites scattered throughout the other twelve territories, because the Levites were the ones who taught the people the Law of the LORD. The people, therefore, must not forget to give generously to the Levites from their fields and their crops, their flocks and their herds. Moses warned the people, "Be careful not to neglect the Levites as long as you live in the land. And do not neglect the Levites living in your towns, for they have no allotment or inheritance of their own" (Deuteronomy 12:19; 14:27). Again Moses said, "The priests, who are Levites—indeed the whole tribe of Levi—are to have no allotment or inheritance with Israel. They shall live on the offerings made to the LORD by fire, for that is their inheritance. They shall have no inheritance among their brothers; the LORD is their inheritance, as he promised them. . . . The LORD your God has chosen them and their descendants out of all your tribes to stand and minister in the LORD's name always" (Deuteronomy 18:1–8). So, once again, the tribe of Levi was counted separately, because they would not receive the same inheritance as the rest of the tribes of Israel. In the first census the total number of Levite males at least a month old was 22,000. In the second census that number was 23,000.

It is interesting to compare the numbers of the first census with the numbers of the second census:

| Tribe | First Census | Second Census, 40 years later |
|---|---|---|
| Reuben | 46,500 | 43,730 |
| Simeon | 59,300 | 22,200 |
| Gad | 45,650 | 40,500 |
| Judah | 74,600 | 76,500 |
| Issachar | 54,400 | 64,300 |
| Zebulun | 57,400 | 60,500 |
| Ephraim | 40,500 | 32,500 |
| Manasseh | 32,200 | 52,700 |
| Benjamin | 35,400 | 45,600 |
| Dan | 62,700 | 64,400 |
| Asher | 41,500 | 53,400 |
| Naphtali | 53,400 | 45,400 |
| **Total** | **603,550** | **601,730** |
| Reuben's Division | 151,450 | 106,430 |
| Judah's Division | 186,400 | 201,300 |
| Ephraim's Division | 108,100 | 130,800 |
| Dan's Division | 157,600 | 163,200 |

What do you notice about these numbers? Here are some questions to ask about these numbers:

Q. *Which tribes decreased in number?*
A. Reuben, Simeon, Gad, Ephraim and Naphtali all decreased.

Q. *Which tribe decreased the most?*
A. Simeon. Simeon had 59,300 soldiers when Israel left Mount Sinai; now Simeon had only 22,200 soldiers. God ordered that this second census be taken right after the plague when 24,000 men died. Zimri, the man whom Phinehas the priest put to death for adultery and idolatry, was a leader in the tribe of Simeon. It might be that Zimri led into that same sin many of his fellow Simeonites, who later died in the plague. That would account for the drastic decrease in the number of soldiers in Simeon.

Q. *Which tribes increased in number?*
A. Judah, Issachar, Zebulun, Manasseh, Benjamin, Dan and Asher all increased in number over those forty years.

Q. *Which tribe increased the most?*
A. Manasseh. In the first census, Manasseh had been the smallest tribe, with only 32,200 soldiers, but by the second census, Manasseh had increased by over 20,000 soldiers. Manasseh now had a larger army than over half the other tribes in Israel. Manasseh's soldiers now numbered 52,700.

Q. *Which tribe was still the largest tribe?*
A. Judah. Judah, which was the largest tribe in the first census, was still the largest tribe in the second census, with 76,500 fighting men counted. All the tribes under Judah's standard had also increased in number, making Judah's division the strongest in Israel's army. Judah's division now numbered over 200,000 soldiers. Judah was the tribe of our Lord, Jesus Christ. It is therefore not surprising that this tribe was so blessed of God even in its early days.

Q. *Had Israel's army increased or decreased in size during the forty years between the first and second census?*
A. After forty years, Israel's army had diminished in size, but this smaller army was a better army, because these men followed their leaders and

the LORD. They obeyed orders. When they received the command to move, they marched forward by faith.

The men recorded in this second census were greatly blessed. They were the ones who would enter the Promised Land and conquer the Promised Land by faith. These men and their families would live in that land and at the end of their days they would rest in that land. Moses himself would not receive so great a blessing. Moses had pleaded with the LORD to allow him to cross the Jordan River to see the Promised Land. Moses begged, "O Sovereign LORD . . . let me go over and see the good land beyond the Jordan," but the LORD was angry with Moses and would not listen to him. "That is enough," the LORD said. "Do not speak to me anymore about this matter" (Deuteronomy 3:24–26). But Moses at least would get to view the Promised Land before he died. The LORD said to Moses, "Go up this mountain . . . and see the land I have given the Israelites." God said, "Go up to the top of Pisgah and look west and north and south and east. Look at the land with your own eyes, since you are not going to cross this Jordan" (Deuteronomy 3:27). "After you have seen it, you too will be gathered to your people" (Numbers 27:13).

Moses was concerned about the people. If he died now, who would lead the Israelites into the Promised Land? Moses spoke to God: "May the LORD, the God of the spirits of all mankind, appoint a man over this community to go out and come in before them, one who will lead them out and bring them in, so the LORD's people will not be like sheep without a shepherd" (Numbers 27:15–17).

So the LORD said to Moses,

> *Take Joshua . . . a man in whom is the Spirit, and lay your hand on him. Have him stand before Eleazar the priest and the entire assembly. Commission him in their presence. Give him some of your authority so the whole Israelite community will obey him. . . . At his command he and the entire community of the Israelites will go out, and at his command they will come in.*
>
> *(Numbers 27:18–21)*

The Israelites would not be left without a shepherd. Joshua was the man. He would be the one to lead Israel into the Promised Land. "Commission

Joshua," the LORD said. "Encourage and strengthen him, for he will lead this people across [the Jordan] and will cause them to inherit the land that you will see" (Deuteronomy 3:28). So Moses did as the LORD commanded. Before the high priest and before the whole congregation, Moses laid his hands on Joshua and commissioned him to be the new leader of Israel.

The LORD then spoke to Moses to remind the people of their first and foremost concern — the worship of God. Moses reminded the Israelites to not neglect the LORD's offerings. The daily sacrifices in the morning and evening, the weekly sacrifices on the Sabbath Day, the monthly sacrifices at the New Moon festivals and all their yearly sacrifices on their special feast days, none of these must be forgotten (see Numbers 28 and 29). When Israel entered the Promised Land, they must not forget to worship the LORD according to all his commands. They must not forsake the true worship of the true God. They must not be seduced into the false worship of false gods. The LORD said to the Israelites through Moses: "When you cross the Jordan into Canaan, drive out all the inhabitants of the land before you. Destroy all their carved images; destroy all their cast idols; demolish all their high places. Take possession of the land and settle in it, for I have given you the land to possess. Distribute the land by lot, according to your clans. To a larger group, give a larger inheritance, and to a smaller group a smaller one. Whatever falls to them by lot will be theirs. Distribute it according to your ancestral tribes" (Numbers 33:51–54).

The LORD then told Moses the exact boundaries of the territory that they would inherit. God mapped out for Moses the southern, eastern, western and northern boundaries of all the land that Israel eventually would possess. The LORD also appointed the men who would be responsible for dividing up this land. Eleazar and Joshua, along with one leader from each tribe (including Caleb from the tribe of Judah) would be the ones to assign this land by lot as an inheritance for the Israelites. Notice their faith. See how certain they were that they would possess the land of Canaan. They were already appointing men to divide up the land, a land that they had not yet even conquered. "Faith is being sure of what we hope for" (Hebrews 11:1) and we see in this an amazing faith in the promises of God.

# THE DAUGHTERS WHO DARED

- **Numbers 27:1–11; 36:1–13**
- **Joshua 17:3–6**

Numbers is a book that is concerned with the counting of the males in Israel, either as soldiers for the army or servants for the priesthood, but Numbers is also a book concerned with the females in Israel. The Book of Numbers ends in an extraordinary way, with the amazing account of five faithful females and God's great LOVE for them. The names of these five girls—Mahlah, Noah, Hoglah, Milcah and Tirzah—are mentioned three times in the Book of Numbers, so that they and their act of faith and God's Word of LOVE to them would never be forgotten. The names of the hundreds of thousands of male soldiers recorded in the census have vanished, but the names of these five faithful females remain to this day, for the Word of the LORD endures forever.

Mahlah, Noah, Hoglah, Milcah and Tirzah were five sisters. Joseph was their great-great-great-great-grandfather; Manasseh was their great-great-great-grandfather, to whose tribe they belonged; a man named Makir was their great-great-grandfather; Gilead was their great-grandfather, to whose clan they belonged; Hepher was their grandfather; and a man named Zelophehad was their father. Sadly, however, at this time in their lives these five girls had no father at all to take care of them. Their own father, Zelophehad, had died in the desert, leaving them as orphans. Not one of these five young maidens had married yet, so there were no husbands to care for them, nor did they have any brothers. These five girls were alone in the world, having to fend for themselves, speak for themselves, plan for themselves. However, they had each other for support, and they had the LORD. God is particularly concerned to "defend the cause of the weak and the fatherless" and to protect the rights of the poor and the powerless (Psalm 82:3). God is called the "helper and defender of the fatherless" (Psalm 10:14, 18). Many times these sisters must have said with joy and thanks, "God is our refuge and our strength, an ever-present help in trouble. Therefore, we will not fear" (Psalm 46:1–2). Many times they must have said, "The LORD is my strength and my shield; my heart trusts in him and I am helped" (Psalm 28:7).

Right now they needed God's help, because the Promised Land, Israel's inheritance from the LORD, was being divided up according to the names on the second census. Their father had died in the desert with that entire generation of men, so his name was not on the second census. They also had no brothers whose names would appear on the new list, which meant their family would have no inheritance in the Promised Land. Was that right? Was that fair? Just because they were all girls, should their father's family not inherit a portion of the Promised Land? Just because they were girls, should they not have a piece of property to call their own?

The girls decided to take this matter to the LORD, not just privately in prayer within their hearts or within their tent, but publicly before the LORD at the Tent of Meeting. It was a very brave thing to do. By faith, these daughters dared to approach the entrance to the Tabernacle to bring their case before the throne of God. By faith, these daughters dared to stand before the most powerful men in Israel—Moses, Eleazar the priest and all the tribal leaders; they also dared to stand before the whole assembly and face the power of all the people. And by faith, these daughters dared to speak. Because they believed in the Word of God, that Israel would surely inherit the Promised Land, and because they believed in the LOVE of the LORD, that he would be fair and just to all his children, these daughters of Israel dared to speak what they believed was right. They said, "Our father died in the desert. He was not among Korah's followers, who banded together against the LORD, but he died for his own sin and left no sons. Why should our father's name disappear from his clan because he had no son? Give us property among our father's relatives."

"Give us property among our father's relatives." This was an extraordinary demand. These daughters dared to say: "Give us property." It was an unspeakable thing which they dared to speak. It was an unthinkable thing which they dared to think. In those ancient times, women usually were not allowed to own property at all. But by faith, these girls brought their case before the LORD. They trusted in God to do what was fair. "Will not the Judge of all the earth do right?" (Genesis 18:25). They also trusted the leaders of Israel to consider with justice and righteousness their claim to property in the Promised Land. In reaching out by faith to grasp God's Promise for themselves, these girls were true daughters of Israel, doing exactly as their forefather Jacob-the-Grasper had done. Like Jacob, they, too, desperately wanted to inherit God's blessing, but unlike Jacob, they acted honestly, openly and righteously, not deceitfully. What these girls wanted was good, and the way they went about getting it was right, but what would God and the leaders of Israel say?

Moses brought their case before the LORD. He stood before the throne of God and presented their case for the great King of all the earth to decide. It was an important case, helping to determine the legal status of women in the nation. Were daughters allowed to inherit their father's property? Were women allowed to own land in Israel? It was not an unimportant issue with the LORD, so God himself spoke to Moses and gave this verdict: "What Zelophehad's daughters are saying is right. You must certainly give them property as an inheritance among their father's relatives and turn their father's inheritance over to them" (Numbers 27:7). Thousands of years ago this was the legal requirement in ancient Israel. By this act of faith, these daughters helped to establish justice in Israel, for what they did benefited not only themselves, but also their whole gender.

Their act of faith also had repercussions beyond the borders of Israel. Because of their petition to own property in the Promised Land, the world now had God's Word on this issue. This law of God was a standard of justice by which to measure the status of women in every nation. (As Matthew Henry so quaintly expressed: "The daughters of Zelophehad consulted, not only their own comfort and the credit of their family, but the honor and happiness of their sex likewise; for on this particular occasion a general law was made." Matthew Henry continued by addressing the common practice of injustice in his own society of 17th and 18th century England: "Those that . . . deprive their daughters of their right, purely to keep up the name of their family, unless a valuable consideration be allowed them, may make the entail of their lands surer than the entail of a blessing with them.") God's Word was clear as to what was just. Ancient Israel was more advanced in its laws than many modern societies, because Israel had the revealed Word of the LORD.

Zelophehad's daughters called on the LORD in their distress, and God answered them, defending their case and upholding their cause. When the soldiers of Israel conquered Canaan, these girls would not be homeless or landless, but they would receive their father's allotted inheritance. This right was guaranteed to them by God's Law. Their claim was protected by the Word of the LORD. How these daughters of Israel must have rejoiced in what the LORD had done for them. They must have sung songs of praise to the LORD, songs that overflowed from their thankful, joyful hearts, songs similar to these psalms:

> I will praise you, O LORD, with all my heart;
>> I will tell of all your wonders.
> I will be glad and rejoice in you;
>> I will sing praise to your name, O Most High. . . .
> For you have upheld my right and my cause;
>> you have sat on your throne judging righteously. . . .
> The LORD reigns forever;
>> he has established his throne for judgment.
> He will judge the world in righteousness;
>> he will govern the peoples with justice.
> The LORD is a refuge for the oppressed,
>> a stronghold in times of trouble.
> Those who know your name will trust in you,
>> for you, LORD, have never forsaken those who seek you.
>
> (Psalm 9:1–2, 4–5, 7–10)

> May the righteous be glad and rejoice before God;
>> may they be happy and joyful.
> Sing to God; sing praise to his name . . .
>> and rejoice before him.
> A Father to the fatherless, a defender of widows,
>> is God in his holy dwelling . . .

*You are awesome, O God, in your sanctuary;*
*the God of Israel gives power and strength*
*to his people.*
*Praise be to God!*

*(Psalm 68:3–5, 35)*

However, not all in Israel rejoiced at what God had done for these young women. The family heads of the clan of Gilead of the tribe of Manasseh (that is, the girls' own close male relatives, their own uncles and cousins on their father's side) opposed the judgment that God had given in the girls' favor. These men thought that the land given to these girls should be divided among the men in the family as part of their inheritance. It is therefore not surprising that they contested the girls' right to own land, which they believed rightfully belonged to them and the other men of the tribe. So they came before Moses and the leaders of Israel to appeal the decision. They wanted the case reopened; they wanted the facts re-examined. They said to Moses, "When the LORD commanded my lord to give the land as an inheritance to the Israelites by lot, he ordered you to give the inheritance of our brother Zelophehad to his daughters. Now suppose they marry men from other Israelite tribes; then their inheritance will be taken from our ancestral inheritance and added to that of the tribe into which they marry. And so part of the inheritance allotted to us will be taken away."

Although one may question the motives of these men, they did present a legitimate concern: What would happen to their tribal territory? If these girls married men from other tribes, then the girls' allotment would be inherited by their children, who would belong to these other tribes. The tribal borders in Israel would be continually shifting. In fact, as the generations passed, there would be no tribal boundaries at all in Israel.

Moses brought this new concern before the LORD. Would God now reverse his former decision? Would the five girls no longer be allowed to inherit the land?

The LORD then gave this order to the Israelites:

What the tribe of the descendants of Joseph is saying is right. This is what the LORD commands for Zelophehad's daughters: They may marry anyone they please, as long as they marry within the tribal clan of their father. No inheritance in Israel is to pass from tribe to tribe, for every Israelite shall keep the tribal land inherited from his forefathers. Every daughter who inherits land in any Israelite tribe must marry someone in her father's tribal clan, so that every Israelite will possess the inheritance from his fathers. No inheritance may pass from tribe to tribe, for each Israelite tribe is to keep the land it inherits.

This was a brilliant resolution to the conflict. Both sides were right in what they presented to the LORD. God said, "What Zelophehad's daughters are saying is right" (Numbers 27:7). God also said, "What the tribe of the descendants of Joseph is saying is right" (Numbers 36:5). They were both right, and God in his great wisdom protected the interests of both sides. The girls would inherit their father's property, but it could not leave the tribe of Manasseh.

If the family heads of the clan of Gilead of the tribe of Manasseh were hoping to gain more land by their appeal, they were disappointed in their attempt. The land was not taken away from Zelophehad's daughters. The five sisters did as the LORD commanded. Mahlah, Tirzah, Hoglah, Milcah and Noah all married men within their tribe. They married their cousins on their father's side (but probably not any of those cousins who had contested their claim to their father's inheritance). God said they could marry anyone they pleased within their father's tribe, and they had considerable choice, for the tribe of Manasseh was a large tribe with many men and many clans (see Numbers 26:29–34).

And so the book of Numbers comes to an end with the story of the daughters who, by faith, dared to ask for an inheritance in the Promised Land. Their request was heard and they received what they wanted by the Word of the LORD. God says, "Ask and it will be given to you; seek and you will find; knock and the door will be opened to you. For everyone who asks, receives; he who seeks, finds; and to him who knocks, the door will be opened" (Matthew 7:7–8). Again the Bible says, "This is the confidence we have in approaching God: that if we ask anything according to his will, he hears us. And if we know that he hears us, whatever we ask, we know that we have what we asked of him" (I John 5:14–15). We all should follow the example of faith set by these daughters of Israel. We should strive with all our hearts to receive an inheritance in the greater Promised Land through faith in Jesus Christ and by believing in him to secure for ourselves an eternal place in the Kingdom of Heaven.

✳ ✳ ✳

W e see, in the final pages of Numbers, that the Israelites had faith in the Word of God. They believed that they would inherit the Promised Land. Their faith was so strong that they were already fighting and quarrelling over their inheritance. That is how sure they were that God would keep his promise and give them the land. "Faith is being sure of what we hope for and certain of what we do not see" (Hebrews 11:1). The Book of Numbers ends with *faith* in the LORD and in his Word.

We see, in the final pages of Numbers, that God made rules and laws to govern the division of the land. Because the LORD loved his people—all of his children, both sons and daughters—he made sure to provide for every single person. No one would be homeless in the Promised Land. If a family lost their father (and there was no son to replace him as head of the family in protecting and providing for the other family members) then the daughters were guaranteed possession of the family property. God said, "If a man dies and leaves no son, turn his inheritance over to his daughter" (Numbers 27:8). Thus the book of Numbers ends with the LOVE of God in caring for all his people.

We see, in the final pages of Numbers, that God was concerned with the equal rights and legal claims of women within the nation. The LORD clearly expressed his will regarding this issue throughout the Scriptures. From the beginning, God blessed both the man and the woman and gave the world to both of them to rule (see Genesis 1:26–28). We read that righteous men divided the inheritance between both sons and daughters. For example: "There lived a man whose name was Job. This man was blameless and upright. He feared God and shunned evil . . . Nowhere in all the land were there found women as beautiful as Job's daughters, and their father granted them an inheritance along with their brothers" (Job 1:1; 42:15). Numbers also declares the right of daughters, as well as sons, to receive an inheritance. The book of Numbers ends with the *justice* of God.

We see, in the final pages of Numbers, God upholding both sides of two parties in apparent opposition. On the one hand, God upheld the claim of daughters to inherit property and the right of women to own land. On the other hand, God upheld the headship of men within a family and the patriarchal system of the tribal territories. The Book of Numbers ends with the *wisdom* of God.

Most importantly, this final account in Numbers foreshadows the grace of God in our time, when he grants his children—both sons and daughters—an equal share in the greater inheritance through faith in Jesus Christ. It was foretold in the Old Covenant when the LORD declared: "And afterward, I will pour out my Spirit on all people. Your sons and daughters will prophesy . . . Even on my servants, both men and women, I will pour out my Spirit in those days. . . . And everyone who calls on the name of the LORD will be saved" (Joel 2:28–29, 32). It was confirmed in the New Covenant: "You are all sons of God through faith in Christ Jesus . . . There is neither Jew nor Greek, slave nor free, male nor female, for you are all one in Christ Jesus. If you belong to Christ, then you are Abraham's seed, and heirs according to the promise . . . God sent his Son, that we [all] might receive the full rights of sons. Because you are sons, God sent the Spirit of his Son into our hearts . . . Since you are a son, God has made you also an heir" (Galatians 3:26–4:7). All who believe in Christ, whether Jew or Greek, slave or free, male or female, receive the full inheritance of a son. God's Word proclaims that men and women are equal heirs—"fellow heirs" of God's "gracious gift of life" (I Peter 3:7). That reality was foreshadowed in God's verdict long ago when he declared to Moses: "You must certainly give [the daughters] property as an inheritance" (Numbers 27:7) in the Promised Land. The book of Numbers ends with the hope of the *grace* of God through our Lord Jesus Christ.

# NUMBERS
# TEACHER'S GUIDE

### Explanation of the Teacher's Guide

I wrote this guide for teachers using the lessons from *Herein Is Love: Numbers*. This manual can be used by any adult involved in teaching children the Bible: Sunday School teachers, Christian School teachers, home school teachers, Vacation Bible School teachers, camp counselors, and parents. Prayerfully study the Scripture references given at the beginning of each lesson. After that, read the lesson carefully. Find the visual aids you need to use for that lesson. Prepare the memory work handouts. Assemble the craft materials. Practice the psalm. Plan your outdoor activity or the route of your field trip, and you're ready to go.

If you have only an hour each week with your class of children (which is all most Sunday School teachers have), you cannot possibly do everything suggested for each lesson in this teacher's manual. However, with one hour you will have time to: teach the lesson (which is your first priority), show and discuss the visual aids (while you are teaching), hear the children's memory work, sometimes do a quick craft, ask a few questions, pray and sing a psalm. If you have a two or three hour block of time, the making of crafts and singing of psalms can be extended. Camp counselors and parent-teachers will find the field trip suggestions particularly useful.

Many Sunday School teachers think that children must have a lesson sheet to take home with them each week. It is nice for the children to have something to take home with them, but it need not be any more than a verse of memory work. What could be more important for the children to take away with them than a jewel from God's Word? However, if you think a parent page is necessary for a lesson review during the week, you can very simply and cheaply make your own by including:

1. The main Bible text (to be read at home).
2. The memory work (to be learned at home).
3. A craft suggestion (if you didn't make one in class).
4. A copy of the main psalm (to be sung daily in family worship).
5. The field trip suggestion (for a family outing).

## VISUAL AIDS

Use *photographs*. Photographs will help connect the Bible to the real world of the children. There are many beautiful and meaningful pictures of enduring significance that will impress the children. Expose the children to the amazing scenes witnessed and captured by the human eye through the camera.

Use *maps*. Whenever possible in a lesson use a map to trace the route of Israel's journey in the wilderness or to point out important mountains and rivers or to show the area of a certain country, etc. Let the children see that the accounts in Scripture are historical events that happened in the real world.

Use *specimens*. Many of the accounts in Scripture have an object in them that is central to the story. It can be something very simple, and yet that object rivets the children's attention to the lesson. For example, in Numbers 13, the spies brought back from Canaan grapes, pomegranates and figs. Bring these fruits for your children to see and taste.

## MEMORY WORK

We should impress upon our children the need to store up God's Word like a treasure in their hearts, which can help them in a time of need. I tell the children that the real reward is knowing God's Word, but I also give them a little incentive by making each child a memory work book. This is quite simple:

1. Make booklets by folding 8 × 12 sheets of construction paper in half. (Make them all the same color with younger children to avoid squabbles.) Make the front cover interesting by pasting on it a slightly smaller rectangle of some sort of picture. (Again, I always make the books identical.) Sometimes I use wrapping paper. I usually make books to last three months for weekly lessons, changing them with the seasons. For example, the memory book for the autumn quarter could have a picture of brightly colored leaves on a yellow background. Often I add a few sparkles to the front cover too. Make sure each child's name is on his/her book.

2. Type out the verse. (I use a 4 × 6 sheet of paper.) Make copies for double the number of children in the class. One copy goes into their book (which you keep until the books are finished). The other copy is handed out to each child to learn during the week. I try to make the hand-out copies interesting: In autumn I make the children's verses in different shades of brightly colored paper cut in the shape of leaves. That way, their weekly Bible verses can make a pretty display on their bulletin boards or refrigerators at home. In winter I hand out white "snowballs." It takes just a few extra moments to trace a circle around the verse before cutting it. In spring you can hand out diamond-shaped "kites" or petalled "flowers" in pastel hues. Be creative. There's more than one way to hand out a slip of memory work, giving the children something special to take home.

3. Buy sheets of stickers, continuing the seasonal theme. (There are usually twelve stickers per sheet, four sheets per package, which costs about fifty cents per quarter per child.) Write each child's name on the back of his/her sticker sheet. For each week's memory work that is learned, they get to choose a sticker from their own sheet to put in their book. At the end of the term, collect all the unearned, unused stickers, but let all the children take their books home.

If you are dealing with a class of children too old for sticker books, give out marks for the memory work. (This can be incorporated into a weekly test with the review questions.)

## CRAFT

For each lesson I suggest one or more simple crafts that in some way deal with what you have discussed in that lesson. Many of the crafts can be easily modified to fit your required time frame. I have not described in detail how to make each item, for this is not meant to be a step-by-step craft book; its purpose is just to give you some ideas.

## REVIEW QUESTIONS

For each lesson I ask a few specific review questions. There are two very important questions, however, that should be asked with every lesson:

1. What does this lesson teach us about God?
2. How does this lesson help us to live our lives?

When I taught classes of older children, I typed these questions each week onto a test sheet, which I then copied and handed out to each child at the end of the class. They had about ten minutes to write the test. Each week each child received a mark, which I carefully recorded in my notebook. At the end of the year the three students with the highest averages received a prize. It is remarkable how this little competition for the top marks and the final reward caused everyone to listen with the utmost attention. (Note: Not all the questions deal with straight information. Some of the questions are just asking for opinions, for which there is no right-or-wrong answer.)

## PRAYER

The application of each lesson to the children's lives is found in the prayer.

## PSALMS TO SING

I list one psalm (or part of a psalm) that is particularly relevant to the lesson, as well as several others that are also related to it. Singing the psalms is an important but simple way for the children to store God's Word in their hearts. "Let the Word of Christ dwell in you richly as you teach . . . and as you sing psalms" (Colossians 3:16). If time permits, I recommend singing the main psalm for each lesson several times, so that the children have already begun to memorize it. The Psalter I have used is *The Book of Psalms for Singing*, published by the Reformed Presbyterian Church of North America, 1973.

## FIELD TRIP

The teaching of the Word of God to our children is not meant to be confined within the four walls of our Christian churches, schools, and homes. Take God's word outside, into the fresh air and sunshine. Teach it in the open fields and the busy streets. Moses says, "Fix these words of mine in your hearts and minds . . . Teach them to your children, talking about them when you sit at home and *when you walk along the road*" (Deuteronomy 11:18–19). How will God's Word be fixed in the hearts and minds of our children? It will happen when we read the Scriptures not only around the family dinner table or when we study the Bible in our Sunday School classrooms or hear the Bible read in church, but it will also happen if we discuss the things of God when we are walking along the road and looking at the world around us.

# GOD'S ARMY

**Numbers 1–2**

*This Student lesson starts on page 8*

## VISUAL AIDS

Look in the back of a big atlas, and you will see lists of countries with their populations. Show these lists to your children and explain to them how a census is taken. Also, you could show your students charts or graphs which depict the sizes of the armies of various nations. Show them the national flags of the world and discuss with them briefly the importance of the colors and symbols on some of these flags.

## MEMORY WORK

Jesus said: "The very hairs of your head are all numbered. So don't be afraid" (Matthew 10:30–31).

## CRAFT

Your students could make banners for the twelve tribes of Israel—a colorful display for your classroom wall.

## REVIEW QUESTIONS

1. Why did God not take the Israelites directly to the Promised Land? What had they been doing in the desert for over a year?
2. In the census commanded by God, who was counted? Why?
3. Which son of Jacob was missing from this census? Why?
4. Which tribe of Israel camped closest to the LORD's Tabernacle? Where did the other twelve tribes camp?
5. Which four tribes were each in command over two other tribes? Why were those tribes chosen as leaders?

6. Do you think it was a good idea to organize the camping and marching of Israel's army? Why?
7. Who was in command of Israel's army? Who set it in order?

## PRAYER

LORD, I pray that each one here is numbered in your army, counted in your records and named in the Lamb's Book of Life. LORD, I pray that by your Grace, each one here might believe in Jesus, the Captain of the Army of the LORD, who defeated Satan on the cross and secured for us the victory forever. May each one of us fight the good fight of faith to the glory of God.

## PSALMS TO SING

115D—and 48B; 56; 80B; 105B; 147A.

Psalm 115D blesses God's people: "May the LORD so add to you that your numbers will abound and as the generations pass may your children still increase. Blessed be you of the LORD."

Psalm 48B and 147A speak of God counting . . . the towers in Jerusalem and the stars in heaven. In Psalm 56, God numbers our wanderings and records our weeping: "Thou numberest my wanderings; not one dost overlook. Within Thy bottle put my tears; are they not in Thy book?"

## FIELD TRIP

It might be interesting to visit your municipal archives and check the census records from years past. Also, as you drive along in your car, note the population recorded on the name sign for each city and town and village.

# GOD'S OWN TRIBE

**Numbers 3–4; 7–8; 18**

*This Student lesson starts on page 17*

## VISUAL AIDS

Show the children pictures of the various carts and frames that nomadic peoples around the world use for transporting their tents and goods when they are traveling. You can show them pictures of Eskimos with their sleds and dogs or Indians with their ponies and travois. You can show them pictures of donkey wagons and ox carts, horses, camels and elephants, all laden with man's burdens. Impress upon your students the difficulty the Israelites would have had in transporting, through the wilderness, a tent of the magnitude of God's Tabernacle.

## MEMORY WORK

I urge you . . . in view of God's mercy, to offer your bodies as living sacrifices, holy and pleasing to God—this is your spiritual act of worship (Romans 12:1).

## CRAFT

Even in modern times we still use simple "carrying frames," such as a stretcher. To make a stretcher would be an easy group project. You will need a strip of canvas, (approximately 3 × 5 feet), ten curtain rings (or more), and two broom handles. Have the children sew the rings securely along two sides of the canvas and then insert the poles. The children can take turns carefully carrying each other on the stretcher.

## REVIEW QUESTIONS

1. How many priests were there at this time in Israel's history?
2. Whom did God give to the priests to assist them in their work?
3. What important work were the Levites called to do?
4. God said, "The Levites are mine!" Why?

5. Where did the Levites camp? Where did the priests camp?
6. How could the Levites carry the most holy things if they were not allowed to touch them or even look at them?
7. How were the Levites consecrated for their new work?

## PRAYER

Heavenly Father, we thank you for calling us and cleansing us through Jesus Christ to be servants in the house of God. LORD, grant us strength that we might not fail at the tasks you call us to do. May we live as Levites, as a tribe of people set apart for the LORD.

## PSALMS TO SING

134AB—and 135AB (1); 135C (4,7,8).

These psalms exhort God's servants—those who guard the house of the LORD, those who render faithful service to him—to praise and bless the LORD! "Bless the LORD, O house of Levi" (Psalm 135C).

## FIELD TRIP

You don't need to go somewhere exotic to see people hauling their bags and bundles from here to there. Just look at all the shopping carts at your local supermarket or the baggage carts at your local airport. How many different carrying devices can you find people using in your own town in just one day? Remember the Israelites who had to transport God's Tabernacle through the wilderness.

# GOD'S SPECIAL SERVANTS

**Numbers 6:1–21**

*This Student lesson starts on page 25*

## VISUAL AIDS

Look in any magazine, and there you will see photos of handsome men and gorgeous women advertising self-centered lives of pleasure and leisure. Their hair is perfectly and expensively styled; they are dressed in fine clothes and rich jewels. The Nazarite, if he/she were pictured on another page, would present the exact opposite kind of person, one who vowed to lead a life of self-denial and service to God. Their hair would not be cut to enhance their looks; their clothes would be plain and perhaps poor; and in their hands they would hold a glass of plain water or a mug of mint tea. The vows that the Nazarites took were not easy.

## MEMORY WORK

1. Come out from them and be separate, says the Lord. Touch no unclean thing and I will receive you. I will be a Father to you, and you will be my sons and daughters, says the Lord Almighty (II Corinthians 6:17–18).
2. I urge you . . . in view of God's mercy, to offer your bodies as living sacrifices, holy and pleasing to God—this is your spiritual act of worship. Do not conform any longer to the pattern of this world, but be transformed by the renewing of your mind (Romans 12:1–2).

## CRAFT

Have the children create an ad for a magazine, promoting a God-centered, service-oriented way of life. Compare their work to the usual worldly advertisements one finds in magazines.

## REVIEW QUESTIONS

1. What were the men and women called who made a special vow of separation to the LORD?
2. How did these Nazarites separate themselves? What three things did God command them to do?
3. Who was a famous Nazarite in the New Testament?
4. Who was a famous Nazarite in the Old Testament?
5. Whose mother vowed that he would be a Nazarite for his whole life before he was even born?
6. Why did God command Samson's mother to drink no wine or other alcoholic beverage before he was born?
7. Why did the Nazarites have to sacrifice a lamb as a sin offering after the completion of their vows?

## PRAYER

O LORD, help us to be holy, even as you are holy. Help us to separate ourselves from sin and dedicate ourselves to you. O LORD, we desire to be like Christ, but we fail in all our attempts. We thank you, O LORD, that we have this hope: You will perfect us through faith in Christ. Even today, O LORD, we pray that you will deliver us from evil. Even today, O LORD, we pray that you will forgive our sins. We thank you, O God, for providing the way for us to be holy, through faith in your Son, Jesus Christ.

## PSALMS TO SING

89D—and 7B (9); 16AB; 19B; 35E; 51B; 56 (6); 61; 65; 66C; 71D; 76AB; 99C; 116C; 119O.

## FIELD TRIP

Just for fun, pretend you are Nazarites. Have the children try to find the places a Nazarite would not go, such as funeral homes and cemeteries, liquor stores and bars, hair dressers and barber shops. As Nazarites, you could go into a grocery store, but which items would you not buy? Grapes and raisins, grape juices and most mixed juices, wines and alcoholic beverages, vinegar and most salad dressings; none of these common items could go into your shopping cart.

# FORWARD MARCH

**Numbers 9:15–10:36**

*This Student lesson starts on page 31*

## VISUAL AIDS

The LORD commanded Moses to make two trumpets of hammered silver. You could show the children pictures of the trumpets and bugles used by armies. If possible, bring a real one for them to see and try. Israel's trumpets of hammered silver must have been very beautiful.

## MEMORY WORK

The LORD will keep you from all harm. He will watch over your life. The LORD will watch over your coming and going, both now and forevermore (Psalm 121:7–8).

## CRAFT

The children could make little wall plaques to hang by their beds. (Something as simple as large paper plates could be used for the bases.) Add pictures of peacefully sleeping children; such pictures can be cut from magazines or drawn by the children themselves. Then add the Word of God to comfort them all through the night: "I will lie down and sleep in peace, for you alone, O LORD, make me dwell in safety" (Psalm 4:8).

## REVIEW QUESTIONS

1. How long had the Israelites been camping at Mount Sinai?
2. How did they know it was time to leave?
3. Whom did Moses ask to go with them? Why?
4. How did the Levites transport the Tabernacle? How did they transport the holy things?
5. Which tribe set out first? Which tribe set out last?

6. Who and what were in the very middle of the procession?
7. How did the Israelites know when to stop and where to camp?
8. What did Moses do whenever the people started or ended a segment of their journey?
9. Why could the people feel safe on their journey?

## PRAYER

Lord, we thank you for watching over us, through the day and night, from the time we enter this world until the time we leave it, and all our comings and goings from the day we are born until the day we die. Thank you for guiding us and guarding us throughout our lives and for loving us both now and forevermore.

## PSALMS TO SING

121ABC; 139A—and 4AB; 5AB (1,3,5); 23ABCD; 31DE; 41B; 46AB; 47A; 68AB; 73C; 78F (23); 97C; 98AB; 107A; 150AB.

Psalm 121ABC tells how the Lord is our protector, watching over us constantly, to preserve our lives. "He who keeps Israel slumbers not, nor sleeps, by night or day." Our daily going out and coming in, "the Lord will keep both now and evermore."

Psalm 139A speaks of God knowing our path—every detail of our journey—whether we are lying down to rest or getting up to run. He is there with us, guarding us and guiding us. "Behind, before me, Thou dost stand and lay on me Thy mighty hand."

Psalms 47A, 98AB and 150AB all deal with trumpets. "Praise him with the trumpet sound!"

The rest of these psalms deal with God guarding us or guiding us.

## FIELD TRIP

Have your children ever heard the sound of trumpets? Take them to, or show them, a band or concert or a military parade where they can hear and see these instruments in action. Remind them that in ancient Israel each of the four main camps set out at the blast of the silver trumpets.

# GRUMBLING AND COMPLAINING

**Numbers 11:1–3**

*This Student lesson starts on page* 37

## VISUAL AIDS

For this lesson you need photos of happy faces—people who are smiling, laughing, singing, praising, rejoicing—people who are shining like stars.

## MEMORY WORK

1. Do everything without complaining or arguing, so that you may become blameless and pure, children of God without fault in a crooked and depraved generation, in which you shine like stars in the universe as you hold out the word of life (Philippians 2:14–16).
2. I will extol the LORD at all times; his praise will always be on my lips (Psalm 34:1).

## CRAFT

Have the children make "blessing books" in which they count and name the blessings in their lives. They can illustrate each page. You could also make a banner with these words on a dark background: SHINE LIKE STARS IN THE UNIVERSE AS YOU HOLD OUT THE WORD OF LIFE. Bright, shiny, sparkly stars can be added to the banner.

## REVIEW QUESTIONS

1. Why did life become harder for the Israelites when they left Mount Sinai?
2. When we face hardships, what should we do instead of grumbling and complaining?
3. What were the blessings that Israel should have counted in the wilderness? Name the many things for which they should have been thankful.
4. What did God hear that aroused his anger?

5. What did God do? What did the people do? What did Moses do?
6. Why do we study what happened to the Israelites so long ago?
7. What are the things in your life for which you can always be thankful and joyful?

## PRAYER

Lord, we do thank you and praise you for all your blessings to us. Forgive us when we grumble and complain. Please, do not hold this sin to our account, and Lord, we thank you for your promise of forgiveness in Jesus Christ. Help us to choose daily to be cheerful and thankful, whatever difficulties we might face. O Heavenly Father, help us to live as children of God and shine like stars before you.

## PSALMS TO SING

34AC; 92C; 106A; 145A—and 9A (1); 30AB; 33A (1); 43; 47A. These are only a few of the psalms that speak of praising and thanking the Lord with cheer and joy.

## FIELD TRIP

I think we all know homes where we can go and, as soon as you enter into them you hear complaining. We also know homes where, in spite of many hardships, the people are joyful, grateful, cheerful and thankful.

An interesting family game might be to keep track of our complaints for just one day. Mark a red X beside each person's name every time they utter some complaint. (Make sure the parents' complaints are recorded too.) How can each complaint be changed into a word of thanks? For example, "I hate this cold winter" can be changed into a prayer of gratitude: "Lord, thank you for giving us a warm house and warm clothes in this freezing weather. Thank you for the chest full of hats and scarves and mitts to keep us warm. Thank you for all those warm coats hanging on their hooks. Thank you for that row of insulated boots, waiting to keep our feet safe from frostbite. O Lord, you have given us everything we need in this cold weather. *Thank you!*" You will be teaching the children the right way to deal with hardships and it will help them throughout their lives.

# WHINING AND WAILING

**Numbers 11:4–35**

*This Student lesson starts on page 42*

## VISUAL AIDS

Do your children know what quail look like? Check out a bird book and show them the pictures. In North America there are all kinds of quail, plump little birds with spots, stripes, crests and plumes. In the Arctic there are even some pure white ones called ptarmigans.

## MEMORY WORK

1. Jesus said, "I tell you the truth: he who believes has everlasting life. I am the bread of life" (John 6:47–48).
2. Jesus said, "I am the living bread that came down from heaven. If anyone eats of this bread, he will live forever. This bread is my flesh, which I will give for the life of the world" (John 6:51).

## CRAFT

On this earth we will never know how manna bread tastes, but perhaps you could make with your children some little loaves of sweet, moist, spicy, nut breads. Use coriander to season your breads, honey to sweeten them and olive oil to moisten them. "The manna was like coriander seed . . . and it tasted like something made with olive oil . . . It was white like coriander seed and tasted like wafers made with honey" (Numbers 11:7–8; Exodus 16:31).

## REVIEW QUESTIONS

1. Why were the Israelites whining and wailing? Did they have any right or reason to complain? Why not?
2. What did the Israelites say? Was it true?
3. How did the Israelites reject the LORD?

4. What kind of "bread" does Jesus call himself? Why?
5. What effect did the Israelites' rebellion have on Moses?
6. What did he want to do? What did he ask God to do? How did the LORD answer Moses' prayer?
7. What effect did the Israelites' rebellion have on God? What did the LORD do? How did the LORD answer the people's wail?

## PRAYER

Heavenly Father, we thank you for providing so abundantly for us, not only our daily bread, but also our daily meat. LORD, we thank you especially for the Bread of Life, Jesus Christ our Lord, who gave himself for the life of the world. May each one of us feed upon Christ—and so live forever. May each one of us believe in Jesus and so not perish, but have eternal life. LORD, we thank you also for the gift of the Holy Spirit, who will lead us into all truth. LORD, we also ask for your forgiveness of our sins against you, for all the times we have failed to thank you and love you and trust you. May we be warned from your Word, O LORD, and never rebel against you. Help us and save us, we pray.

## PSALMS TO SING

78C; 145C—and 22H; 34AC; 85B; 104B; 107A; 111A; 136A (1, 2, 13); 146AB.

## FIELD TRIP

Great flocks of birds are an impressive sight. If you know of a place where birds congregate in vast numbers, you could take your children there to see them. To find flocks of quail might be difficult; where I live, to find even one wild quail would pose a problem. Perhaps you know a place where the children could see some real, live, quail-type birds.

Another outdoor activity would be to build a campfire and roast thin pieces of chicken (or other quailish meat) over the flames. Eat these with your home-made breads, and you will be eating a meal quite similar to an Israelite family's dinner in the wilderness so long ago. Cool fresh air and warm wood flames always give food a special flavor, and should add a special fervor to your thanks before the meal.

# A HIDEOUS SIN, A HIDEOUS PLAGUE

**Numbers 12**

*This Student lesson starts on page 52*

## VISUAL AIDS

Show the children pictures of the world's people of color, especially pictures of beautiful black women. Photography books have exquisite pictures, but even ordinary magazines now display beautiful black models.

## MEMORY WORK

Man looks at the outward appearance, but the LORD looks at the heart (I Samuel 16:7).

## CRAFT

Make two kinds of masks, blacks ones and white ones. When the masks are all decorated, the children can wear any of them. It doesn't matter what color their face masks are; they are still the same people on the inside, whatever color is on the outside.

## REVIEW QUESTIONS

1. Why did Miriam and Aaron oppose Moses' marriage to a Cushite? Did Moses do anything wrong in marrying a woman of another race? Who sinned in this situation?
2. Moses' sister and brother began to speak against Moses. Why was this so wrong?
3. Did Moses defend himself? Who vindicated Moses?
4. Was Moses a proud man? What does the Bible say? Was Moses a faithful man? What does God say?
5. God struck Miriam with leprosy. God is a righteous judge and all his judgments are just, but in this case, how did the punishment so perfectly fit the sin?

6. What sins are warned against in this portion of Scripture?
7. How did God demonstrate his LOVE in this story for the Cushite woman, for Miriam, for Aaron, for Moses, and for Israel?

## PRAYER

O Heavenly Father, help us to be fair and just in our dealings with all people. Forgive us when we sin, when we do not love others as we love ourselves, when we do not esteem others better than ourselves. LORD, we thank you that you alone are the Judge, and that you judge righteously. We thank you that you love us, defend us and vindicate us when we are innocent; we thank you that you love us, confront us and discipline us when we are guilty. LORD, we thank you for the forgiveness of our sins in Jesus Christ.

## PSALMS TO SING

96B; 103A—7AB; 17A; 26A; 35E; 50A; 67AB; 72A; 75 (1–4); 94A; 98AB; 99C. Many of these psalms deal with the just judgments of God:

"For you it is who tries the minds and hearts; O righteous God, you are the Judge of men" (7A). "A righteous judge, God judges righteously" (7B). "Thou wilt judge the peoples in truth and righteousness and o'er the earth shall nations, Thy leadership confess" (67A).

## FIELD TRIP

People of color have enriched our world and our lives. They have made enormous contributions to the nations, and they have greatly influenced American culture. Perhaps you can visit an exhibit at a museum, where the children can view African art, or perhaps you can attend a concert, where the children can hear African music. Where can you go to see the amazing athletes and musicians and artists that the black peoples have produced? Sadly, sorrowfully, there are also exhibits, to our shame and guilt, that show how the black peoples have been mistreated. Use this lesson to impress upon the children the evil of racial prejudice.

# EYES OF UNBELIEF

**Numbers 13**

*This Student lesson starts on page 59*

## VISUAL AIDS

Use a map to trace the route of the Israelites' journey through the wilderness, pointing out the places where they stopped along the way. Also show where the spies went in the Promised Land.

Have your children see (and taste) the fruit that the spies brought back to Israel's camp. You will need a large luscious cluster of grapes, some pomegranates and some figs.

## MEMORY WORK

1. The LORD is my light and my salvation. Whom shall I fear? The LORD is the stronghold of my life. Of whom shall I be afraid? Though an army besiege, my heart will not fear; though war break out against me, even then will I be confident (Psalm 27:1, 3).
2. God . . . when I am afraid, I will trust in you (Psalm 56:3).
3. In God, whose Word I praise, in the LORD, whose Word I praise—in God I trust! I will not be afraid. What can man do to me? (Psalm 56:10–11).
4. I sought the LORD and he answered me; he delivered me from all my fears (Psalm 34:4).

## CRAFT

In Canada we often have sets of stamps depicting our beautiful maple trees or our wild flowers, but one day I saw three very interesting stamps from Israel, showing the fruit that the spies brought back from the Promised Land. Perhaps your children can design three large postage stamps—one with grapes, one with pomegranates, and one with figs. You can make their pictures look like stamps, simply by leaving a white border around the four sides and then trimming the edges with pinking shears.

## REVIEW QUESTIONS
1. What hindered the Israelites' progress on their journey to the Promised Land?
2. At last the Israelites reached Kadesh Barnea. Why was it exciting for them to arrive at that place?
3. God said, "Go and take possession of the land!" Moses said the same thing. What did Israel's army want to do first?
4. How many men did Moses send into the land as spies?
5. What two things did Moses instruct the spies to bring back to Israel's camp?
6. The spies traveled all the way to Hebron. Why did they go there? What did they find there?
7. What three fruits did the spies bring back with them?
8. Ten spies spread an evil report about the land. What did they say? Was it true?
9. Ten spies said: "We cannot do it." Who were the other two spies? What did they say? Whose words would you believe? Why?

## PRAYER
O LORD, help us to trust you always. Help us to have faith, instead of fear. Keep us from seeing with eyes of unbelief. Keep us from thinking thoughts and speaking words of doubt and discouragement. O LORD, guard our hearts and our minds in Christ Jesus. Please deliver us from every evil. LORD, we thank you for your Word, which brings us comfort and courage.

## PSALMS TO SING
27AD—and 3; 23; 27E; 31DG; 34AC; 56; 62C; 64AB; 112AB (1,4).

## FIELD TRIP
The spies reported that the cities were fortified, with "walls up to the sky." Are there any old fortresses with high walls that your children can visit? The spies also reported that they saw "giants," powerful people of great size, who were stronger and taller than they were. Perhaps you could take your children to see some modern giants such as NBA basketball players, Sumo wrestlers or NHL hockey players. Imagine if you had to fight such men who were armed for battle with deadly weapons?

# ISRAEL'S CHOICE

**Numbers 14**

*This Student lesson starts on page 64*

## VISUAL AIDS

Show the children some contrasting landscapes, both desert wastelands and fertile farmlands. Israel must choose between them; they must advance in faith to the good land or retreat in fear to the badlands. For this lesson, you could also bring pictures (or specimens) of various bones, skulls and skeletons.

## MEMORY WORK

1. See to it . . . that none of you has a sinful, unbelieving heart that turns away from the living God (Hebrews 3:12).
2. We also have had the gospel preached to us, just as they did; but the message they heard was of no value to them, because those who heard did not combine it with faith (Hebrews 4:2).
3. Imitate those, who through faith and patience, inherit what has been promised (Hebrews 6:12).

## CRAFT

When my daughter, Shoshannah, was a little girl, she went through a phase of being fascinated with skeletons. These ancient bones inspired her "Skeleton Book," a series of remarkable pictures of all kinds of skeletons.

God said to the Israelites, "In this desert your bodies will fall . . . They will meet their end in this desert; here they will die" (Numbers 14:29, 35). Their bones remained in the wilderness; they were not carried, as Joseph's bones were, into the Promised Land. No, their skeletons lay buried beneath the desert sand.

Perhaps your children would like to draw some bones, skulls and skeletons. These can be animals, as well as humans, for the Israelites traveled with flocks and herds. Then you can make a somber mural for your classroom wall. Just get some sort of sand-colored paper for the background. Cut out the children's various drawings of white bones and skulls and arrange them on your desert landscape.

## REVIEW QUESTIONS

1. The people responded to the spies' report with weeping and wailing. How did Moses respond?
2. Moses tried to encourage the soldiers to go forward and fight for the Promised Land by faith. How did the soldiers respond to Moses? What did they say?
3. Why was their idea to go back to Egypt stupid?
4. Two other voices tried to calm the crowd. Whose voices were they?
5. How did the Israelites respond to these two good and faithful men? What did the Israelites say?
6. What did Moses and Aaron do that showed how upset they were? What did Joshua and Caleb do to show how upset they were?
7. What did Moses do when God threatened to destroy the Israelites? What did Moses say, when he argued in prayer to God? What reasons did Moses give God not to destroy Israel?
8. God said about the rebellious Israelites: "They will meet their end in this desert. Here they will die." Whom did God exclude from this punishment? Whom did God execute immediately? How?
9. God said, "Turn back tomorrow and set out towards the desert." What did the Israelites do instead?
10. The Israelites tried to take the Promised Land. Why were they not successful?
11. What very important lessons can we learn from the Israelites? Do they set a good example or a bad example for us? Can we learn from their mistakes and failures? Whose example should we follow?

## PRAYER

O LORD, help us to live by faith, not by fear. Forgive us, we pray, when we fail. Help us to seek you and trust you and love you always. We thank you, God, for your mercy to us and your LOVE for us, in sending your Son to die for our sins. For this we praise you forever and ever.

## PSALMS TO SING

95BC; 106D (18, 19)—Psalm 95BC and 106D (18, 19) deal explicitly with this account.

## FIELD TRIP

This might be a good time to visit a museum and view the various skeletons, many of which were preserved in desert badlands.

# A TRAGIC EXPERIMENT

**Numbers 16**

*This Student lesson starts on page 75*

## VISUAL AIDS

In photographs of Hasidic Jews you can see the tassels hanging beneath their jackets. Thousands of years later they are still obeying God's command about the tassels. If you have a Jewish friend, perhaps you can borrow a fringed prayer shawl, which has the tassels on the corners, to remind the Jews to obey God's Law.

## MEMORY WORK

1. A heart at peace gives life to the body, but envy rots the bones (Proverbs 14:30).
2. Rid yourselves of all malice and all deceit, hypocrisy, envy, and slander of every kind (I Peter 2:1).
3. Godliness with contentment is great gain (I Timothy 6:6).

## CRAFT

Tassels are easy to make. Have the children wind white yarn or string around small (2x4-inch) rectangles of cardboard. Loop a piece of blue cord under the white yarn at one end and tie it. Cut the yarn at the other end. Take out the cardboard and then wind yarn or string around the tassel about half an inch from the top, securing the end. The children can pin these tassels on the edges of their garments or hang them on their walls, to remind them how the Israelites were reminded to obey God's Law in the wilderness.

## REVIEW QUESTIONS

1. The Israelites made it to the edge of the Promised Land, but then God made them turn back to wander for forty years in the wilderness. Why must they do this?

2. How do we know that God still loved the Israelites during those forty years of punishment? How did God bless them?
3. During those forty years there was a great rebellion. How did it begin? Who was the ringleader of the rebellion?
4. Who joined Korah in this rebellion? Why? What was their grievance?
5. Who were the two competing sides in the contest that Moses arranged?
6. How did God show that Aaron alone was his holy high priest?
7. What happened to the 250 rebels? What happened to their censers?

## PRAYER

LORD, let us be content with the work and the place you provide for us. Let us serve you with joy and thanks, whatever we do, wherever we are. LORD, may envy never be a sin that ensnares us; may jealousy never be a sin that destroys us. O LORD, deliver us from evil, we pray. May we never join in any rebellion against you or your servants. O LORD, grant us peace.

## PSALMS TO SING

37AB; 52AB—and 1AB; 5AB; 7AB; 31C; 34BDE; 35AB; 36A; 37CEF; 43; 54AB; 55C; 59B; 70ABC; 71B; 92B; 94B; 101; 109AC; 119P.

Psalms 37 and 52 are about wicked men, like Korah and his followers, who "love evil more than goodness, lying more than truthful speaking." But God will destroy them: "God will break you down forever. He will pluck you from your dwelling; he will lift you by your roots, from the land of living men" (52B).

Many of these psalms deal with liars, just as Korah was a discontented deceiver. "O let the lying lips be dumb, which speak with arrogance, whose haughty words against the just, contempt and pride advance" (31C). "Because of sin within their mouths and words their lips let fly, let them be caught in their own pride, because they curse and lie" (59B).

## FIELD TRIP

Perhaps you could take a walk through an orthodox Jewish neighborhood (especially on a Saturday morning), when you can see the fringed and tasseled prayer shawls beneath the men's ordinary street clothes.

# SOMETHING TOTALLY NEW

**Numbers 16**

*This Student lesson starts on page* 82

## VISUAL AIDS

This is a truly terrifying lesson, and perhaps the words in it need nothing else to impress this vivid image upon the children's minds. I still remember as a small child seeing a picture of the earth opening its fiery jaws and swallowing dinosaurs alive. For many weeks following exposure to that picture, I piled all my stuffed animals upon my bed. My small self reasoned that, if the earth opened up in the darkness and swallowed me whole along with my bed and my house in one great gulp, I at least wanted the comfort of my teddy bears. I do not necessarily advise this, but you could show the children photos of the devastation of earthquakes, especially when the ground opens up.

## MEMORY WORK

To him who is able to keep you from falling and to present you before his glorious presence without fault and with great joy—to the only God our Savior be glory, majesty, power and authority, through Jesus Christ our Lord, before all ages, now and forevermore! Amen (Jude 24–25).

## CRAFT

Maybe for this terror-filled lesson, your children can make little cuddly teddy bears. Make sure the children know that clinging to teddy bears in times of terror will do nothing, but clinging to Christ will save them forever.

## REVIEW QUESTIONS

1. Who else joined in Korah's rebellion? What were their names? To which tribe did they belong?

2. What was the grievance of these Reubenites? Why did they oppose Moses and Aaron?

3. Dathan and Abiram accused and slandered Moses. What lies did they speak against him? How did Moses respond?

4. Moses said that God was about to do something totally new. What was it?

5. How did Moses warn the Israelites? What did he say? Who listened to him? Who did not listen to him?

6. What happened to Korah, Dathan, Abiram and all who remained with them?

7. Who is the Prophet greater than Moses? Who is the Priest higher than Aaron?

8. Who has testified that Jesus is the Christ, the Son of God? Name ten witnesses.

9. If the people who rebelled against Moses and Aaron did not escape punishment, what will happen to those who rebel against the Son of God?

10. Do you believe that Jesus Christ is the Son of God?

## PRAYER

O LORD, open our minds to understand the Scriptures. O LORD, open our hearts to believe all that has been written about the Son of God. May we believe in Jesus this day and every day of our lives. May we never rebel against him. May we never reject his LOVE—your LOVE, O LORD—demonstrated by Christ's death upon the cross for us. O LORD, we thank you and praise you for saving us from destruction.

## PSALMS TO SING

106C (11–14); 140B—1B; 7AB; 21BD; 35AB; 52AB; 54AB; 55BC; 56; 57AB; 73B (7); 88AB; and 92AB; 101.

Psalm 106C speaks of this tragic event: "The op'ning earth on Dathan closed; Abiram's band entombed. A fire blazed in their company and wicked ones consumed."

## FIELD TRIP

There may be in your area some great crevice for the children to see, an enormous crack where the earth's surface opened up long ago. There also may be an earthquake exhibit at your local museum that shows the awful destruction when the earth trembles and opens.

# AARON'S CENSER

**Numbers 16:41–50**

*This Student lesson starts on page 90*

## VISUAL AIDS

Once again, pictures of censers would be useful for this lesson.

## MEMORY WORK

There is one God and one mediator between God and men, the man Christ Jesus, who gave himself as a ransom for all men (I Timothy 2:5).

## CRAFT

It would be simple to make small censers from tuna fish cans. Buy some cone incense for each child's censer.

## REVIEW QUESTIONS

1. How did God execute Korah, Dathan, Abiram, and all their followers?
2. What should have been the people's response to the death of these rebels? What was their response the very next day? What did the people do? What did the people say? Was it true?
3. The people accused Aaron and Moses by saying, "You have killed the LORD's people!" In what two ways was this statement not true?
4. How did God respond to this rebellion of the people? What did God say? What did God do?
5. What did Moses and Aaron say? What did they do?
6. How many people died of the plague that day? How did the ministry of Aaron save the rest of Israel?
7. How did Aaron's ministry of life foreshadow Jesus Christ?

## PRAYER

Heavenly Father, we thank you for Jesus Christ, our Great High Priest, whom you have appointed to bring us life. May we always believe in him. May we always honor him. LORD, deliver us from the Evil One, we pray, and grant us your Grace.

## PSALMS TO SING

115B—and 99C; 118A; 133AB; 135C (4,7,8).

All these psalms mention God's high priest, Aaron.

## FIELD TRIP

The prayers of God's people rise before the LORD "like incense" (Psalm 140:2). God's people are a kingdom of priests, whose invisible prayers are like the smoke of Aaron's incense wafting up to heaven, bringing life to many who are facing death. If you want to show your children the powerful, life-giving, priestly incense, show them God's people on their knees in prayer.

# AARON'S STAFF

**Numbers 17**

*This Student lesson starts on page 94*

## VISUAL AIDS

Aaron's staff was made from an almond branch. If you live in a place with a warm climate, you could bring a real almond branch to show your children. Otherwise, use pictures of the almond tree, which show in detail its beautiful, pinkish-white blossoms and its long, pointed, curved leaves. Wherever you live, you can bring samples of its fruit, both the almond stones and the almond nuts.

## MEMORY WORK

1. Jesus said, "I am the vine; you are the branches. If a man remains in me and I in him, he will bear much fruit; apart from me you can do nothing" (John 15:5).
2. Jesus said, "I am the Resurrection and the Life. He who believes in me will live, even though he dies; and whoever lives and believes in me will never die" (John 11:25–26).

## CRAFT

You could cut out large, brown, cardboard staffs for each child. Have them print Aaron's name on them. The children can then make the staffs "sprout" by pasting onto them green tissue-paper leaves, pink tissue-paper blooms and real almonds for the fruit.

## REVIEW QUESTIONS

1. How had God demonstrated in the past that Aaron was his appointed priest?
2. What did God do to prevent another rebellion against Aaron's priesthood in the future?

3. What happened to Aaron's staff overnight in the Tabernacle? Why was this a miracle?
4. What was done with Aaron's staff after the over-night miracle? What was done with the other eleven staves?
5. God said he had done this so that the Israelites would not die. What did the Israelites say?
6. How was Aaron's staff a sign of life?
7. Who was called the "Branch of the LORD" and the "Righteous Branch"? Why was he called by these names?
8. What did Jesus mean when he said, "I am the vine; you are the branches"?

## PRAYER

O LORD, we thank you for your greatest miracle, which was not the sprouting of Aaron's staff, but your bringing forth life from death. We thank you for raising Jesus' dead body to everlasting life. We thank you that the grave had no lasting grip upon him, nor could the tomb hold him. LORD, we thank you for the promise of eternal life in him! May we ever trust and hope in that promise. Amen.

## PSALMS TO SING

1AB—and 23ABCD; 52AB; 92BC; 96B; 128AB.

Many times the righteous are compared to living, growing, fruit-bearing trees: "He shall be like a tree that grows set by the water side, which in its season yields its fruit and green its leaves abide" (1A). "In God's house I am growing like a green tree bearing olives. In the steadfast love of God I am trusting evermore" (52B). "Those planted by the LORD shall in God's courts be seen; when old they'll still bear fruit and flourish fresh and green" (92C).

## FIELD TRIP

You never know what will appear on seemingly dead branches. Go for a winter walk with your children—a branch-hunting, branch-cutting expedition—and then place the branches in water in your warm house. In just a few days, there are sure to be some signs of life and eventually there should be some interesting surprises. Remember, the staves that Moses placed in the Tabernacle were not placed in water and they were only in there for a few hours in the night. It was truly amazing that Aaron's staff, without time or water, not only sprouted, but also budded, blossomed, and produced almonds.

# THE MISSING MIRACLE OF MERIBAH

**Numbers 20:1–13**

*This Student lesson starts on page 98*

## VISUAL AIDS

Water is so precious, and a drop of water is like a jewel. Pictures of water drops and waterfalls would be useful for this lesson. You could also show the children pictures of arid wastelands, where nothing grows and few things live, because there is so little water. How amazing that God "opened the rock and water gushed out; like a river it flowed in the desert" (Psalm 105:41). How amazing that God "split the rocks in the desert and gave them water as abundant as the seas; he brought streams out of the rocky crag and made water flow down like rivers" (Psalm 105:15–16).

## MEMORY WORK

Jesus said, "If anyone thirsts, let him come to me and drink. He who believes in me, as the Scripture has said, out of his heart will flow rivers of living water" (John 7:37–38 NKJV).

## CRAFT

Cut out large drop-shapes, one for each child. Let the children draw in their "water drops" some of the many living and growing things that depend upon water. The Israelites complained that they had neither grain nor fruit in that waterless wasteland. They feared that both animals and people would die of thirst.

## REVIEW QUESTIONS

1. Miriam died. Who was she? Tell three good things about her.
2. God gave the Israelites a re-test. What was it?
3. How did the people respond to this crisis? What three stupid and wicked things did they say?

4. How did Moses and Aaron respond to their quarrelling? What did they do? Where did they go?
5. What did God tell Moses and Aaron to do? Did they obey God?
6. Why was it especially important for Moses and Aaron to do exactly what God told them to do?
7. Tell five ways that Moses and Aaron sinned.
8. How did God punish Moses and Aaron? Why was their punishment so severe?
9. What was the "missing miracle" because of Moses and Aaron's disobedience?

## PRAYER

LORD, we thank you for providing for us all the necessities for life, especially our daily food and drink. May quarrelling and complaining be far from our lips. Instead, may praise and thanks fill our hearts and our lives. LORD, we ask that we would be careful to obey all your commands. We also ask that you would forgive our sins, for the sake of your Son, Jesus Christ.

## PSALMS TO SING

36B—and 23ABCD; 42AC; 46ABC; 63AB; 65B; 78B (8); 81AB; 95BC; 104B; 106E.

Many of these psalms speak of God providing water for people to drink. "They with the bounty of Thy house shall be well satisfied; from rivers full of Thy delights Thou dost their drink provide. Because the fountain filled with life is only found with Thee. And in that purest light of Thine we clearly light shall see" (36B).

Some of the psalms speak directly of this miracle, of God giving them water from the rock: "He split the rocks and gave them drink, as from great deeps below; he from the rock brought running streams, like floods made waters flow" (78B).

## FIELD TRIP

There are many water places that you could visit, where your children can participate in all the water activities that humans like to do. You could visit lakes, rivers, rapids, fountains, geysers, waterfalls, waterslides, swimming pools, etc. Sometimes water is just interesting to watch, like gazing at the huge waves crashing and splashing on an ocean shore. Even pumping water from an old-fashioned pump or playing in a water sprinkler on the lawn are fun activities for children. Water! People love it, need it and want it.

# GRIEF UPON GRIEF

**Numbers 20:14–29**

*This Student lesson starts on page 106*

## VISUAL AIDS

For this lesson, a Bible map would prove very useful, to point out Kadesh, the short route through Edom and the long route around it, and Mount Hor where Aaron died.

All Israel mourned for the loss of their high priest, Aaron. Pictures of nations mourning for their beloved leaders would also be of interest to the children. For example, you could show them pictures of the funeral processions of President Kennedy, Martin Luther King or Princess Diana.

## MEMORY WORK

Men are not cast off by the LORD forever. Though he brings grief, he will show compassion, so great is his unfailing LOVE. For he does not willingly bring affliction or grief to the children of men (Lamentations 3:31–33).

## CRAFT

Do you know someone who is grieving the loss of a loved one? Perhaps the children can make cards or bake cakes or do something to express their sorrow or to offer their comfort.

## REVIEW QUESTIONS

1. The Israelites were nearing the end of their journey. What three things would impede their progress? Would anything be able to stop them from eventually entering the Promised Land? Why not?
2. The Israelites again found themselves on the southern border of the Promised Land. Why would they be hesitant to attack Canaan along this border? What did they want to do instead?

3. Moses hoped that the Edomites would let the Israelites use their highway to pass through their territory. Name five good reasons why the Edomites might be persuaded to help the Israelites. Unfortunately, what was their response? How did they back it up?
4. What two ways would Edom have benefited greatly by allowing Israel to pass through their land?
5. Why did the Edomites not help them? What possible reasons could they have for their obstinate refusal?
6. Why did the Israelites not attack the Edomites and force their way through their country?
7. How was this a test of faith for Israel? Did they pass the test?
8. The time had come for Aaron the high priest to die. What was so very sad about his death? Nonetheless, what seven circumstances surrounding Aaron's death made it as good a death as anyone could have?

## PRAYER

LORD, we thank you for being with us throughout life and even through death. We thank you that, through faith in Jesus Christ, it is not the grave that awaits us, but eternal life with you. LORD, help us to trust in you, whatever we face. May we be faithful to you as we live and even as we die.

## PSALMS TO SING

25D—and 6; 13; 22H; 31BF; 39AB; 73C; 90CD; 102A; 116AC; 119DU.

These psalms are about grieving and dying: "My groaning ever wearies me, through every night till morn appears. My grieving makes my bed to swim and waters all my cot with tears" (6). "O LORD, have mercy on me, for anguish fills my life; my eye, my soul, my body are all consumed with grief. My life is drained by sorrow, my years with sighing spent. I've lost my strength by sinning; my bones are weak and bent" (31F).

## FIELD TRIP

You could suggest that your children watch a funeral procession as it approaches a cemetery. Point out the black hearse, the line of cars with their lights on, the people dressed in black, the wreaths of flowers, etc., all the ways in which our culture honors the death of a loved one.

# A TASTE OF VICTORY

**Numbers 21:1–3**

*This Student lesson starts on page 112*

## VISUAL AIDS

"V" is the sign for victory. During World War II you can see old photographs of the allied leaders making a "V" with their fingers to express their hope for victory. You can also see pictures of Olympic athletes making this same sign with their fingers. NIKE is the Greek word for victory and the Nike Company uses a "V" as their trademark, (because in Greek, their "V" equals our "N"). The children would be familiar with the Nike symbol on shoes, shorts, shirts, hats, etc.

## MEMORY WORK

1. Thanks be to God! He gives us the victory through our Lord Jesus Christ (I Corinthians 15:57).
2. This is the victory that has overcome the world, even our faith. Who is it that overcomes the world? Only he who believes that Jesus is the Son of God (I John 5:4–5).

## CRAFT

Make large cardboard V's for each child in your class to decorate. You could also write the two victory verses from their memory work, one of them going up each side of the "V".

## REVIEW QUESTIONS

1. God was watching over Israel. Whose unseen eyes were spying on Israel?
2. Who was the king of Arad? What did he do? Why was he important in the history of Israel?
3. When the king of Arad attacked the Israelites and captured some of them,

what was Israel's response? To whom did they plea for help? What did they vow to do?

4. Did God hear Israel's prayer? Did God give them success? Why was this an important victory?

5. The king of Arad was not only wicked; he was also stupid. In what two ways did his attack on Israel prove to be very foolish?

6. Why was the region of this king's cities named Hormah?

7. The Israelites were fighting against human enemies, but their battle was not simply against flesh and blood. Against whom were they also fighting? Why did Satan want to keep Israel out of the Promised Land?

## PRAYER

Our heavenly Father, we thank you that in every time of trouble and battle, we can turn to you for help. Thank you for hearing and answering our prayers. O LORD, deliver us from our enemy, the Evil One, and keep us from every harm and sin. LORD, we thank you for Jesus, who defeated the devil forever on the cross. O God, we thank you for giving us the victory, through our Lord Jesus Christ.

## PSALMS TO SING

98A—and 2; 7A; 9A; 18EJK; 31E; 44A; 45A; 47A; 54AB; 56; 59B (7,12,13); 92AB.

Psalm 98A is perfect for this lesson: "O sing a new song to the LORD for wonders he has done. His right hand and holy arm the victory have won, the victory have won, the victory have won!"

The other psalms are also about God's deliverance of his people and triumph over his enemies. "You chided the nations; the wicked destroyed. Their names you erased and forever made void. The foe is consumed, is completely erased, their cities destroyed and their memory effaced" (9A).

## FIELD TRIP

Do you want the children to see people expressing the exaltation of victory? Suggest they see an athletic event where they will see a runner cross the finish line first with a shout of victory or a whole team exult triumphantly at the end of a game over the defeat of the rival team.

# SERPENTS

**Numbers 21:4–9**

*This Student lesson starts on page 116*

## VISUAL AIDS

You could show the children pictures of venomous snakes and poisonous scorpions. That dreadful desert where the Israelites walked was crawling with these creatures.

Also, I think the children would be very interested in seeing the symbol for medicine—a serpent on a cross—a very strange sign indeed to signify healing, unless you know its Biblical roots.

## MEMORY WORK

1. Just as Moses lifted up the serpent in the wilderness, so the Son of Man must be lifted up, that everyone who believes in him, may have eternal life (John 3:14–15).
2. Everyone who looks to the Son and believes in him shall have eternal life (John 6:40).

## CRAFT

Moses had to make a fake snake and for some reason children like to make snakes too. Give a child a lump of molding material, and probably the first thing he will roll out is a snake.

## REVIEW QUESTIONS

1. As the Israelites trudged the long way through that dreadful desert, they grew discouraged. What should they have done in their discouragement? What should we do when we are discouraged?

2. The Israelites did not pray to the LORD. They did not thank God for their many blessings, nor did they ask God to help them. What did they do instead?

3. For forty years God had protected the Israelites from something horrible hiding in the rocks? What was lurking there? What did they do to the Israelites?

4. Now the people turned to God for help and Moses prayed for them, but the LORD did not take the venomous vipers away. What did God tell Moses to do instead?

5. What was the only way a person who had been bitten by a poisonous snake could be saved from death,? What was God trying to teach the Israelites?

6. How have we all been bitten by a serpent? What fatal venom is within us all? There is only one cure for sin. What is our only hope for healing?

7. How did Moses lifting up the serpent in the wilderness point us to Jesus Christ?

## PRAYER

O LORD, may each one of us believe in you and obey your Word. May each of us look to Christ on the cross—and so be saved from sin and death. O LORD, deliver us from evil and that ancient serpent, Satan, who leads the whole world astray. Keep us safe from the devil, that we may never be led astray. LORD, we praise your holy name, for your LOVE, your mercy, your forgiveness of our sins. May we turn to you in every time of trouble, with pleas for help and prayers of thanks upon our lips. May we live that life of faith, which is pleasing in your sight.

## PSALMS TO SING

30AB—and 22ABCG; 58AB; 91A; 103A; 140A.

Psalms 30 and 103 give praise to God for healing us: "O LORD, my God, I pleaded that you might heal and save. LORD, you from death have ransomed and kept me from the grave" (30AB).

Psalm 22 is a description of Christ Jesus on the cross.

Psalms 58, 91 and 140 speak of snakes and their venom.

## FIELD TRIP

You can have the children visit the snake pit at your local zoo.

# WAR AND PEACE BY THE WORD OF THE LORD

**Numbers 21:10–35**

*This Student lesson starts on page 121*

## VISUAL AIDS

A map, showing the lands through which Israel traveled and the lands which Israel conquered, would be very useful for this lesson. Show the children the countries, the river borders, the cities, the mountains. You can also show them photographs of these geographical regions and landmarks.

## MEMORY WORK

1. I call to the LORD, who is worthy of praise, and I am saved from my enemies (Psalm 18:3).
2. No king is saved by the size of his army; no warrior escapes by his great strength ... But the eyes of the LORD are on those who fear him, on those whose hope is in his unfailing love (Psalm 33:16, 18).

## CRAFT

For this lesson you can have the children draw or trace maps, then color and name the different landmarks and regions. Rivers, mountains, cities and countries can all be identified. Add the points of the compass too. If you want a more complicated group project, you can make a topographical model of the region (including Canaan), showing the deserts, rivers, valleys, gorges, mountains, cities, plains, etc. Make sure to show the boundaries of the different countries. This model will be useful for future lessons also.

## REVIEW QUESTIONS

1. Why were the Israelites taking a long detour and traveling south, away from the Promised Land?
2. Why did the Israelites not fight against the Edomites?

3. Why did the eastern Edomites allow Israel to pass through their territory? How did this benefit the Israelites? How did this benefit the Edomites?
4. What restrained the Israelites from fighting against Moab and Ammon? From whom were these nations descended?
5. Why were the Israelites without water in Moab? What two things did Israel do to get water in Moab?
6. Why was God giving the land of the Amorites to the Israelites?
7. Who were the two mighty kings of the Amorites?
8. If God found even one righteous person in a city doomed to destruction, he rescued that person. Name two people who were spared, and name their cities which were destroyed.
9. Moses gave the land of the Amorites to three of Israel's tribes. What did the men of these tribes have to do before they could settle in their new homes, farms and towns?

## PRAYER

LORD, we thank you that we have peace in our land and we pray for the peoples and nations who are at war. Have mercy on them, we pray. We thank you that you are the king of all the earth, that you control all nations. Heavenly Father, we pray for the spread of the gospel; we pray that the good news of Jesus Christ and the forgiveness of sins would go forth in power throughout the world. We pray for our enemies, for all those peoples who hate Christians and Christ, that they will be converted to the one true God and so be spared from everlasting judgment.

## PSALMS TO SING

47A; 135B; 136A (1,2,9–12)—2; 5AB; 9AB; 24ABC; 33C; 44AD; 45A; 76AB. Psalms 135 and 136 speak particularly of God defeating the two Amorite kings of this lesson.

## FIELD TRIP

Who are the rulers and monarchs of the nations today? Their power and splendor will come to nothing. Visit a museum, where you can view the vanished glory of ancient civilizations. All their majesty has been reduced to a few artifacts in some glass cases. But the LORD's kingdom endures forever and his glory is eternal.

# A FALSE PROPHET AND A WICKED KING

**Numbers 22**

*This Student lesson starts on page 129*

## VISUAL AIDS

Horses are powerful and majestic beasts, but it is the lowly little donkey that has been chosen by God for special missions and extraordinary favors. The LORD opened a donkey's mouth, not to hee-haw, but to speak in human words. It was also a donkey that carried our Lord Jesus Christ in his triumphal entry into Jerusalem. You could show the children some pictures of donkeys.

## MEMORY WORK

1. Godliness with contentment is great gain. For we brought nothing into this world, and we can take nothing out of it (I Timothy 6: 6–7).
2. People who want to get rich fall into temptation and a trap and into many foolish and harmful desires that plunge men into ruin and destruction. For the love of money is the root of all kinds of evil. Some people, eager for money, have wandered from the faith and pierced themselves with many griefs (I Timothy 6:9–10).
3. Jesus said, "No one can serve two masters. Either he will hate the one and love the other, or he will be devoted to one and despise the other. You cannot serve both God and Money" (Matthew 6:24).

## CRAFT

Donkey puppets would be simple to make from grey felt. If you make them so the mouths can open, the children can make their donkeys talk.

## REVIEW QUESTIONS

1. When the Israelites returned from their northern conquests, where did they camp? What could they see facing them? What could they not see facing them?

2. Why was the king of Moab worried? What should he have done for Israel? What two things did he do instead because he was afraid of them?

3. Who was Balaam? He claimed to be a prophet of God. Was he? What made him a false prophet, rather than a true prophet?

4. In the night, God really did speak to Balaam. Was Balaam pleased with God's Word? Why not? What did Balaam want, more than anything else in the world?

5. Who stood in Balaam's way on the road to Moab? Who was this Angel of the LORD? What did he have in his hand? Who saw him standing there? What did the little donkey do each time? How did the donkey save Balaam's life? What was Balaam's response when his donkey stopped?

6. How was it possible for an animal to speak? What was God showing this stupid and wicked man? How did his little donkey have more sense than he did?

7. Balaam said to the Angel of the LORD, "I have sinned." Balaam also offered to return home. Why does this not impress us as real repentance?

## PSALMS TO SING

7B; 12AB; 36A; 52AB—and 5AB; 10AB; 19B (5–7); 19D; 26A; 31ACG; 37C; 49B; 59B; 62AB; 63AB; 101; 109ABC; 119IMPQV; 120 (1,2,4).

Many of these psalms speak of evil men with their cursing, lying lips: "See how the wicked evil thoughts conceives, is pregnant with ill-will and brings forth lies" (7B). "They empty falsehood speak to one another; with flattering lips and double heart they speak" (12B). "The words he utters with his mouth are wickedness and lies; he has refrained from doing good and ceases to be wise. His thoughts and plans upon his bed iniquity invent; he sets himself in ways not good, from evil won't relent" (36A).

## FIELD TRIP

Perhaps you know a farm that has little grey donkeys grazing in the fields. Maybe you know a place that gives children rides in donkey carts. Alas! These adorable donkeys will not speak one word to the children.

# A SIGN OF GOD'S LOVE

**Numbers 23–24**

*This Student lesson starts on page 137*

## VISUAL AIDS

You can show the children photos of the morning star (or the picture entitled "The Bright Morning Star," which is on the cover of this book.)

## MEMORY WORK

1. No weapon forged against you will prevail, and you will refute every tongue that accuses you (Isaiah 54:17).
2. The LORD your God . . . turned the curse into a blessing for you, because the LORD your God loves you (Deuteronomy 23:5).
3. Jesus said, "Love your enemies. Do good to those who hate you. Bless those who curse you. Pray for those who mistreat you" (Luke 6:27–28).

## CRAFT

The cover picture on this book is from an original piece of art in pastels. Perhaps the children would like to make a pastel picture also, depicting the bright morning star. The scenes and the hues should be as varied as the children in your class.

## REVIEW QUESTIONS

1. How do we know that King Balak was waiting anxiously for the prophet Balaam to arrive? What did he do? What did he say? Who had detained Balaam on his way to Moab?
2. Balaam had a plan to turn God against Israel. What was it?
3. Why was Balaam so determined to place a curse on Israel? Why was Balak so determined to place a curse on Israel?
4. How many altars did they build? How many bulls and rams did they slaugh-

ter? Was God impressed with their offerings? Why not? How many times did the prophet and the king try to get God to curse Israel?

5. Why did God change the curses meant for Israel into blessings?
6. Balaam's fourth and final oracle was like a riddle. He said, "A star will come out of Jacob. A scepter will rise out of Israel." What did this mean? Of whom was he speaking? Of whom was this a prophecy?
7. What was the greatest blessing that God gave to his people that day?

## PRAYER

Our Heavenly Father, we thank you for changing our sorrow into joy, for changing the curses of our enemies into blessings upon us. Truly you are a great and loving God. Please, LORD, deliver us from evil this day and forever. Keep us from harm and from sin. May we guard our mouths. May we be people who always bless and never curse. We thank you for the Bright Morning Star, even Jesus Christ our Lord.

## PSALMS TO SING

67AB; 110 (1,3); 115BD—and 3 (5); 5AB (5); 28A (8); 29A (1,6); 33B; 40ABE; 65A; 72C; 84AB; 89D; 109C; 112AB (1); 116A; 118C (14–17); 119AI (1); 128AB; 134AB.

These are just a few of the psalms that speak of God blessing his people: "O God, to us show mercy and bless us in Thy grace. Cause Thou to shine upon us the brightness of thy face . . . God, our own God will bless us. Yea, God will blessing send, and all the earth shall fear him to its remotest end" (67A). Balaam prophesied concerning Christ: "A scepter will rise out of Israel." Psalm 110 is a Messianic Psalm, which proclaims: "Jehovah shall from Zion send the scepter of thy power. In battle with thine enemies, be thou the conqueror" (110).

## FIELD TRIP

You could climb to the top of a high hill, which overlooks the houses of a village or city far below you. Imagine going up there to curse the people living there. But that is exactly what Balaam and Balak tried to do. Instead, pray for the people living in the town below you. Ask God to bless them.

Another outdoor adventure with the children would be to wake them at dawn to see the bright morning star. Remind them of the prophecy: "A star will come out of Jacob." Jesus was that brilliant star.

# ONE LAST TRY

**Numbers 25**

*This Student lesson starts on page 145*

## VISUAL AIDS

The army that Moab and Midian sent to Israel was very unusual. The glamorous female models in any magazine will serve to illustrate the beautiful "soldiers" that Balak and Balaam used to capture and conquer the Israelites.

## MEMORY WORK

Charm is deceptive and beauty is fleeting, but a woman who fears the LORD is to be praised (Proverbs 31:30).

## CRAFT

Let each child make a "praise" card for some faithful woman, who has had a good and godly influence in his/her life, some woman who fears the LORD and loves the child. The "praise" card could be for a mother or grandmother, an aunt or godmother, a neighbor or teacher, etc. "Her children arise and call her blessed" (Proverbs 31:28).

## REVIEW QUESTIONS

1. Why was Balaam sad as he rode home from Moab? Although Balaam did not receive his handsome reward of much money, why should he have considered himself blessed? What better things did Balaam receive? What had he heard and seen and done that should have caused him to rejoice?
2. How could this have been a new beginning for Balaam? Of what sins would Balaam have to repent in order to lead a new life? What evil practices would he have to forsake in order to follow God? What did Balaam choose to do?
3. As Balaam rode his little donkey home, he realized there was a better way to get God to curse Israel. What was Balaam's new plan? Balaam and Balak had

been unsuccessful in attacking God's LOVE for Israel; they had failed in bribing God to forsake his people. Whose love and faithfulness would they attack now? What was their plan to entice Israel to forsake God?

4. What kind of army did Moab and Midian send against Israel? Were they successful in capturing and conquering the Israelites? What did the beautiful women entice them to do? How did God respond? What did God do?

5. Who was Zimri? Who was Cozbi? What did they do? Who was Phinehas? What did he do?

6. Phinehas killed Zimri and Cozbi. Why was this not wrong? Why was this not considered murder? How do we know that God approved what Phinehas did?

7. How many Israelite men died in the plague because of their adultery and idolatry? Do you think Balaam and Balak were pleased with the results of their new scheme? Do you think Balaam at last received his handsome reward?

## PRAYER

O LORD, lead us not into temptation, but deliver us from evil, we pray. May we never be enticed to forsake you and may we never entice another person into sin. O LORD, may we always hate what is evil and love what is good. Keep us from the Evil One, we pray. And LORD, we thank you that nothing can separate us from the LOVE of God, in Christ Jesus our Lord. Forgive our sins, for his sake, and keep us close to you.

## PSALMS TO SING

106D—and 16AB; 31E; 44F; 73C; 81B (4); 96A; 97ABC; 115C.

Psalm 106D speaks of this exact incident in Israel's history.

Some of these psalms speak of the evils involved in worshipping idols and the necessity of trusting and serving God alone: "Those worshipping other gods multiply griefs" (16B). "I hate those serving idols. My trust is in the LORD" (31E). "If we have forgotten the name of our God or unto an idol our hands spread abroad, shall God not search out and uncover this sin, who knows every heart and the secrets within?" (44F)

## FIELD TRIP

Tonight, enjoy the peace, quiet and sanctity of your own home, which are the blessed benefits of a holy life devoted to God. Hopefully, you need not go beyond your front doorstep for the children to experience such a shelter.

# BALAAM RECEIVES HIS REWARD

**Numbers 31**

*This Student lesson starts on page 150*

## VISUAL AIDS

For this lesson you could bring "crafted articles" of gold (or pictures of such jewelry), items similar to the plunder that the Israelite officers took from the war and then gave to God as a freewill offering.

## MEMORY WORK

1. A faithful man will be richly blessed, but one eager to get rich will not go unpunished (Proverbs 28:20).
2. An evil man is snared by his own sin, but a righteous one can sing and be glad (Proverbs 29:6).

## CRAFT

You could have the children make some sort of "gold" jewelry. (A very simple craft idea: crowns and chains can easily be made from gold paper or pendants can be made from glittery gold cardboard shapes attached to a gold cord.) You could also have the children make necklaces, threading "gold" beads.

## REVIEW QUESTIONS

1. Do you think Balaam at last received his handsome reward from Balak? Why? What did Balaam do that helped Balak?
2. Why did the Word of the LORD go out against the Midianites? Why did God command them to be killed?
3. A foreigner was found with the Midianites. Who was it? Why was he there? What did the Israelites do to him? Why should Balaam have known not to be in league with Israel's enemies?
4. The Israelites killed the soldiers and burned the cities of Midian. Whom did

the Israelites not put to death? Why did Moses say that the women, too, must be executed? Of all the prisoners of war, who were the only ones allowed to live?

5. The Israelites plundered the Midianites. What did they take? How was it purified? How was it divided? Did Israel's army officers keep the gold for themselves? What did they do with it? Was God pleased with their offering? Why?

6. How many Israelite soldiers died in this war? Why do you think their casualty list was so low? How did Israel's army officers explain this amazing protection?

7. What happened to Balaam's "wages of wickedness?" What probably happened to Balaam's little donkey? How did Balaam's donkey fare better than her master?

## PRAYER

Our merciful Heavenly Father, we thank you for protecting your people in amazing ways. We thank you for rescuing us from harm and sin throughout our lives. We pray that, even this day, you will deliver us from evil. LORD, please keep us from the love of riches. May we seek always to glorify your name and not ourselves. LORD, forgive our sins for the sake of your Son.

## PSALMS TO SING

62C—and 18CI; 20AB; 28AB; 31D; 58AB; 79B; 91AC; 109B.

Many of these psalms speak of God rewarding both the righteous and the wicked: "According to my righteousness I am rewarded by the LORD. According as my hands were clean, he gives to me a just reward" (18C). "Repay them justly for their deeds and evil of their way, and for the work done by their hands a due reward repay" (28A). "O love the LORD, ye godly ones! The LORD the faithful guards; and he the proud and haughty ones abundantly rewards" (31D). "There surely is reward for righteous ones of worth. There surely is a living God, who judges in the earth" (58AB).

## FIELD TRIP

The Israelite army gave all the gold they plundered to God. Museums sometimes have special exhibits of ancient gold artifacts, but even a trip to a fine jewelry store to see real gold necklaces and bracelets would be interesting for a child.

# PREPARING FOR THE
# CONQUEST OF CANAAN

**Numbers 26; 27:12–23; 34**

*This Student lesson starts on page 155*

## VISUAL AIDS

A map of ancient Israel is needed for this lesson to show the boundaries of the land (as described by God in Numbers 34:1–12). Another map could show how the land was eventually divided between the twelve tribes. (Discuss why there is no territory named Levi or Joseph.) Give each child in your class a copy of the comparison between the first census and the second census, so that they can ask and answer questions about these two lists.

## MEMORY WORK

1. Evil men will be cut off, but those who hope in the LORD will inherit the land" (Psalm 37:9).
2. Those the LORD blesses will inherit the land, but those he curses will be cut off (Psalm 37:22).
3. Wait for the LORD and keep his way. He will exalt you to inherit the land (Psalm 37:34).

## CRAFT

God said, "Distribute the land by lot . . . Whatever falls to them by lot will be theirs" (Numbers 33:54). One way we now have of casting lots is by rolling dice. Each child could make a pair of dice by using small wooden square blocks and marking each side with the right number of dots. This can be a simple project, or more involved by sanding, varnishing and marking the cubes with a wood-burning "pen."

## REVIEW QUESTIONS

1. Why was it necessary for another census, a second census?

2. What two names appeared on both lists? Why? What happened to all the other names and all the other men on the first list?
3. This second census recorded the names of every soldier in Israel's army. What other great purpose did this list have?
4. The names from the tribe of Levi were not recorded on this list. What would happen to them? Would they receive an inheritance? How? Where?
5. Why was it good that the Levites were scattered throughout the whole land of Israel?
6. Which army was larger, the first one or the second one? Which army was better? Why?
7. Which tribe in Israel still had the greatest number of soldiers? Why was this tribe so blessed by God?
8. Moses was concerned that when he died, the people of Israel would be "like sheep without a shepherd," with no one to lead them into the Promised Land. Whom did God choose as the new leader? Why?
9. What preparations were made by God for dividing up the land?

## PRAYER

Our heavenly Father, we thank you that we also have the hope of an inheritance, kept in heaven for us who believe in Christ. We thank you that our inheritance from you can never perish or vanish, that it endures forever. O LORD, help us to live by faith in the Son of God all our days upon this earth, that we might at last receive this eternal reward.

## PSALMS TO SING

47A—and 16AB; 37BCE; 69E; 78F (23–26).

These psalms all speak about the inheritance of God's people: "My lot you maintain and the lines fell to me in pleasant lands; I have a good heritage" (16B).

## FIELD TRIP

Is there a lookout on a high hill in your community? Take your children somewhere they can see how land is divided, where they can see the boundaries of fields and farms, where they can see the roads or rivers that divide townships, counties and nations.

# THE DAUGHTERS WHO DARED

**Numbers 27:1–11; 36:1–13**

*This Student lesson starts on page 161*

## VISUAL AIDS

In many Islamic countries women are denied basic human rights. They are not allowed to attend school, to own property, to earn a living. They are prisoners in their own homes, unable to leave them or to walk freely without a "guard." They are not even allowed to feel the sun or the wind upon their faces, which they must keep hidden behind black veils. Show the children some pictures of these poor people, who live their lives shrouded in darkness. Women had equality in ancient Israel, guaranteed by God's Law. They had the right to own land and inherit property.

## MEMORY WORK

The LORD declared: "I will pour out my Spirit on all people. Your sons and daughters will prophesy . . . Even on my servants, both men and women, I will pour out my Spirit . . . And everyone who calls on the name of the LORD will be saved" (Joel 2:28–29, 32).

## CRAFT

Your children could make black veils and wear them outside. It may be interesting for a change, but how would it feel to always look at the world through such a veil?

## REVIEW QUESTIONS

There were five sisters in Israel, whose father had died. Did they have another Father who would take care of them? Who was their help and their strength in times of trouble?

1.  The Promised Land was being allotted according to the names on the second census. Why did this concern the five girls?
2.  What brave action did these five daughters dare to take? What clear demand did they dare to make?
3.  How did their demand show that they had amazing faith in the Love of God, the justice of God and the promises of God?
4.  Do you think it was right that they asked for property in the Promised Land? How do we know that what they asked for was good in the eyes of God? What was the Lord's answer to their request?
5.  Who opposed the idea of these girls receiving an inheritance? Why did they say they were opposed? Was this a legitimate concern? Might there have been another reason for their opposition?
6.  Whom did God say was right in this contest? How did God take care of both sides in this case?
7.  Whom did the five girls marry? Why?

Does God give an equal inheritance to both his sons and daughters in Jesus Christ? Should earthly fathers follow God's example in dealing with their children? How does this final story in Numbers display the amazing grace of God?

## PRAYER

Our loving heavenly Father, thank you for giving us an inheritance through faith in your Son Jesus Christ. Thank you that this promise of eternal life to all who believe in Christ is certain. Thank you for your justice and fairness; thank you for not discriminating against anyone because of their sex or their age or their race. We praise you, O Lord, for your great Love.

## PSALMS TO SING

48B—and 9AB; 45BC; 97BC; 144BD.

All these psalms speak of daughters.

## FIELD TRIP

Visit the homes or view the works of some great women in our society, women who were given the freedom to make a contribution.

# *About the Author*

Nancy Ganz has spent the last twentyfive years in her native land of Canada, helping her husband, Dr. Richard Ganz, in church-planting work and home-schooling their four daughters. She received her formal theological training from the University of Toronto prior to her conversion to Christ at L'Abri in the Netherlands. However, it has been the many years of Bible study since that time which has produced her *Herein Is Love* commentaries on the Old Testament. Currently, most of her time is spent studying the Scriptures, writing various books, and taking long walks along the country roads and woodland paths near her home.